The Battle of the Airfields

1st January 1945

NORMAN L. FRANKS

GRUB STREET · LONDON

Published by
Grub Street
The Basement
10 Chivalry Road
London SW11 1HT

British Library Cataloguing-in-Publication Data
A catalogue record is available on request from the British Library.

ISBN 1 898697 15 9

Typeset by Pearl Graphics, Hemel Hempstead

Printed and bound in Great Britain by Biddles Ltd,
Guildford and King's Lynn

2520

Contents

MAPS

The Airfields

B56	–	Brussels – Evere
B58	–	Brussels – Melsbroek
B60	–	Grimbergen
B61	–	St Denis Westrem
B65	–	Maldegem
B67	–	Ursel
B70	–	Antwerpe – Deurne
B77	–	Gilze Reijen
B78	–	Eindhoven
B79	–	Woensdrecht
B80	–	Volkel
B83	–	Knokke
B88	–	Heesch
A89	–	Culot
A92	–	St Trond
Y29	–	Asch
Y32	–	Ophoven
Y34	–	Metz-Frescaty

Acknowledgements

Whilst writing and researching the 'Battle of the Airfields' I have been privileged to meet or correspond with a number of men who 'were there'. All have made a useful contribution to the story and I wish to thank each one of them for their kind help.

Volkel

Group Captain J.B. Wray DFC, Leader No 122 Tempest Wing
Pilot Officer R.W. Pottinger, 3 Squadron
LAC D. Brooks, 6022 SE, 122 Wing
LAC D.N. Macdonald, 125 Wing

Eindhoven

Air Chief Marshal Sir Harry Broadhurst GCB, KBE, DSO, DFC, AFC, AOC 83 Group, 2nd TAF
Colonel R. Preston OBE, GC RAF Regt, 83 Group
Air Commodore C.D. North-Lewis DSO, DFC, Leader 124 Typhoon Wing
Wing Commander G.J. Gray DFC, OC 182 Squadron
Wing Commander L.H. Lambert DFC, AFC, OC 168 Squadron
Squadron Leader G. Clubley DFC, 137 Squadron
Squadron Leader H.G. Pattinson DFC, OStJ, 182 Squadron
Flight Lieutenant H. Beechens, 404 Air Stores Park
Flight Lieutenant A.C. Simon, HQ 83 Group
Wing Commander M.M. Kaye OBE, HQ 83 Group
Warrant Officer F.R. Newall, 83 Group Comm Squadron
Cpl. E.W.J. Sadler, 403 R & S U
LAC L. Collier, 124 Wing
LAC G.H. Davis, 403 R & S U
LAC D.C. Shepherd, 137 Squadron

Ursel
  Sergeant P. Crowest, Airfield Controller
  LAC E.H. Green, MT Section
St Denis Westrem
  Flight Lieutenant W. Link, 308 Polish Squadron
  Flying Officer T. Szlenkier, 308 Polish Squadron
Grimbergen
  Group Captain A.K. Gabzsewicz DSO, DFC, VM, KW, OC 131
  Polish Wing
Melsbroek
  Group Captain M.J.A. Shaw DSO, OC 69 Squadron
  Group Captain H.M.H. Tudor DFC, AFC, 140 Squadron
  Group Captain R.D. Walton, 140 Squadron
  Wing Commander E.R. Dutt AFC, 16 Squadron
Gilze Reijen
  Flight Lieutenant A.D. Mercer, 268 Squadron
Deurne
  Group Captain D.E. Gillam DSO, DFC, AFC, Leader 146
  Typhoon Wing
  Wing Commander S.J. Eaton DFC, 257 Squadron
  Wing Commander A.G. Todd DFC, OC 257 Squadron
  Flight Lieutenant J.G. Simpson DFC, 193 Squadron
  Flight Lieutenant R.E.G. Sheward DFC, 263 Squadron
  LAC J.B. Hopley, 341 Squadron
  LAC C.R. Southgate, Mobile Signals Unit
Woensdrecht
  Captain H.R. Lea DFC, 127 Squadron

Wing Commander R.P. Beamont CBE, DSO, DFC, Flight Lieutenant
J. Mierzejewski, Captain W. Milewski of the Polish Institute &
Sikorski Museum Ltd, Air Vice Marshal H.A.C. Bird-Wilson CBE,
DSO, DFC, AFC, M.C. de Penaranda, Herr Konrad Dammeier of
JG6, Herbert Kirchner – German Fighter Pilots Association, Mr
R.W. Cole DFC, FBOA, MoD (AR8b RAF), Edward H. Sims, Major
Reed Hansen USAF – Maxwell Air Force Base, Mr Kenn C. Rust,
Mr C.F. Shores, Martyn Ford-Jones, Imperial War Museum,
Keeper of the Public Records Office and staff; Kew, Miss Yvonne
Martin, Mr Chaz Bowyer, Mr Don Caldwell, Mr Eric Mombeek,
Mr Chris Thomas and Mr Dilip Sarkar.

CHAPTER ONE

The Last Gamble

As the Allied armies advanced relentlessly across western Europe following the breakout from the Normandy beach-head, their air cover was always with them. The Royal Air Force's Second Tactical Air Force (2nd TAF), commanded by Air Marshal Arthur Coningham, comprising 2, 83, 84 and 85 Groups, was, weather permitting, constantly on hand to support the men on the ground. Its fighters covered them, its bombers hit strong-points and lines of communications, its reconnaissance aircraft kept watch on German activities behind the front lines, while its fighter-bombers blasted ways through defensive positions.

With almost total Allied air superiority the retreating German soldiers rarely saw their once victorious Luftwaffe in the skies above them, only the seemingly endless armadas of British and American aeroplanes. They were bombed, strafed, rocketed and watched wherever they tried to make any kind of defensive stand.

The Luftwaffe was short of aircraft, short of petrol, short of experienced air leaders and more often than not was outnumbered. Yet the leaders that continued to survive and the youngsters that still came from the training units, fought on doggedly. In many ways the Luftwaffe was still a very dangerous adversary even now, the winter of 1944.

*

On the ground the land battles moved on towards the River Rhine in the north. Across it lay the German homeland. Brussels, the capital of Belgium, had been liberated. Operation Market Garden – the ill-fated Arnhem raid – had been tried and lost. Southern Holland was taken and then the advance embraced the sea port of Antwerp and the Scheldt Estuary.

As the armies moved up so too did the Allied air units. Mobile wings using bases in Belgium, Holland and France, so recently the homes of the Luftwaffe, were taken over and used to continue the support so valiantly given since D-Day. The only limiting factor was the weather which proved very bad as winter took its grasp. Airfields and landing grounds became unusable as rain, flooding and mud turned them into quagmires. So, as the advance came to a halt for the winter, the squadrons consolidated on more permanent airfields around Brussels and Antwerp, and at Eindhoven and Volkel.

This situation might well have continued until the weather improved, perhaps until early in the new year of 1945, had not the Germans decided to launch a major offensive in the Ardennes which opened on 16th December 1944. As it happened, the Allies too had planned a thrust under Field-Marshal Bernard Montgomery in late December, but the Germans, under Feldmarschall von Rundstedt, struck first. Thrusting through the woodland of the Ardennes, against positions held mainly by the American 1st Army, von Rundstedt's fourteen infantry and ten armoured divisions, comprising the 5th and 6th (SS) Panzer Armies and the 7th Army, achieved complete surprise in bad weather. Snow and fog kept air forces on both sides on the ground after an initial flurry of activity on the first day. On this first day the Luftwaffe put up over 500 aircraft, more than had been seen for a very long time. Then the weather clamped down.

No sooner had the surprise attack been mounted than the 8th Panzer Army broke through the American lines to push towards Liége, the plan being for it to head for Antwerp, thereby cutting the British 21st Army off from the Americans. To face this threat, the more northerly American troops came under Montgomery's command while the American XXIX Tactical Air Command, part of the US 9th Air Force, came under the command of Air Marshal Coningham.

The weather changed on 23rd December, allowing 2nd TAF to give support to the American front, and helped to stop the Germans reaching Malmédy and Bastogne, which left them only the bottleneck at St Vith to use as a line of support and communication. Thus the German attack began to falter and stop.

*

Earlier, the Luftwaffe High Command, in conjunction with the planning for the Ardennes offensive, had been requested to husband its fighter strength. Reichsmarschall Hermann Göring himself had already devised a plan to use the maximum number of his fighter force against the Allied air forces in one mighty blow as early as October 1944. At least 2,000 fighters were to be employed and it was to be the largest air battle of the war. General of Fighters, the successful German fighter pilot Adolf Galland, had the entire fighter arm in the West ready for action by mid-November, and a total of 3,000 fighter aircraft. Now all that was needed was suitable weather to unleash them, and sweep the RAF and USAAF from the skies.

It was then that the Ardennes battle plan called for air support and Galland's fighter reserves, so carefully built up, were used not for a great blow in the air, but for action in support of the offensive. Forced into this situation Galland left two fighter groups in Germany when ordered to send his force to the West in December. Over the period just before, during and immediately after Christmas 1944, the mass of fighters were employed in offensive and defensive actions which reduced its strength, increased aircraft unserviceability and generally watered down its fighting potential. Some of these offensive actions occurred on 17th December as recalled by the wing leader of the Tempest wing at Volkel, Wing Commander John Wray DFC:

> About two weeks before the end of 1944 the Luftwaffe launched a fighter sweep over our forward airfields but unfortunately for them nearly all the squadrons on those airfields had just got airborne, and one of my squadrons was on its way back from a visit to Osnabrück. The Hun caught a real packet including those who fled running into the returning Tempests. No 122 Wing had a tally of eleven that day, with other wings also making their contributions.
>
> *Wing Commander J.B. Wray, OC 122 Wing*[1]

[1] All ranks given are those held on 1st January 1945.

Wing Commander Wray himself shot down a Messerschmitt 262 jet on the 17th.

*

To support now the Ardennes offensive totally, the remaining fighter force was gathered together for another 'Great Blow' plan – a blow against the Allied air forces in Belgium and Holland. The task of planning this assault against the Allies was handed to Generalmajor Dietrich Peltz, commander of II Jagdkorps, and responsible for air operations over the Ardennes. At thirty years of age, Peltz was the holder of the Knight's Cross with Oak Leaves and Swords. He had begun his flying career as a Stuka pilot, flying in Poland and France before flying Ju88s against England, and later flew on the Russian front. He became an outstanding leader, his ability gaining him high rank, and taking him to almost every German battle area. He had successfully attacked Allied air power before – on the ground. The plan now was to hit the Allies on the ground – on their home airfields.

A secret conference was convened on 15th December at the Headquarters of II Jagdkorps, in an inn near Altenkirchen, east of Bonn. Peltz assembled his air commanders including Obersten Grabmann, Hentschel and Gotthardt Handrick, commanders of Jagddivisionen 3 and 5, and the Jagdabschnitts Führer Mittelrhein respectively. Also in attendance were Geschwaderkommodeuren of all Western-based Jagdgeschwader. Peltz outlined the plan, showing his audience a very detailed plan of the battle front and the planned target airfields. His plan called for ten major Jagdgeschwader to attack sixteen Allied airfields in Belgium, Holland and a base in France, at Metz.

Three code words were assigned to this secret operation. 'Varus', followed by a number, would confirm the operation was to go ahead, and the date. 'Teutonicus' would confirm the first signal and give permission to brief all pilots. Finally 'Hermann' would give the actual time of the attack. The whole operation was given the code-name 'Bodenplatte' – ('Baseplate').

*

As the weather improved on Christmas Eve, so the Americans'

mighty 8th Air Force re-opened operations over Germany, forcing the Luftwaffe to engage and continue to smash itself against the huge air armadas. In December the Luftwaffe lost 535 fighter pilots killed, missing, or as prisoners, with nearly 200 more wounded. The loss of aircraft was a disaster for Bodenplatte, and sufficient for some of the German air leaders to believe it must be cancelled or at the very least postponed. But then, on the afternoon of 31st December came the code-word 'Varus 1.1.45', closely followed by 'Teutonicus'. There followed some very hurried organising of air units. Aircraft were prepared and ground staff were urged to get the maximum number of aircraft serviceable, and to this end they worked into the night. There would be very little time for New Year celebrations among the groundcrews, while pilots were virtually forbidden to celebrate.

Finally the last code-word, 'Hermann', was received and the attack time given as 9.20 a.m. With no New Year parties in Luftwaffe Messes, there was the slight consolation that the British and American airmen might well be celebrating and, therefore, be at a disadvantage the next morning. That the German air assault was planned for New Year's Day was coincidental. It was merely that it was the first day that the weather cleared and a cold but bright dawn was forecast.

*

Activity on Luftwaffe airfields was tremendous. Briefings were held at various times depending on how a commander interpreted the need for secrecy. Some held briefings in the early evening, others nearer dawn.

Some fighter units who were to fly in company with another unit had to fly to a new base, others had to co-ordinate briefings with these other units. There was even one group of long-nosed Focke Wulf 190 D9s airborne and about to do battle. III/JG54 took off from its base at Varnelbusch to fly a patrol behind Bastogne and had found a formation of American B24 Liberators. They jettisoned their long-range tanks but then received the order to return to base. Owing to weather, most of these pilots landed at Achmer from where they had then to fly to Furstenau where they were to join and fly with I/JG26. Once down they were driven to

I/JG26's monastic HQ at 10 p.m. where they and JG26 pilots were briefed by Major Karl Borris, a Knight's Cross holder and Commanding Officer of JG26's I Gruppe.

The pilots of JG3 were briefed in the late afternoon at their bases at Paderborn, Lippespringe and Gütersloh. Wine and drink was forbidden, many pilots simply going to bed to grab what rest they could. Their ground crews prepared their Messerschmitts and Focke Wulfs, even taking out the FuG 25 sets (the German equivalent of the RAF's IFF – identification-friend-or-foe) on grounds of security.

II/JG54 pilots were briefed at 6 p.m., great care being given on the route to be flown to their target airfield. On the airfield stood a Ju88 night-fighter, the reason for its presence being now understood. This was duplicated on other airfields, for within the plan was a scheme for each fighter group to be led towards its target by Ju88 night-fighters. Their job was to navigate the fighters to a jumping-off point. As the whole attack was to be flown in silence and at low level, this navigational help was an important factor.

Oberstleutnant Johann Kogler briefed his JG6 when his orders were received. He used the aid of a table-top model of the target, which as events were to prove, was to be a complete waste of time.

The last few days of 1944 and the first few in the new year brought us pilots a few surprises. Early one afternoon curfew and prohibition were ordered. No New Year celebrations were to take place either. After our evening meal our group was called to a meeting. The squadrons were assigned operations; JG6 got Volkel for its destination. The squadrons leaders instructed their flight leaders. I was one of Oberfeldwebel Rieper's crew. Rieper was an old hand of the former ZG/26 Gruppe. Our part of the mission was to hold off any enemy aircraft. After the meeting we all went to bed.

Leutnant Konrad Dammeier, JG6

The Richthofen Geschwader, JG2, were briefed in the early hours of 1st January with little time to go into too much detail. It was a case of 'Follow me and stay with me!'

So the briefings went on. Some better than others, but often quite detailed. Maps had been prepared in quantity and given out to the pilots. Many of these were later found by the RAF after the raid and it seemed obvious that a good deal of effort had gone into their production. The RAF also found several printed cards on dead or captured Luftwaffe pilots which, depending on the translation, read:

To be carried in aircraft:
1. Everything counts!
2. At the jumping off point switch on your radio.
    Switch on station keeping lights.
    Switch on armament.
3. Maintain discipline in the attack.
4. Pay particular attention for damaged and burning aircraft! Count them in your score!
5. Do not forget before every run-up to test your weapons!
6. Keep a sharp look-out for airfields during your approach and return flights and make a note of their location!

Thus the scene was set for the Germans' great air battle on the British 2nd TAF and American 9th TAF bases. The great gamble was on. Those Luftwaffe pilots who were able, slept, while others waited restlessly for the time to go out to their aircraft. Take-off was scheduled for dawn. They would be called shortly beforehand.

At least one Gruppe of JG26 had a party – they were going to celebrate the New Year come what may. Leutnant Gunther Bloemertz recorded this in his book.[1]

We danced, laughed and drank until quite suddenly – on a gesture from the Kommandeur – the orchestra stopped playing: the saxaphone's sweet sensual notes died away, but the drummer, who was dull with drowsiness, continued for a few seconds to beat out his ominous rhythem.

'*Meine Herren,*' the Kommandeur's voice rang out across the silent room, 'we will check our watches. Take-off in fifty minutes!'

[1] *Heaven Next Stop*, William Kimber, 1953.

Leaving the girls where they were, we walked in silence to the cars. There were no heartrending scenes – nothing more, perhaps, than a hurried kiss, or a tragic look exchanged! Outside on the airfield our aircraft, sixty in all, stood waiting in the fresh, powdery snow as if on parade. In the control room we heard the Kommandeur's final briefing. It was a small room and we had to crowd round the tactical chart to find out what we could about the plan. Among the unfamiliar faces of several airmen who had landed here the day before, I noted the child-like features of a seventeen or eighteen-year-old, and reflected that some of the new pilots whom the Kommandeur had brought in for this operation would not return from it either. I stamped the features of this seventeen-year-old on my mind, to remember him if he didn't come back.

Changing into our leather flying suits, we stood drawing nervously at our cigarettes, only Vogel and Meyer II having come on from dinner in their Mess uniforms. These two now climbed into their aircraft in white shirts, patent leather shoes and white gloves. 'If we have to stay behind on the other side,' Vogel called irrepressibly, 'the Tommies'll know they have to deal with superior people. Oh yes, they'll admit all right that the Knights of Abbeville are still going strong.'

'X' minus 30 – the moment of take-off was approaching. Soon a hundred and twenty thousand horse-power from sixty aircraft thundered across the airfield, blowing the virgin snow of New Year's Eve into whirling clouds with their take-off.

The pilots of the III Gruppe of JG54 were in bed early but most were unable to sleep. All knew that something really big was about to begin and that on the following day a number of them were sure to die. Willi Heilmann recorded:[1]

We were woken at 3 o'clock in the morning and half an hour later all the pilots of Fighter Wing 26 and III Fighter Wing 54 were assembled in the messroom. Captain Worner came in with the ominous envelope already open in his hand.

[1] *Alert in the West*, William Kimber, 1955.

'To make it brief, boys, we're taking off with more than 1,000 fighters at the crack of dawn to prang various airfields on the Dutch-Belgium border.' Then followed details of take-off, flying order, targets and return flights. Brussels was the target for III/JG54. The whole mission was to be carried out at less than 600 feet until we reached the targets so that the enemy ground stations could not pick us up. To this end radio silence was the order until we reached the target.

We were given a magnificent breakfast, cutlets, roast beef and a glass of wine. For sweets there were pastries and several cups of fragrant coffee. The last minutes before we were airborne seemed an eternity. Nervous fingers stubbed out half-smoked cigarettes. In a scarlet glow the sun slowly appeared above the horizon to the east. It was 8.25 a.m. And then the armada took off ...

*

Not every take-off was perfect. II/JG4 at Babenhausen lost a FW190 A-8 on take-off. As Feldwebel Altpeper's FW190 D-9 (Yellow 4) became airborne at Ettingshausen, it developed engine trouble. Black smoke poured from it, followed by flames. Fritz Altpeper of the 4th Staffel of II/JG2 did not break radio silence nor did he bale out, but crashed to his death near Dierdorf. At Delmenhorst Oberleutnant Pfeiderer, Yellow 1, of I/JG6, took off in his FW190 A-8, lost flying speed and dived into the trees surrounding airfield being killed instantly.

Finally all were airborne and setting courses for their assigned targets. The fighter formations latched onto their Junkers 88 or Junkers 188 'pathfinder' aircraft and later a handful of Me262 jets joined some of the formations. As the watery winter sun began to make its slow climb into the sky, its gentle rays gleaming on the Christmasy snow-covered landscape, the fighters flew towards Belgium and Holland. Operation Bodenplatte was about to begin.

CHAPTER TWO

Happy New Year

Despite its being New Year's Day and the celebrations that had occurred the previous evening and night, for the pilots of the RAF and USAAF in Europe Monday, 1st January 1945, was treated little differently from any other day. Indeed, with the danger of the Ardennes offensive uppermost on everyone's mind from air commanders down to squadron personnel, the desperate needs of the soldiers on the battlefront were of paramount importance.

The recent bad weather had now begun to clear. Although in some parts of Holland and Belgium the bad weather lingered on, on this first day of the year it was rapidly clearing elsewhere. During the night of the 31st it was predicted that in some areas the next day, though not perfect, the weather would be good enough to get aircraft into the air. Missions needed to be flown over the Ardennes and Allied air presence needed to be in evidence elsewhere, especially in dealing with German road and rail transport supporting the battle zone.

On the majority of 2nd TAF and 9th TAF bases men were rising early in anticipation of a day's operational flying. At Volkel the Tempest pilots of No 3 Squadron were shaken out of their slumbers at an early hour and they would be the first RAF squadron airborne on this day. One pilot woken early was Pilot Officer R.W. Pottinger.

Ron Pottinger was nearing the end of his tour with 3 Squadron, having been with it for nearly two years. He had flown all through the V1 threat in the summer of 1944 and had shot down six of these dangerous flying bombs. He had been on Christmas leave in England, and like others fortunate enough to get UK leave in England over the festive season, found some difficulty in getting back to his unit. The usual way was to travel to and from Eindhoven to RAF Northolt by Dakota but the bad weather stopped this method of travel. Therefore, he was left to get back as best he could, managing to hitch a lift by Naval MTB to Ostend and thence by road back to Volkel.

He finally arrived at 3 Squadron's billet – an empty seminary in Uden, some ten miles out from Volkel airfield – and following his long and tiring journey, wanted little else but to get to bed. He also found that news of the end of his tour had been received, so could look forward to returning home within a day or so. For the time being his war was over!

However, he was allowed little rest that night. There was a squadron party in full swing and at midnight he was pulled out of his bed and made to join in the singing before being allowed to slip away back to his bed. Early the next morning he was roused by a Tasmanian pilot, who, feeling the effects of the party, asked Ron to take his place on a dawn show that had been called. Despite being tour-expired, he agreed to fly for his colleague, but when the CO found out, he put Ron down as spare pilot. Spare pilots were needed in case any of the other aircraft developed engine trouble on or before take-off. This was not an uncommon occurrence with the Tempest V which was also a cow to get started. Only a few weeks earlier Squadron Leader Johnny Heap DFC, the experienced CO of 274 Squadron and his Number 2, both suffered engine failure on take-off. His No 2 did the unforgiveable, turned back, bellied in, skidding along on his two underwing drop tanks and survived. Johnny Heap did the correct thing, attempted a straight-ahead forced landing, hit a low wall and was killed.

Shortly after 8 a.m., Squadron Leader K.F. 'Jimmy' Thiele DSO, DFC and bar, the New Zealand CO of 3 Squadron, led eight Tempests out onto the runway and took to the air. All eight aircraft roared into the dawn sky, leaving Ron Pottinger to taxi the spare kite back to the dispersal area. Jimmy Thiele was a former bomber pilot, having received his decorations during two operational tours with 467 (NZ) Squadron. He was now on his first tour as a fighter pilot. His squadron's assignment on this morning was to fly an armed reconnaissance mission to the Paderborn area.

*

Some ninety miles to the south-west of Volkel, at the base at St Denis-Westrem, near Ghent, the Polish pilots of 308 Squadron were preparing to take-off on an early show. Flying fighter-bomber Spitfire IXs, all three squadrons of Group Captain Alexsander Gabszewicz's 131 Polish Wing were due off soon after dawn. 308, under Squadron Leader Karol Pniak VM, KW, DFC, were first off at 8.15 a.m. to attack a ferry and buildings near Wounstrecht. One pilot who stood down was Flying Officer Wlodzimierz 'Jimmy' Link, who had gone down with a cold and sore throat, and so stayed in bed. His place was taken by Flying Officer Tadeusz Szlenkier.

Number 308's sister squadrons, 317 and 302, commanded by Squadron Leader Marian Chelmecki KW and Squadron Leader Marian Duryasz KW, DFC, took off at 8.35 and 8.40 a.m. respectively. 317 was to attack targets at Werkendam on the Waal, 302 to fly an Armed Recce: to the Lyons-Amersfoort-Zwolle-Appeldoorf areas.

Meanwhile, at Eindhoven, air activity was also beginning. At 8.20 a.m. Flying Officer R.H. 'Bob' Laurence led four Typhoons of 439 Canadian Squadron away from the airfield to fly a weather reconnaissance to the American battle front at St Vith.

Back at Volkel, the Typhoon wing (No 121) commanded by Wing Commander W. Pitt-Brown DFC, was starting their day by sending 175 and 184 Squadrons out to do battle. They began to taxi out shortly before 8.30. Six of 175 Squadron took off on an armed recce: to Osnabrück, and although Flight Sergeant Ashman's engine cut out, Warrant Officer R.H. Webber (in MN988) took his place. A short while later Flying Officer H. Pearce (MN425) dropped out and had to return to Eindhoven. 184's six Typhoons all got away on another armed recce: to the Enschede-Rheine-Osnabrück and Münster area at 8.35.

At the Canadian base at Heesch, 2nd TAF's most northerly airfield, 402 RCAF Squadron put up two Spitfire XIVs to fly a defensive patrol towards Volkel, while 411 Squadron prepared to fly an armed recce-cum-fighter sweep, over the Osnabrück-Münster area.

Sixty miles due south, at Ophoven, 41 Squadron under Squadron Leader D.I. Benham DFC, AFC (RM791) were airborne at 8.35 a.m. to fly down to the Rhine north of Coblenz, looking for road transport or railway targets. The Spitfire XIVs of 610 and 350 Belgium Squadron were also airborne at between 8.50 and 9 a.m. to fly fighter patrols to the Malmédy region.

*

Reconnaissance missions too were under way. No 2 Squadron at Gilze-Reijen, a few miles north west of Eindhoven, sent off two Spitfire XIVs at 8.29 on a tactical reconnaissance (Tac/R) mission to the Leeuwen-Hilversum-Arnhem areas, the two pilots being Flight Lieutenant J.M. Young (RM805) and Flight Lieutenant E.J. Packwood (RM708). At 8.32, 268 Squadron sent out two Mustangs, piloted by Flight Lieutenant A.D. Mercer (FD560) and Flight Lieutenant J.B. Lyke (FD558), to fly a Tac/R mission towards Utrecht.

> I was called around 6.45 a.m. (wonder if we had a hangover after New Year's Eve?). I'm not a breakfast eater in the early morning, so except for a couple of mugs of tea had nothing else. We were living in the old German officers' mess, about two miles from the airfield. Probably briefed around 7.30. It would have been early on 1st January in case any specific target information came in overnight. John Lyke and I were the first pair off (I believe the only pair in the morning) and the general idea was to cross into enemy territory as soon as it was light enough to see.
>
> *Flight Lieutenant A.D. Mercer, 268 Squadron*

Meantime, at Melsbroek, just outside Brussels, the Mitchell wing, comprising 98, 180 and 320 Squadrons, were all airborne to attack the road communication centre at Dasburg. Also at Melsbroek was 69 Squadron flying night reconnaissance Wellington XIIIs, commanded by Wing Commander M.J.A. Shaw. He too had been in England over the Christmas period but had arrived back on the 31st December.

> I had flown back to Melsbroek on the 31st having spent Christmas at home in England. I wasn't on operations that night probably because of the bad weather – we had had a lot of bad

weather. The announcement of the award of my DSO came through that evening and so we had a bit of a party – to put it mildly!

Wing Commander M.J.A. Shaw, OC 69 Squadron

Mike Shaw may have been rather apprehensive about the morning of 1st January, for he had, in a moment of weakness, agreed to air test a Short Stirling four-engined bomber. This particular Stirling had flopped down badly shot-up on Melsbroek after the Arnhem do back in September. For three months the ground crews had been working on it to get it airworthy again. The work had finally been completed by the 31st but it needed air testing. Although Mike Shaw had never flown a four-engined aircraft, he had read through the pilot's notes and felt he could manage it. Mike Shaw recalls:

By the end of the year the Stirling was repaired and rebuilt. On my return to Melsbroek, the MU people said they were going to give it an air test. Nobody was forthcoming so I said I didn't mind having a go. I'd never flown one, never flown anything larger than a Wellington, but they had some pilot's notes. So I got in and started up the engines and taxied it round from our dispersal, where it had stood since September, (we had actually built our dispersal around this drunken-looking Stirling) to the Repair and Inspection hangar for it to have its final service checks. It was agreed that I'd fly it the next morning – 1st January.

Flight Lieutenant Hugh Tudor was at Melsbroek with 140 Mosquito Squadron. He had been grounded since Christmas Eve through bad weather, indeed had been lucky to get down at Melsbroek on that night.

I landed in thick fog when everyone else was diverted, but I wanted to go to a party! I pretended I had radio failure and landed entirely on a time circuit and they took thirty minutes to find where I came to a halt on the airfield, as there was no way of taxi-ing in.

Flight Lieutenant H.M.H. Tudor, 140 Squadron

With the weather clearing, Hugh Tudor planned an early flight on the morning of 1st January, a flight to England.

*

With air activity over several Allied air bases increasing as it became lighter, other units were ordered to prepare for operations. At Eindhoven six rocket-armed Typhoons of 137 Squadron took off at 8.50 a.m. led by Flight Lieutenant G. Clubley DFC, detailed to carry out an armed recce over the Minden area. It was George Clubley's first operation with 137 Squadron, for he had left 181 Squadron (in the same 124 Wing at Eindhoven) only the day before to take command of a flight in 137. He was an experienced Typhoon pilot, having flown with 181 Squadron since before D-Day.

Number 168 Squadron was another Typhoon unit on Eindhoven, commanded by Squadron Leader L.H. Lambert DFC. He too had only just returned from England.

> We'd been moved into the Convent on the outskirts of Eindhoven with the nuns still in residence, although we never saw them at all. They occupied the entire upper floor, we the lower. They would come down when we had left for the airfield, and clean up everything and go into our rooms. Any socks or bits of underwear left about were taken and washed etc. From time to time we'd leave items of food for them, as food was still in short supply for the Dutch population.
>
> I arrived back from England on the night of 31st December, having had to hitch-hike back because of the weather. There was a bit of a party going on but being tired I was in bed by midnight, but nobody was really in the mood for a big party, for everyone felt pretty tense about what was going on in the Bastogne salient. It was thought that the Germans might break through unless the weather cleared and we could give the ground troops the air support we'd been able to give them from Normandy onwards.
>
> The weather signs seemed good and most people were prepared for an early call the next morning. In the event, we were called at 4 a.m. and told that the weather was clearing. We

had a very careful briefing because none of us had been to the attack area before owing to the fog. We were told where we would find an American liaison officer, and given radio frequencies etc, and prepared for take-off.

Squadron Leader L.H. Lambert, OC 168 Squadron

The Typhoon squadrons at Antwerpe Deurne too were up and preparing for early operations:

On the 1st January all our squadrons had been called for an early morning briefing and I recall that it was still dark when we made our way to the briefing room. I believe that a Wing target had been selected but that briefing was interrupted by a power failure and all but one squadron left the room to be briefed in turn by temporary lighting.

The next unexpected delay was due to the one runway being covered with ice and all take-offs were held up. Most pilots remained around the briefing area or their squadron's accommodation very nearby. The briefing room was almost at the foot of a railway embankment which ran east of the airfield on the side where the Typhoon squadrons were parked, not particularly well dispersed, because of the number of aircraft (80 Typhoons) and the very poor state of the grass areas due to a great deal of rain.

Flight Lieutenant S.J. Eaton, 257 Squadron

Back at Volkel, the Tempests of 56 Squadron took off at 8.55 a.m. to fly an Armed Recce: over the Paderborn region while the New Zealanders of 486 (NZ) Squadron prepared to fly their Tempests on a similar operation to Hanover. They were due to take off shortly after 9 o'clock. Their CO was Squadron Leader A.E. Umbers DFC, who had previously flown with 3 Squadron and been a very successful pilot against V1 flying bombs the previous summer. Umbers had personally destroyed twenty-eight of them. He led eight of his men off just minutes before the Germans were reported at nearby Eindhoven.

At Maldegem airfield, the New Zealanders of 485 (NZ) Squadron were due to take their Spitfire IXs off on a mission at

8.45 but the airfield was declared unserviceable and ice-bound at daybreak and so the show was cancelled. As it proved, it was just as well for they would have been taking off just as the Germans struck.

It was not only at squadron level that men were up and about. Air Vice-Marshal Harry Broadhurst DSO, DFC, AFC, commanding 83 Group, was up early that morning, like every morning.

My home was in the Philips House in Eindhoven and my Fieseler Storch was kept on the first fairway of the Golf Course outside the house. My office was in a Philips building near the airfield. Everything was Philips at Eindhoven.

I would normally be called just before dawn and would be given a run-down on the weather forecast and proposed operations for the day. After a cup of tea I would either drive to my office or get into my Storch and fly to see the Wings, the GCC (Group Control Centre), or Army HQ (General Dempsey) etc: On 1st January I went to my office, arriving between 7.30 and 8 a.m. We had no party on New Year's Eve – we had celebrated two days earlier after a conference at my HQ!

Perhaps it was just as well he went to his office and was not flying between airfields in his German Storch aeroplane on this day of all days.

*

Across the Channel in England, other air operations were being implemented. New Year's Day or not, the air war was still being taken to the Germans.

RAF Bomber Command had planned a raid on the Dortmund-Ems canal with over 100 Lancaster heavy bombers, Take-off times were set at around 7.30 a.m. – the raid would take place in daylight. Mosquitos of 8 (Pathfinder) Group were to attack railway tunnel targets in the Bonn-Coblenz area. No 9 Squadron at Bardney briefed ten of its crews as part of the major raid of the day. On the ground there was a moderate frost at first with light winds. As the Lancasters took off, two crashed. Lancaster NG252, piloted by Flying Officer C. Newton, exploded, killing all except Pilot Officer R.C. Flynn, the Canadian bomb-aimer. PD368, with Flying

Officer J.W. Buckley (Australian) at the controls, also came to grief but the crew escaped with the exception of Sergeant K.E. Dawes, the flight engineer.

Number 467 (RAAF) Squadron at Waddington was also part of the Lancaster force. They had had a party the night before and those who actually got to bed were not woken but rather pulled from their beds when the operational orders came down from Group.

The 8 Group Mossies took off earlier than their big brothers, around 6.30-6.40 a.m. 128 Squadron at RAF Wyton lost one of its sixteen aircraft on take-off. PF411 (M5-B) blew up killing its crew of Flight Lieutenant L.C.R. Wellstead and Flight Lieutenant G.P. Mullen.

These operations from England did not affect nor were they affected by the Luftwaffe's attacks but were part of the day's air activities. Yet these operations had caused the first RAF deaths of 1945 – there were more to come.

The first Luftwaffe losses had already occurred some hours earlier. Over the Continent American night-fighters were in action in the early hours. Between 00.25 a.m. and 3.25 a.m. Lieutenant Eugene D. Axtell of the 422nd Night Fighter Squadron had attacked and destroyed a Junkers Ju188 bomber, and Lieutenant Edward A. Schlueter of the 415th NFS had destroyed a Messerschmitt 110 night fighter.

Back at Eindhoven, Corporal Ted sadler, i/c the guard detail at dispersal, heard the Canadians from their part of the airfield celebrating by shooting small arms fire into the air. As he listened and watched the dark sky:

I heard the sound of a very low-flying, slow moving aircraft approaching, and it passed within feet of myself and LAC Osborne. We were able to see it was a Fieseler Storch. Unfortunately my sten-gun was in the guard hut, so it passed over unmolested, but it seemed quite feasible to have shot down this spy 'plane'.

Corporal E.W.J. Sadler, 403 R & S Unit.

CHAPTER THREE

Volkel

The time planned for the German attack to begin was 9.20 a.m. It is fairly obvious that even with the best will in the world it was not going to be possible to keep to this time at every target airfield. RAF records too do not make it absolutely clear when each base was attacked; times, even by units on the same base, recorded by either wing or squadron diarist vary – sometimes considerably. What is attempted here is to record the best time from the available evidence.

Number 121 Wing at Volkel records that German fighters and fighter-bombers appeared over their airfield shortly after nine o'clock, while 122 Wing stated that the attack began '... around 9 a.m., when the airfield was beaten up in a half-hearted fashion by Me109s, FW190s and Mean262.'

Volkel was the assigned target for Oberstleutnant Johann Kogler's JG6. All three Gruppen were involved, I and II with Focke Wulf 190 A-8s, III Gruppe flying Messerschmitt 109 G-10s and G-14s. They were based in the north of Germany, the three Gruppen commanded by Hauptmann Ewald Trost, Hauptmann Johannes Naumann (Knights Cross) and Major Helmut Kuhle. Trost was to lead the attack as first wave, Naumann would be the second wave, while Kuhle's fighters would act as top cover, then be the third wave.

I really cannot remember what time the alarms were set for but I can remember that the U v D went over and the roll-call was an hour later. After that I said to my room-mate, 'Now the whole thing will go wrong.' When we were woken up the next morning we were lively very quickly. Whether the technical staff got any

sleep at all is questionable. While we were eating breakfast the machines were being prepared and run-up. After a long wait the green flare at last went up, giving the go-ahead to start. While the (Pathfinder) Ju88 circled above, our FW190 A-8s soared into the air. Until now everyone had been preoccupied with his particular job in the aircraft and the Ju88 was there to navigate and show us the way.

Leutnant Konrad Dammeier, JG6

After losing Oberleutnant Pfleiderer on take-off, the fighters assembled over Quakenbrück, then headed westward – about seventy machines, height 500 feet. Reaching the southern tip of the Zuider Zee, Oberfeldwebel Walter Jung went down, possibly after collision with another aeroplane. Following the Ju88 night-fighter they carried on to Spakenburg but 'the Junkers' crew made a navigational error and missed the turning point, taking the whole Geschwader too far to the west. When the error was discovered and still being under radio silence, the German formation began to split up. Few actually found Volkel. The pilots flying low over the dawn countryside were soon lost. Some found Eindhoven, others stumbled upon Heesch. Volkel was almost untouched and according to one report only nine German fighters and one Me262 put in an appearance over the airfield.

As the Ju88 came to the end of its assignment it gave us the signal and turned back. After being on our own for a short while, we soon saw an enemy aircraft. It was flying very low. Then somewhat to my right an aircraft fell to the ground in flames. That could have been the actual enemy aircraft. With a feeling deep down that we had lost the actual enemy aircraft we were pursuing, we proceeded on our way towards Volkel.

The first confusion soon came. As it turned out later, we had made some mistakes with our navigation. What had gone wrong up till now had caused us unnecessary losses and the real mission hadn't even begun yet. Now an airfield was in sight. We flew in and attacked. According to our briefing our ceiling of 109 metres should have been higher than the enemy would be at. Instead, Spitfires were on the spot and we had counted on an element of surprise! This was not to be. Even the gunners were in for a few surprises. We were then being fired on from all sides. It was complete chaos. After two further attempts with varying success, Ofw Rieper turned us away in the direction of Gartenzaur. There was no disturbance from the enemy on the journey home. During the course of the day the rest of the fighters returned in dribs and drabs; of the nine pilots that set out from my Staffel, only three returned.

Leutnant Konrad Dammeier, JG6

On the airfield, Ron Pottinger, the spare pilot for 3 Squadron's early patrol, had returned to dispersal. Climbing down from his Tempest, he stood chatting to the ground crews when the handful of German fighters came in. Everyone dived for cover, few having experienced a strafing attack before. Ron dived into a tent, grabbed a rifle and came out again, but by the time he had done so the attack seemed to be over. His lasting recollection is of a seemingly very large Focke Wulf fighter roaring low over his head.

Two other pilots of 3 Squadron, Pilot Officer R.S. Adcock and nineteen-year-old Pilot Officer H.J. 'Bill' Bailey,[1] both Australians, were in their Tempests on the airfield and had the nasty experience of being strafed by a FW190, but neither was hit.

Working on the airfield was LAC Donald Macdonald, a Fitter IIA with No 121 Wing.

During the winter of 1944-45 I was stationed at Volkel – a former German airfield near Nijmegen, with Eindhoven the nearest town. My job was in R & I (Repair and Inspection) and did major overhauls and damage repair on 'Rockphoons' of the Wing.

On the morning of New Year's Day I had arrived at the blister hangar on a clear frosty morning. It was just after nine o'clock when the first wave of Messerschmitts came over, strafing the kites on the ground. By the time they turned to make their next attack, I had taken shelter in an old large bomb hole, the water in the bottom having frozen and was covered in ice. As they came

[1] Bailey had scored 11 V1 victories over England, Adcock 2.

back and forth I cross the ice and took cover from the direction they were coming. There seemed to be no opposition and when they left, it was with a sigh of relief that I again recrossed the ice, but this time the ice gave way and I went straight through, being immersed in cold, muddy water almost to the waist!

A short time after the attack a strange aeroplane passed over, being engaged by our AA guns. We were informed that this was a German jet – the first one I had seen.

Leading Aircraftman D.N. Macdonald, R & I, 121 Wing

Twenty-year-old Dennis Brooks was an instrument repairer, attached to 6022 Servicing Echelon in 122 Wing at Volkel. He remembers:

The wing was flying Tempests and on 1st January they were due for a long range armed reconnaissance into Germany. As our planes were due to take off early, the duty crew were up early, sanding the runway because the weather, although fine, was very cold and icy. In fact I slipped off the wing of one aircraft on which I was doing a DI because the wing was covered with a thin sheet of ice.

After we had finished the daily inspections and the aircraft had taken off, I was charging up some oxygen cylinders – out in the open by the dispersal because things were a bit primitive. A friend of mine passing by stopped to ask me if I could sell him a postal order. While we were talking about this he looked over my shoulder and said something like, 'My God, a Jerry.' I said, 'Don't be stupid, it's a Tempest.' The FW190, that it actually was, proved me wrong by opening fire on us both. We both crashed to the ground and, with true survival of the fittest, tried to elbow each other out of a shallow depression that we were both trying to get into.

Some moments later all hell was let loose when Me109s and FW190s began attacking from different directions; the Bofors AA gun just by us was firing non-stop, and our Tempests were jettisoning long range fuel tanks full of petrol all over the 'drome.

Deciding that I had better get on with charging the oxygen bottles although I was more than a little scared as the oxygen rack was just standing out in the open near the main runway. It was just off the perimeter track and had no shelter whatsoever except for a small ditch. As I stood there an Me109 made a strafing run over our dispersal and I promptly dived into the ditch and crashed through the ice and into about nine inches of cold water. While I was laying there trying to make myself as big as a frog, an RAF sergeant from the AA gun, started to shake me by the shoulder and ask me if I could confirm that he had shot down the Me109. He seemed quite oblivious to the bullets (both ours and theirs), and the shrapnel that was falling about. His only concern was to claim a kill.

Soon our own planes were overhead and the Germans were quickly shot down or driven off, and soon our Tempests were coming in to be re-armed, refuelled and fitted with new oxygen bottles, so I was kept really busy. Our pilots told us that the whole German air force was in the sky and they were shooting them all down.

Some time later I met a cousin of mine stationed at Eindhoven and he gave me a graphic description of an airman standing and shooting at low level strafing Germans with a sten gun.

Leading Aircraftman D. Brooks, 6022 SE, 122 Wing

Damage to Volkel was practically nil, but with aircraft of the Tempest wing airborne it was a simple matter of calling them up on the radio to tell them of the presence of enemy aircraft. Having taken to the air only minutes before the attack began, 486 Squadron were quickly recalled having only reached Arnhem, the message initially informing them that many enemy fighters were over the Eindhoven area.

Squadron Leader A.E. 'Spike' Umbers (in EJ577) received the call from Kenway control telling him of eight FW190s on the deck in the Deurne area, then giving their location as Eindhoven. Dropping their jet (jettison) tanks, he led his men towards Eindhoven in a gradual descent from 9,000 feet. On approaching the area they could clearly see the airfield under attack and almost at once spotted three FW190s – two at 6,000 feet, the third on the deck, flying east towards Helmond. Ordering Green Section after the higher two, Umbers broke downwards to chase the lower 190.

He found himself closing too quickly and had to weave to reduce his approach speed. At 300 yards he opened fire, seeing strikes on the German's wing root and fuselage. The 190 began to stream smoke, white and black, then began to slow, Umbers having to pull up violently to avoid hitting it. As the New Zealander pulled up, he saw the 190 hit the ground and burst into flames.

As he then climbed away to the left he saw a Me109 about 1,500 yards away at 10 o'clock, flying east. The German pilot saw the Tempest and dived for the ground. Umbers followed and overtook it, closing to 600 yards, but then up ahead and a little to the left a gaggle of twenty Me109s came into view, also on the deck. The lone 109 turned to join these but as he did so, Umbers fired two short bursts from 400 yards. The 109 straightened up with the other formation but then it did a violent break to the right, then to the left. Umbers stayed with the weaving Messerschmitt, firing again, his bullets striking the fighter's cockpit, fuselage and wing root. Its starboard wheel flopped down as Umbers overshot it and when Umbers turned he saw the 109 hit the ground and explode.

Now out of ammunition, Umbers turned for Volkel, leading his Red Section home. As they arrived over their home field he saw a FW190 at zero feet crossing the aerodrome. Umbers ordered his Number 3, Flying Officer W.A.L. Trott (EJ606) to attack and as Bill Trott dived down from the sun, he saw the 190 firing into the middle of the airfield. Trott opened fire at 250 yards from behind, firing again at 150 yards and at 100 yards, seeing strikes all around the cockpit, starboard wing root and port side of the fuselage. As he hauled his Tempest over the German fighter, Trott saw its right wing crumble as it turned over onto its back and hit the ground where it exploded. It had probably been Bill Trott's successful combat that was mentioned in 121 Wing's diary: 'A Tempest patrolling to the east gave a superb demonstration of the fighter pilot's art, slowly turned and dived on a FW190. One short burst and the FW raised its nose, turned over and dived into the ground.' 174 Squadron also mentioned this action: 'A Tempest gave a perfect example of how it should be done.'[1]

[1] Bill Trott later received the DFC but was badly wounded in an attack on a train. A piece of shrapnel entered his lower abdomen, but despite the pain he flew more than 100 miles back to base. Spike Umbers was shot down and killed on 14th February 1945.

A few moments later Trott spotted a Me109 south of Volkel
flying east on the deck. He and his wingman, Pilot Officer C.J.
Steadman (EJ711) dived after it. Trott opened fire from 350 yards,
conserving his ammunition by firing in short bursts, but finally his
guns fell silent, though not before the 109 began to trail
white smoke – probably glycol. 'Butch' Steadman too was out of
ammo having attacked three Me262 jets which he saw flying near
the enemy fighters that Umbers had attacked earlier. The jets had
left him standing and then he had used up his ammunition firing at
a low flying FW190, which he damaged but then had to leave when
two other 190s attacked him. Now out of ammunition, both he and
Trott could only watch as the damaged Messerschmitt flew on,
even though Bill Trott tried to force the pilot down by flying low
over it.

Green Section, meantime, had gone after the other 190s, Pilot
Officer J.G. 'Gus' Hooper (EJ750) closing to 200 yards behind one
to fire. He saw no hits and his starboard guns stopped. Firing again
at point blank range with his port guns, he passed over the 190, he
saw a puff of smoke come from near the cockpit, then as he curved
round, saw the 190 explode in a field. Immediately he was attacked
by a Messerschmitt 109 but after a couple of turns with it, the
German pilot broke away. Hooper hit him with two bursts
which produced white smoke from its right wing, but then his
ammunition gave out.

Green Three, Pilot Officer C.J. 'Jim' Sheddan (EJ748) arrived
back in the circuit at Volkel when bursting AA shells at low altitude
in the direction of Nijmegen attracted his attention. Flying north on
the deck, he saw two FW190s and a 109 in line abreast flying north-
east at zero feet. Shedden closed in and fired at one of the Focke
Wulfs seeing his cannon shells explode around the cockpit and on
its right wing. The 190 pulled up into a steep turn and after a
complete turn straightened out as it attempted to crash land, but it
hit the ground violently, exploded and blew up into small pieces.

*

There were three Royal Air Force Regiment Squadrons defending
Volkel, 2809, 2834 and 2874. Initially they were unable to engage
the attacking fighters owing to RAF fighters taking off and others,

like 486 Squadron's Tempests, being overhead. Squadron Leader E. Whitehead's 2809 Squadron finally got going and one gun in B Flight under Sergeant Lawton, firing single rounds, hit a Me109 which appeared to be in difficulties as it flew out of range. Squadron Leader Neill's 2834 Squadron opened fire from all guns as targets presented themselves and claimed three destroyed and two damaged, recording that it was a 'wonderful tonic after months of no action'.

The Number Three gun post of 2874 Squadron saw AA fire to the south-west of the airfield and then an Me109G flew across the 'drome at a height of twenty to thirty feet dropping two bombs. It then flew off to the north but none of their guns was able to fire. At 9.25 a.m. an Me262 jet flew across Volkel from south to north at 5,000 feet. No 3 gun fired fifteen rounds but the jet flew off unscathed. Five minutes later a 109G came in from the south-west, its cannons blazing. Numbers 10 and 12 guns fired and the former gun crew claimed one hit, the 109 flying off losing height and leaving a smoke trail. It disappeared behind some trees and later a search revealed a crashed Messerschmitt. At 9.35 a FW190 was seen flying towards Volkel from the east at zero feet which appeared to be carrying one large bomb. No 3 gun obtained a hit on this fighter and as it went into a steep righthand climbing turn to the left, rising to 600 feet, several of the squadron's guns opened up on it, 7 and 8 guns claiming hits. Smoke poured from it and then a Tempest attacked it; it turned upside down and exploded in the air. A few minutes later five Me109s came in from the south-west at zero feet but only No 3 gun fired.

Little else occurred until 10.20 a.m. when another Me262 flew over the airfield at 10-12,000 feet, engaged again by No 3 gun but without success.

*

Jagdgeschwader 6's attack plan against Volkel completely miscarried owing to the navigational error and the fighters being split up all over Holland. Some reports indicate only three fighters actually located Volkel, and all were shot down. From RAF and RAFR reports there were clearly more than this, but whether all were from JG6 or from other units also unsure of their location will never be known. None of the attackers caused much damage in any event.

The New Zealand Tempest pilots had claimed five enemy fighters destroyed, one probably destroyed and three damaged, although not all over their base. Other Tempest squadrons scored combat kills but, as we shall see, these were all some distance away from Volkel.

Because it was only lightly attacked, it enabled aircraft of the Typhoon Wing to mount ordered missions. 174 Squadron were able to get a six-man armed recce sortie airborne at 9.15 a.m., their aircraft loaded with rockets and long range fuel tanks, heading for Osnabrück.

Nearing the bomb-line, Yellow One had a problem with his D-Door and with his No 2 returned to Volkel. As the other four 'Tiffies' crossed into Germany they spotted a lone Me262 jet streaking low towards Rheine. North-west of Osnabrück they found a train standing in a station and Flight Lieutenant B.F. Proddow and Flying Officer G.B. Chapman went down to score near misses with two rockets each. Pulling round for a second attack, the train moved forward under some trees. The two pilots raked the area with cannon fire which hit the waggons and set fire to a nearby signal box. Meanwhile, Flight Lieutenant H.R. Irwen and Flying Officer J.S. Kennon went down on a train further south and saw strikes during two passes. Later rockets were fired into a railway yard packed with locomotives and goods waggons, then Irwen and Kennon shot up another train near Münster. Kennon even spotted a Me109 and had a quick but ineffectual shot at it.

Number 274 Squadron got its Tempests off at 9.50, led by Squadron Leader A.H. Baird DFC, to fly out to the Paderborn area but this proved uneventful. The Typhoons of 175 and 184 Squadrons had got off before the German attack, and each unit blasted trains successfully. 175 claimed three at least, 184 badly damaging another near Enschede.

While this was going on the Tempests of 3 and 56 Squadrons which had also flown out on armed recces before the attack, were on their way back to Volkel when they heard of the problems back at base.

Four aircraft of 3 Squadron had already headed home with

empty guns from actions against trains and ground targets in the Paderborn-Bielefeld area, and Blue Section was now approaching Volkel at 2,000-3,000 feet. Blue Leader, Flying Officer D.J. Butcher, saw two columns of smoke when about five miles south-west of base. As the Tempest went down to investigate, control radioed to tell them to watch for eight enemy aircraft near Helmond. Butcher led his men in that direction and almost immediately spotted at least four Me109s flying south away from them, going through flak, on the deck. Even as he watched, Butcher saw one Messerschmitt hit by ground fire and go down. Butcher selected one of the other Messerschmitts while Flight Sergeant M.J.A. Rose went after another.

Butcher's 109G was flying to the extreme left and it broke to the left and headed east on the deck. Butcher followed and closed in to 200 yards, flying at 440 mph but not closing further. Opening fire from that range he saw strikes on the 109's fuselage which caused white smoke to stream back. The 109 now slowed, allowing Butcher to get in close to fire again. As he then broke hard to the right, the 109 hit the ground and caught fire. Behind Butcher came Warrant Officer D.R. Worley and he too opened up on the German fighter when Butcher broke away; Worley was also under fire from the ground, with tracer shells whistling past his Tempest, obviously directed at the Messerschmitt but close enough to be dangerous to the British pilot.

Maurice Rose spotted enemy fighters attacking ground targets and being engaged by ground fire. Rose circled above the flak and identified the Germans as Me109s. Selecting one he dived down as it flew out of the flak at low level. Closing to 200 yards he fired but saw no hits. With little ammunition left, Rose closed right in to 100 yards and let go the rest of his shells. As he then called up on the radio for anyone with ammo left to come and help him, the 109 pulled up to 1,500 feet, rolled over onto its back and the pilot baled out. The 109 crashed into a field near Lieshout and caught fire.[1]

Flight Lieutenant J.D. 'Jock' Ross, leading 56 Squadron's recce

[1] Maurice Rose had shot down 12 V1s in 1944. He was shot down and taken prisoner on 24th January 1945. Butcher was reported missing on 17th January.

to Paderborn, was also on his way home after strafing several
locomotives when he heard over the radio that 486 Squadron were
in action near Volkel. They opened up and returned towards Volkel
in a gradual descent. At 3,000 feet to the east of base they could see
no signs of the reported enemy. Pilot Officer D.E. Ness, a Canadian
(EJ536 US-B), dived to zero feet and saw two Tempests chasing a
109G southwards. As he watched he saw the 109 break away and
Ness opened up to go after it, chasing the 109 due south towards
Helmond. Closing in the 500 yards Dave Ness aimed a burst ahead
of the German trying to make the pilot turn, but the German kept
going. Gradually closing the gap, Ness fired at 200 yards and his
next burst produced strikes on the 109's fuselage and black smoke
poured from the engine. Ness continued firing but oil covered his
windscreen, forcing him to pull up.

Also in this chase was Pilot Officer H. 'Artie' Shaw (EJ548 US-
G) and as he saw Ness pull up he closed in and fired, seeing the
109's cowling had already been ripped open by Ness's fire. He fired
again as flames spurted from the rear engine; then he watched as
the pilot pushed the canopy open as his fighter's propeller began to
windmill. The German pilot, now too low to bale out, then
attempted to force-land but just as the 109 hit the ground it tore
through a row of trees, it turned over and broke up.

*

Volkel's Tempest pilots had destroyed a total of eight German
fighters, probably one more and damaged four others. Had other
returning Tempests not had empty guns from their train shoots
they would undoubtedly scored further successes. As it was, it was
a victory for Volkel with the bonus that little damage had been
inflicted to the base. Other airfields were not to get away so lightly.

*

The day was really a non-event for me. I seem to recall leading a
sortie to the Osnabrück area. Because of our high cruising speed
and ability to get up to 500 mph plus, very quickly in a dive, we
were used a great deal against German jets.

In the air we heard that the airfields were being attacked and I
felt a bit cheated at missing them because Huns were becoming a

rare sight at that time.

Volkel was lucky. We had several squadrons there, with aircraft packed together because the airfield had been heavily bombed by the Americans when it was occupied by the Germans and so it was a mass of bomb craters off the runways, perimeter track and hard standings.

As a sideline, as with a number of German airfields, there was a railway loading station in the area where their stores had been. The railway line ran from here absolutely straight and into Germany. Having been in the low-level business for much of the war I had a bee in my bonnet that one day the Luftwaffe would attack us low level down this railway line, so I always tried to ensure that three of my five squadrons were off the ground at first light on some operation or other, provided we were not involved in a Group operation. On the morning of 1st January, I myself was airborne and when I got back the show was over.

Wing Commander J.B. Wray, Leader 122 Wing

CHAPTER FOUR

Prelude at Eindhoven

Probably the first pilots on the Allied side to see the raiding German fighters were the Tac/R men of 35 Wing from Gilze-Reijen. It will be remembered that Flight Lieutenant J.M. Young and Flight Lieutenant E.J. Packwood in their Spitfire XIVs had taken off at 8.29 a.m. to recce the Leeuwen-Hilversum-Arnhem areas. From 268 Squadron, Flight Lieutenant A.D. Mercer and Flight Lieutenant J.B. Lyke had been airborne at 8.32 a.m., heading for Utrecht in their Mustangs.

At 9.05, Packwood was flying at 5,000 feet west of Amersfoort with his leader when he spotted two Ju88s with what he assumed was an escort of thirty plus Me109s and FW190s flying west. The two Spitfire pilots immediately turned up-sun of the enemy formation, then dived down on the rear section. Packwood attacked a Messerschmitt from dead astern and from slightly above. The German pilot took no evasive action as Packwood closed in from 400 to 150 yards and pumped a five-second burst of cannon and machine-gun fire into him. Packwood saw his fire striking the cockpit and fuselage of the 109 and then it began to disintegrate; the right wing broke away. Then the 109 flicked over onto its back and hit the ground in flames. Already Flight Lieutenant Young had put a call to base warning them of this enemy raiding force which at this stage, looked obviously like a small bombing force strongly escorted by fighters.

This was exactly the same thought that passed through the mind of Dave Mercer when he spotted three Ju188s escorted by five FW190s over Utrecht, at zero feet, at 9.15 a.m.

We were operating initially around 5-6,000 feet and north of

Utrecht when I spotted a formation of aircraft flying very low –
three Ju188s escorted by five FW190s. I informed my base
(Longbow) at Gilze-Reijen of these aircraft which was probably
the first indication of what was to come. I then dived into the
attack and shot down one of the 188s, confirmed by my No 2. We
stayed down very low and headed back towards our own lines –
could not see any sense in sticking around with the 190s after us.

After a few minutes our base called on the radio – 'Action over
base', repeated several times. I saw lots of smoke in the distance
and headed towards it; this was not my base but another airfield
in the area which I believe was Eindhoven. They were getting a
real pasting, the airfield was covered in smoke, Bofors guns going
full blast, and FW190s buzzing around like flies. John Lyke lost
contact with me in the mêlée. I picked up a 190 and closed in on
him. He still had his bomb aboard, but when I pressed the
trigger nothing happened – used all my shells on the 188. He had
not seen me coming and as I had excess speed I went alongside
him and when he saw me I remember giving him the V-sign. He
broke away and tossed his bomb off, harmlessly into a field; he
probably never realised how near he had been to getting the
chop.

John Lyke returned to base and landed. Things seemed to
have quietened down by then, though not quite, as John was
promptly shot up on the runway. He jumped out smartly and
escaped injury although his Mustang was damaged. By the time
I got back to base things had finished and I landed without any
problems apart from being a bit low on fuel. However, I had
finished up way south of my airfield (and my map!) and when I
was returning, having got a 'steer' and flying for endurance – low
revs and lean mixture, I nearly got clobbered by four American
Mustangs, who probably had heard of the troubles and were
coming for a look-see, too late by then of course, all the activity
had died down. They were the Mustangs with the Packard
engine, all silver, and me being an Allison Mustang, all
camouflaged for low level, they must have thought I was a
Me109. I had to do a lot of wing waggling and showing of
roundels before they left me alone.

Flight Lieutenant A.D. Mercer, 268 Squadron

Dave Mercer's Ju188 had crashed into a wood with its right engine burning fiercely. What his recollections do not mention is that after scaring the 190 pilot, he chased three more Focke Wulfs away from the airfield. Luckily they were not inclined to stay and fight. His whole impression was that the Germans' attack was without any kind of co-ordination and each fighter he saw seemed to go in individually.

*

At Gilze-Reijen itself, an estimated sixteen German fighters made an attack some time after nine o'clock – Me109s, FW190s and Me262s.

RAF Regiment AA Squadrons timed the attack as 9.22, lasting until 10.05. Eighteen guns of 2736 and 2845 Squadrons fired 806 rounds, claiming three destroyed and five damaged, including two Me109s whose remains were found soon after the attack, on the south and south-west sides of the base, and one Me262 jet. One 109 hit had been the fighter which had strafed John Lyke's Mustang. Damaged in its left wing, the 109 continued away to the west. No 4 Squadron RAF recorded seeing one Me109 hit by the cockpit as it went over the airfield and seen belching smoke as it flew off. One German airman baled out and was locked up in the guardroom.

Number 2736 Squadron was commanded by Squadron Leader J.F.A.H. Lindsay DCM, MM. Regiment gunners suffered three wounded, one officer and two other ranks. Some damage was also done to Regiment motor transport.

Anti-personnel bombs were dropped on the aerodrome, some landing close to flying control. No 123 Wing was in the process of moving from Gilze to Chièvres on 1st January and, of the holding party still there, seven men received slight injuries during the attack. One of the wing's Typhoons was also damaged.

No 164 Squadron, commanded by Squadron Leader Remy van Lierde DFC (Belgian), had landed its Typhoons at Gilze on the 31st, and was in the process of going to Chièvres, but some of its Typhoons were caught on the ground, one of which was destroyed. A few others received minor damage but one was Category B. 183 Squadron moved early and missed the attack and the third squadron in the wing, 198, were already at Chièvres which was not attacked. In fact 198 flew an operation to Euskirchen at 9.20 a.m., led by the CO, Squadron Leader N.J. Durrant (JR505). They shot up a train and later found a lone FW190. Flight Lieutenant F.B. Lawless (MN951 TP-A), a New Zealander, closed in but before he could open fire on the German fighter it was hit by ground fire, bursting into flames as it hit the ground. Everyone sympathised with the New Zealander for had he only fired his guns, he could have shared in the claim for one FW190 'confirmed'.

A small convoy of vehicles of the wing, moving by road from Gilze to Chièvres was machine-gunned from the air by a German fighter looking for an airfield. Corporals Eastwood and Bunyard were both injured in its attack.[1]

*

Jagdgeschwader 3 (Udet) had as its main target the large Allied airfield at Eindhoven, the home of eleven 2nd TAF Squadrons and 82 Group's Communication Squadron. JG3's three Gruppen, I, III and IV were based at Paderborn, Lippespringe and Gütersloh, led and commanded by Oberstleutnant Heinz Bär, one of the Luftwaffe's top *Experten* who to date had scored 202 victories in air combat. 'Pritzl' Bär had been in action since the start of the war, flying against the British in the west and in North Africa, and then on the Russian front. He held the Knight's Cross with Oak Leaves and Swords.

Acting CO of I Gruppe (FW190s) was Oberleutnant Seidel, III Gruppe's CO was Hauptmann Karl-Heinze Langer, Knight's Cross, and IV Gruppe was led by Leutnant Müller as acting CO. Both latter units had Me109Gs. The Jagdgeschwader pilots had their final briefing at 7 a.m. with take-off at 8.30. The aircraft formed up over Lippstadt before heading west at low level, picking up their Ju88 pathfinder before crossing the Rhine into Holland, fifteen miles north of Venlo with Helmond to the south. When the seventy-odd fighters reached Sonse Heath they turned south to

---

[1] The Wing Leader of 123 Wing was the legendary Wing Commander W. Dring DSO, DFC. He was killed returning from a weather recce on 13th January 1945; his wheels caught a bank of snow as he landed and his Typhoon turned turtle.

make a wide sweep round Eindhoven to come in from the south-west. It was here that a small unit broke away to make an attack upon Gilze-Reijen.

Despite Gilze control having been warned of many aircraft in the vicinity by both 2 and 268 Squadrons only a short time before, nothing had filtered down to the operational units who even now were either in the air, or, more importantly, on the ground preparing for take-off.

There were three wings on Eindhoven on 1st January: 124, Typhoons; 143, also Typhoons and 39 Reconnaissance Wing flying Spitfires. Several units were already operating aircraft, missing the attack by minutes in some cases. LAC Desmond Shepherd, a Fitter/Armourer with 137 Squadron recalls:

> Our aircraft were rocket-firing Typhoons and I think our dispersal was about halfway up the airfield, a place we shared with the other three Typhoon squadrons in our wing. At the bottom end of the runway were three Canadian squadrons and I believe one British squadron of bomb-carrying Typhoons. Over on the Zeelst side were three squadrons of PRU Spitfires.
>
> There were plenty of other aircraft visiting – spotting, transport and others being repaired after forced landings. The airfield was full of aircraft, not dispersed but almost wing-tip to wing-tip. We didn't really expect a massive enemy strike at that late stage of the war.
>
> The first hours of 1945 was spent letting in the New Year, wishing each other all the best and having a few beers. I sat with a young chap, AC1 Norris, who was to die as a result of the raid.[1]
>
> *Leading Aircraftman D.C. Shepherd, 137 Squadron*

Squadron Leader L.H. Lambert DFC, the CO of 168 Squadron at this time, and the squadron had been called at 4 a.m. for an early mission to St Vith in the Ardennes. The squadron had one flight of British pilots, one of Australians and New Zealanders. Six Typhoons took off at 9 a.m.

---

[1] AC1 Ronald Arthur Norris, aged twenty, came from London. 6137 SE also lost Flight Sergeant Reginald Bazley (37) from Denbighshire, with Corporal Wattercamps and Leading Aircraftmen Hockaday and Dughan seriously wounded.

We were sent to do what we could for the 101st US Parachute Brigade who were stuck near St Vith. We had contact with a very good American Liaison Officer.

The brief was to go low level as this was the only way to get through, and we plotted a course down the river valleys which, provided the cloud base stayed above 800 feet, would be all right. The cloud was beginning to break over Eindhoven but there was still thick cloud over the Salient. We got a good start but the cloud got lower and lower as we approached the Salient. We found our way following a little single track railway down the valley and kept radio silence until we reached the area, when we immediately picked up the American ALO who told us there was a lot of targets available and asked what our armament was – it was just cannon.

He said he'd fire smoke shells. We saw the smoke and just beyond where the ALO was, the valley opened up quite wide and there was just enough room for us to get into line astern and turn round to carry out our first attack. We picked up several targets and also a mobile radar post which we picked off. There was quite a lot of anti-aircraft fire about and I was hit in one wing.

Finally, four of us formed up and climbed up through the cloud and on top found the other two pilots. It was then, as we climbed into radio range, that we began to hear all the garbled messages and gathered that a massive air attack was taking place. Yet we didn't know what was really going on until we met enemy aircraft being led by a Mustang!

Squadron Leader L.H. Lambert, 168 Squadron

At one minute to nine o'clock, Squadron Leader G. Wonnacott DFC, CO of 414 RCAF Squadron, took off to fly a Tac/R mission to Cologne, his No 2 being Flight Lieutenant S.C. Chapman (Spitfire IX MJ677). Another pair, Flight Lieutenant J.H. Donovan (MK924) and Flight Lieutenant P.W. Grier (MJ732) went towards München where at 9.20 a.m., Grier saw two speeding Me262 jets at 500 feet. A third pair of Spitfires, Flying Officer L. Woloschuk with Flight Lieutenant W.C. Sawers, went out towards Neus-Cologne.

Two Canadian pilots of 430 RCAF Squadron were in their Spitfire XIVs just after 9 a.m. Flight Lieutenant R.F. Gill and

Flying Officer W.P. Golden. The third squadron in 39 Wing, 400 RCAF, also equipped with Spitfires, were preparing for a day's flying, its pilots proceeding to the airfield from their billets shortly after 9 a.m.

In 124 Wing, six aircraft of 137 Squadron were airborne on an armed recce to Minden, as previously related. Flying Officer H.G. 'Pat' Pattinson in 182 Squadron was also up early.

New Year's Eve involved a party in the Mess, but as I was on first standby on 1st January at 5.30 a.m., I was not late in going to my camp bed. Following an early call, I and seven other pilots went to our dispersal at 5 a.m. to get our things together for the first op. of the day. Having done that and imbibed a mug of tea made by our telephone operator, we dozed and waited, as usual in war, for first light and a scramble. Our dispersal, as I recall, was on the north-west side of the airfield and was, officially, a marquee. That winter was one of the coldest I have ever experienced, with heavy snowfalls which necessitated taxying in narrow tracks between banks of snow to the take-off point, sometimes with airmen sitting on the wing-tips to signal clearance. The marquee proved to be inadequate protection against the below zero temperatures so we had built a wooden hut between the marquee and the adjoining wood. This was equipped with a drip-feed heater which gave off a good supply of heat but which was a fearsome device manufactured out of an oil drum and was in constant danger of exploding.

It must have been a little after nine o'clock and we were thinking about being relieved for breakfast when there was a very rude awakening.

Flying Officer H.G. Pattinson, 182 Squadron

The wing leader of 124 Wing was Wing Commander C.D. 'Kit' North-Lewis DFC who recalls:

The wing had moved up to Eindhoven from Brussels in September 1944 and consisted of four squadrons: 181, 182, 137 and 247, each of twenty rocket Typhoons. In addition, there was an Auster and I had a private Hurricane which I had acquired during the campaign.

As we were the first inhabitants of Eindhoven, the wing was relatively well dispersed and my wing headquarters was accommodated in a hut which was surrounded by a large revetment. In addition to 124 Wing which was in 83 Group, there were two other wings, a Canadian bomber Typhoon wing of 84 Group and the Spitfire PR recce wing of 83 Group. Neither of these wings was well dispersed and, in fact, the Canadian Typhoon Wing was drawn up in lines in front of the hangar. Eindhoven at this time consisted on a single tarmac runway but the grass areas were heavily cratered.

The officers of 124 Wing had planned a big New Year's Eve party for the 31st December. However, when the party took place we were somewhat depleted as, during the German offensive in the Ardennes a few days before in which the wing had been heavily engaged, we had lost the Group Captain – Charles Green[1] – and three of the four squadron commanders! None of these had been replaced by 1st January and thus there was only one CO and myself to run the entire wing. Nevertheless, as far as my memory goes, a riotous time was had by all on New Year's Eve.

January 1st 1945 dawned bitterly cold. It had been an exceptionally cold winter in Holland and when I went up to Wing HQ soon after first light I remember that I had to break the ice in the washbowl in my room of the small cottage in which I was billeted. However, in spite of the previous evening's revelries, I had despatched two squadrons before breakfast to fly armed reconnaissances across the Rhine north of the Ruhr. Although these aircraft were airborne, we still had some sixty aircraft on the ground.

Wing Commander C.D. North-Lewis, Leader 124 Wing

In the Canadian Wing, Flying Officer Bob Laurence, Flying Officer Hugh Fraser and two other pilots of 439 RCAF Squadron, were returning towards Eindhoven just after 9 a.m. In 439's crew room, the other pilots were waiting their return and their report on the weather over the Ardennes.

[1] Group Captain Charles Green DSO, DFC was shot down on 26th December but Pat Pattinson of 182 Squadron saw him bale out.

On the airfield itself, eight Typhoons of 438 RCAF Squadron were preparing for their first operation of 1945, being led by Flight Lieutenant Peter Wilson. Pete Wilson had been appointed CO of 438 two days earlier and this was the first chance he had had to lead his new command. Shortly after 9, these eight Typhoons, engines roaring, were in the process of taxying towards the take-off point. 440 Squadron too had eight Typhoons at the take-off point alongside 438.

In the final minutes of peaceful activity on Eindhoven aerodrome (peaceful that is, except that aircraft were about to fly war sorties) Flight Lieutenant H.P. Gibbins, a married man from Berkshire, aged twenty-four, a member of 168 Squadron, strapped himself into the cockpit of a squadron Typhoon, started the engine and he too taxied towards the runway. His duty was peaceful – he was down to fly an air-test on this particular aircraft.

As he reached the runway just ahead of the two flights from 438 and 440 Squadrons, and prepared, he asked control for permission to take-off. As he sat waiting, Oberstleutnant Heinz Bär's JG3, coming in fast and low, were just seconds away. The time was 9.20 a.m.

CHAPTER FIVE

Eindhoven

Wing Commander Marcus Kaye (Org 1 at 83 Group HQ), a veteran flyer from WW1 was in the Hotel Concorde, Valkensward in Eindhoven. The Administration part of 83 Group HQ was established in the hotel which was about five kilometres from the airfield.

I was coming out of the Concorde with the intention of setting off to visit some units when I saw large enemy formations (all fighters) coming over very low, flying roughly north-west. After the first wave, some more came over. There was no firing, presumably because they had not reached their target which clearly must have been Eindhoven airfield and the aircraft based there. Later that morning I drove past that airfield and saw the remains of several of our own fighters which had been shot-up.

Wing Commander M.M. Kaye, 83 Group HQ

On New Year's Eve, one had been celebrating and my personal story is that I had a slight 'head', so I said to my driver, 'I'm going out to have a look at my Regiment squadrons and wish them a Happy New Year.' We took the road to Eindhoven aerodrome which was a few miles away from my HQ. We arrived all right but suddenly I saw a number of German aircraft going over my head and the next moment everything was let loose. I saw one Typhoon squadron taking off and the Germans got them as they were leaving the ground. One of the chaps I saw killed was the son of the High Commissioner of Canada, who I think had been cox of the Oxford boat at one time.

Colonel R. Preston, RAF Regiment

Some time after nine o'clock, I happened to look out of the

window of my HQ and I saw eight to twelve strange aircraft in line astern passing. As I registered that they did not belong to us, I realised that they were Me109s. I remember wondering what in the hell they were doing at Eindhoven, for throughout the campaign from the beach-head in Normandy to Holland, our airfields had never been attacked.

Having realised that a German fighter force was over the airfield at low level, I dashed outside to see what was going on. To my amazement I saw that not only was there a force of 109s, but a force of FW190s as well. I think there must have been about twenty to twenty-five German aircraft circling the airfield. They immediately started to make low level attacks on the parked aircraft.

The Canadian wing had their aircraft drawn up in lines outside the old German hangars. At the moment of the German attack they had one squadron fully bombed up and one squadron just getting up to take off. The Germans concentrated on these aircraft and few of those waiting to take off escaped. The squadron commander made a brave attempt but when I last saw him with his wheels still down, he had a couple of German aircraft queuing up behind him to shoot him down.

Wing Commander C.D. North-Lewis, Leader 124 Wing

The pilot seen by both Colonel Preston and Kit North-Lewis had been the new CO of 438 Squadron, Flight Lieutenant Pete Wilson, leading his eight-man section off. However, it would appear that the first Typhoon away was that being air-tested by Flight Lieutenant H.P. 'Gibby' Gibbons of 168 Squadron.

'Gibby' had been left behind that morning and was doing an air test. The story I got from a flight sergeant was that just as he was halfway down the runway the first of the attacking aircraft came in. I'm not sure if he got a radio warning or simply saw them, but he whipped round in a very tight turn into them. Gibby was in a mêlée with them and immediately shot down a 190 which crashed behind our dispersal but Gibby went down beside it. Both aircraft hit belly down but both pilots had been killed in the air. It was a very valiant effort indeed.

Squadron Leader L.H. Lambert, 168 Squadron

Gibbons was flying QC-D and was seen by Leading Aircraftman R.W. Whitfield to attack one Focke Wulf 190 and blow its tail off before he himself was hit by 190s and shot down.

> After breakfast I was crossing the runway, going towards the armoury and keeping a sharp look-out for our aircraft, as some were already out on ops. and others were taking off. At that moment I heard gunfire. Looking up the runway I saw what looked like an Me262 jet go streaking above my head. This was closely followed by several FW190s, and coming almost in the opposite direction were several Me109s.
>
> I threw myself down onto the grass at the side of the runway. Looking back at the centre of the runway, I saw what I think were the lead planes of each German section collide with each other. They burst into flames and locked together they came spinning down a few feet above my head, giving off tremendous heat. One of the pilots was struggling to get out, then the aircraft broke apart and exploded in the woods beyond dispersal.
>
> *Leading Aircraftman D.C. Shepherd, 137 Squadron*

The Canadian Typhoons were in the process of starting down the runway as the attack began, Pete Wilson leading in his Typhoon F3-Q. Seeing the Germans approaching he apparently throttled back and pulled to the end of the runway where he climbed out of the cockpit. He had been hit in the stomach, either when in the aircraft or as he climbed out. He died a few minutes after being admitted to sick quarters. Flying Officer R.W. Keller (F3-R) in the second Typhoon, became airborne but was hit and crashed, Keller being found later still in his burnt-out Typhoon.

The pilots in the other Tiffies were extremely lucky. Pilot Officer Don Campbell (F3-K) was unable to get out of his aircraft due to the intense strafing, so he remained in it, crouched down in his seat behind the armour plate until the attack was over. His machine took several hits but he escaped unhurt. The other five Canadians, Pilot Officer F.R.F. Skelly (F3-S), Pilot Officer W.L. Beatty (F3-T), Pilot Officer J.A. Lord (F3-G), Pilot Officer A.B. Harle (F3-F) and Flight Lieutenant F.X.J. Regan (F3-Y), all scrambled out of their Typhoons and lay on the ground. Two found a slit trench, two others found cover behind a small pile of sand while the fifth huddled down in a frozen wheel track in the mud. Of the eight Typhoons, three were burnt out, one crashed and broke up and two others were shot up and damaged. Only Pilot Officer Harle was slightly injured. He ran into the adjutant's office of 440 Squadron to telephone dispersal and was hit by flying glass when a 1,000 lb bomb exploded nearby.

Another of 438's pilots, Pilot Officer B.J. Macklon, was awaiting transportation back to England and was at the ADRU, when he was hit and wounded in the shoulder by a stray bullet. The squadron's senior armourer NCO, Flight Sergeant Ron Beatty, operating a Bren-gun, claimed to have shot down one of the attacking fighters.

> I recall several incidents. I saw several Typhoons shot up as they were taking off, slewing off the runway in all directions and then colliding with other aircraft. Some were shot down whilst only a few feet in the air.
>
> I saw Flight Sergeant Burrows of my squadron shot up and killed whilst taxying. Burrows had asked our Rigger NCO to make a cross to his design should he be killed. The NCO carried out his wish, making a most beautiful cross. I wonder what happened to it?
>
> *Leading Aircraftman D.C. Shepherd, 137 Squadron*

The pilots of 439 RCAF Squadron were sitting around in their crew room awaiting the return of the weather recce flight when they heard gunfire and low flying aeroplanes. Immediately the pilots rushed to the door to see what was happening. They saw a FW190 coming straight at them from across the aerodrome. Everyone grabbed their .45 pistols or .38 revolvers and began to fire at the fighters as they swept over them. Focke Wulfs and Messerschmitts came in and several of 439's pilots identified American Mustangs with German markings among them.

Everyone was diving for cover, including some of the pilots who dived into a trench behind the crew room, which they discovered had three feet of water with a top layer of ice. Pride was cast aside as Sergeant King, one of 439's maintenance NCOs, led a disorganised rabble into the trench, only to be trampled down into the ice and water as other men dived in on top of them.

The CO of 439, Squadron Leader R.G. 'Bing' Crosby, was in his jeep, driving from the Mess with Flight Lieutenant Johnny Carr. They only got as far as the Salvation Army building before 'baling out' into a ditch. Leading Aircraftman Len Weir was driving Flying Officer Johnny Johnson and Flying Officer Jack Roberts to the Maintenance hangar in a three-tonner when the attack began. They, too, quickly sought cover, Johnson squatting down behind one of the lorry's wheels. Then a bullet hit the tyre which caused the Canadian no small consternation.

Corporal M. Singerman was wounded when lying flat on the ground beside a newly erected toilet which was hit by a 20 mm cannon shell. Another 20 mm shell crashed through the wall of the pilot's crew room, piercing an Irvine jacket and slicing through the peak of Flying Officer Lyal Shaver's cap.

Flight Lieutenant H.A.V. 'Art' Massey, the squadron's Intelligence Officer, was hit while he was in his shack, being wounded in the head, chest and posterior. Two other airmen were wounded, Leading Aircraftmen J.T. Bews and Crinklaw. Only one of 439's Typhoons was set on fire and destroyed, another being damaged.

Most of the pilots of 440 Squadron were in their orderly room when the attack started. Although it was well protected by a blast-wall, it still seemed to get the full blast of an exploding bomb which smashed every window, flying glass inflicting cuts on hands and faces of several of the occupants. The whole place became a shambles as desks, tables and chairs were blown over. At the same time, eight pilots of 440's Typhoons, seated in their machines at the end of the runway were, like 438, shot up by JG3's fighters.

Pilot Officer R.A. Watson, seated in his cockpit, opened fire with his cannons from the ground as a 190 came straight at him, damaging it before his Tiffie was set on fire. All eight pilots jumped clear unharmed with the exception of Pilot Officer E.T. Flanagan who received several shrapnel wounds and a damaged eye. In addition, three of 440's service echelon were wounded.

Number 430 RCAF Squadron also had aircraft and pilots caught on the ground. Flight Lieutenant R.F. Gill suffered a slight head

wound in his Spitfire and, as he clambered out, slipped and broke
an arm. Flying Officer W.P. 'Bill' Golden was wounded in the body
when a cannon shell exploded in the cockpit of his Spitfire.

Meanwhile, 124 Wing's squadrons were also receiving attention.
Two aircraft of 137 Squadron were hit by cannon and machine-
gune fire and as witnessed by Des Shepherd, 23-year-old Flight
Sergeant L.A.V. Burrows, who was taxying his Typhoon to
dispersal, was hit and killed. The squadron's 'Chiefy' fitter, Flight
Sergeant R. Bazley, was killed in his office. He was wounded in the
German's first pass and then hit again by a cannon shell in the
head and in the stomach. Nine other airmen were admitted to
hospital with injuries, some serious. Corporal Myers and Corporal
Oakley had lucky escapes in the crew room which was heavily shot
up, cannon shells and machine-gun bullets fairly buzzing around
the place.

Still lying out on the middle of the airfield was Des Shepherd of
137 Squadron, taking in all the events that were happening about
him.

Many pilots were jumping out of their (parked) aircraft and I
saw a German aircraft crash into a row of parked Spitfires,
causing more fires. Lorries were being shot up, including the
'breakfast special' resulting in Leading Aircraftman Norris, one
of our armourers, dying from his wounds the following day.
Many aircraft were burning, a petrol bowser exploded, huts and
other buildings were shot up.

One of our NCO's came out of our flight hut looking for a first-
aid box because our Chiefy, Flight Sergeant Bazley, had been hit
in the hand, but when the NCO returned he found our Chiefy
dying after being hit further. Air battles were taking place
around the airfield as more RAF planes joined in. German
cannon shells were hitting the ground around me and one grazed
my right knee-cap, so I was unable to run for cover, although the
main cause was probably being paralysed with fear. I even tried
to dig myself into the ground with my hands but the ground was
frozen hard. An empty German cannon shell case with links
attached, fell onto my head (no tin hat with me). When it cooled
off I put it inside my battle-dress blouse thinking that if I

surivived this day I would keep it as a reminder of New Year's
Day 1945 – I still have it.

Leading Aircraftman D.C. Shepherd, 137 Squadron

Number 181 Squadron was luckier than most, having only one
Typhoon destroyed – EL-H, which was totally burnt out, but they
had no personnel casualties. 182 Squadron was not so fortunate.

As far as I recall, we had just dressed, on the second floor of a
commandeered school just to the south of the aerodrome, when it
started. I and five other pilots dashed in my jeep to the airfield. I
remember my fitter beside my aircraft 'G', which he had started
up, when a 190 came in very low – firing. He blew-up two of my
aircraft and shot the propeller boss and prop. off my aircraft –
which caused it to rev-up uncontrollably and then seize. My fitter
then did a splendid spring into the nearest slit trench!

Squadron Leader C.J. Gray, CO 182 Squadron[1]

The squadron had two casualties, Corporal Rabbitt was caught in
the open and fatally wounded while Leading Aircraftman Hodges
had one foot shot away by a cannon shell.

Pat Pattinson was still at readiness when the raid began:

It must have been a little after 9 a.m., and we were thinking
about being relieved for breakfast when there was a very rude
awakening. All hell broke loose with the noise of a large number
of aircraft diving on us with the accompanying noise of machine-
gun and cannon fire. The attack was carried out by Me109s and
FW190s and we even saw some jets giving top cover but not
participating directly in the attack. Fortunately our wooden hut
escaped unscathed as it was invisible to the German pilots
situated as it was between the marquee and the wood.

I was told later that a little Welsh batman, still in a euphoric
state from the previous evening's revelry was up on the roof of the
Mess, firing away with a .303 rifle, thoroughly enjoying himself

[1] Gerry Gray's bar to his DFC was announced on 1/1/45. He
commanded 182 from August 1944 to March 1945.

endeavouring to shoot down the enemy but not endangering them in the slightest!

Flying Officer H.G. Pattinson, 182 Squadron

For the next half-hour – it certainly seemed as long as that but it may well have been shorter – the Germans circled the airfield as they made incessant attacks on the parked aircraft. I had a grandstand view as I was able to watch the proceedings in comparative safety protected by the revetment. I had to run from one side of the revetment to the other in order to ensure that I was protected as the German aircraft dived over it as they attacked the airfield.

The Canadian squadrons, bombed-up in front of the hangar, caught fire and blew up one by one as their 500 lb bombs detonated. The squadron was almost totally destroyed. It was difficult to see what was happening elsewhere as the smoke obscured one's vision.

We made attempts to recall our squadrons which were already airborne but by this time they were too deep into Germany to get the message. As all the other British airfields were under attack we received no fighter protection from them. However, the Germans did not escape entirely without loss. One of the Typhoons managed to get airborne and he shot down one German fighter.

Wing Commander C.D. North-Lewis, Leader 124 Wing

I was in rather a bad temper with some of my guns as I thought they were being a trifle slow firing, so I was talking to one squadron commander, asking him what the hell was going on, whereupon there was a bomb dropped nearby which blew in the window and window frame. The frame landed squarely around my neck and so there I was trying to curse my men like hell with this frame around my neck. Suddenly we all burst into peals of laughter at the ridiculous situation.

Colonel R. Preston, RAF Regiment

Flight Lieutenant A.C. Simon, a Typhoon pilot of 137 Squadron, temporarily attached to 84 Group HQ, was at dispersal when the

Germans came in. Tony Simon had just arrived and immediately all pilots there grabbed a few sten-guns that were available, while others pulled out revolvers, etc: With these they began to open fire on the diving fighters. Simon and the others lay on their backs, spraying the air with their gunfire, all feeling certain that they had inflicted some damage on the attackers. Tony Simon also saw two Ju88s fly across the airfield and felt certain they had dropped delayed action bombs.

Also at Eindhoven was 82 Group's Communication Squadron, this unit having moved there on 3rd October. Freddy Newell was one of its pilots.

> Of the actual raid I did not see very much, being pinned in the Mess throughout, with German fighters flying past the door at low level attacking our Ansons and Austers at one end of the road, and the R & SU (Repair and Servicing Unit) at the other end.
>
> We were asleep when it began, the noise waking us up. Without a word Warrant Officer Basil Mills and I, still in pyjamas, rushed to the door, looked out and saw German fighters, very low down, whipping along the road by our building. Still without saying a word, Basil and I turned, rushed back inside and each returned to the door wearing a tin helmet. The Mess building had been built by the Germans, with very thick walls and a solid roof, so we felt pretty safe.
>
> The Communication Squadron's aircraft were dispersed at the far end of Eindhoven airfield near the Tiffie's R & SU area. We also had Broadhurst's personal Spitfire kept there, also his Miles Messenger. His German Storch was also there on occasion as it was serviced by us, but it wasn't there that morning.
>
> *Warrant Officer F.R. Newell, 83 Group Communication Squadron*

*

Leading Aircraftman George Davis was a Fitter II stationed at Eindhoven while serving with No 403 R & SU. He recalls:

> We were situated on the north-west corner of the perimeter of the airfield with planes for repair on either side of the track. When

they left, the Germans had blown up every hangar to render them useless, and the particular 'gang' to which I belonged, used some of the T & G wood to build ourselves a shed in which to spend the winter. Across the track from us was a hangar 'space' housing the CO's trailer-caravan, one Tempest and one Typhoon for repair. To the side of these was a guardroom of the same sort of wood as our shed. Under the Tempest was a quantity of drained-off oil.

When the attack started there were several bods in the guardroom, including the CTO. At some stage during the period of the attack, one chap thought that he would have a look outside to satisfy his curiosity, and lo! he saw the oil under the Tempest on fire! He promptly ran back to the guardroom, grabbed a fire extinguisher and put out the fire. Upon his return, the CTO asked him what he thought he was doing. He then said, 'The next man who embarks on similar or like actions will be court-martialled immediately.' – or words to that effect. It seems he was worried about obtaining a replacement for him!

The aeroplanes for repair were placed at ninety degrees to the 'peri' track on either side (an ideal situation for an air to ground sweep for the enemy). The only way for an airman engaged on fuselage repair who wished to gain access to the inside of the said fuselage was to remove the panel which covered the W/T set, remove the set, then climb in. I am told that this operation took the best part of twenty minutes. Work started at 8 a.m. and since the attack started some time after 9 o'clock, some of our chaps were already inside these Tiffies. I was told that the time taken to extricate oneself that morning was cut by a factor of ten!

The MT Section was situated nearer to the centre of the airfield and one corporal by the name of Job, was on his Coles crane and was promptly shot up. He nipped smartly down to the ground and ran for the trees by the MT site. He was followed by this same German pilot, who missed him. Job was known as a very quiet person before this episode, but his incident certainly set him talking! Another corporal, Gerald 'Jerry' Porter, happened to have his greatcoat hanging in the billet, and had the misfortune to have two holes burnt through it by tracer shells. There was no suitable replacement in the stores for him so he went on leave wearing it. During his stay at home, one little old lady asked about the coat, so he explained what had made the holes. She said, 'You poor man, did you have it on at the time?'

There was a man in the cookhouse – 'Taffy'. He had long service stripes occupying most of his sleeve it seemed; I think he had spent many years in the army. The cookhouse itself was a portable one, made out of wood and brand new, situated on the side of another track nearer the centre of the airfield and parallel to the perimeter. During the attack, Taffy grabbed a Bren gun and saying, 'Who do these people think they are?' promptly leaned out of a window and started to blaze away! He was hit of course, and taken to hospital and I never saw or heard of him again. This action in my view, was a brave thing to undertake.

Leading Aircraftman G.H. Davis, 403 R & SU

About two miles from the airfield stands the village of Zeelst. Leading Aircraftman Lawrence Collier of 124 Wing's MT Section was billeted, in a cigar factory. He had just returned to the village following duty with the night shift. No sooner had he arrived that German fighters came roaring overhead which co-incided with women and children coming out of the village church after Mass. As bullets started hitting the rooftops, Collier and his pals started to grab the children and put them under their three-tonners. There was a moment of panic as a couple of fighters appeared to be dropping bombs but these proved to be jettisoned long-range fuel tanks.

As the attack ended, Collier and the other men of the section, raced back to the aerodrome. As they reached the main gate they could see the damage. Burning aeroplanes littered the airfield and one crashed Typhoon lay just inside the gate, its nose facing them as they drove in. Bell tents next to the runway were burning and Collier and the others helped by taking injured men to the local military hospital in their trucks. When this was done, Lawrence and the others assembled at one of the dispersal areas where they were issued with rum – the first time he for one had ever tasted rum.

Lawrence had organised a party in Eindhoven for the night of the 1st and asked his officer if he should cancel it. The officer said it must be held – 'It would help morale,' he said!

Just a mile from the airfield, in the grounds of a church school, was No 404 ASP (a Mobile Air Stores Park) which serviced 121 and 124 Wings, and commanded by Squadron Leader R. 'Dick' Landon. The adjutant was Flying Officer Harry Beechens who made the following entry in the unit's Record Book:

> Today the Luftwaffe staged its attempted 'come-back'. Although the Park was not attacked, the enemy being too intent on the airfield a mile away, we were interested spectators. For some twenty minutes enemy planes flew by and over us at tree-top height, their swastika markings shining in the morning sunlight.

The Canadian Air Stores Park No 406 was also near Eindhoven. All ranks were intensely excited watching the German planes bombing and strafing the airfield soon after their reveille. German aircraft came zooming over their heads en-route. Fortunately for them they were only concentrating on the airfield and made no attempt to attack either them or similar units scattered around the area. Only one of its people was injured. Leading Aircraftman A.G. Douglas, a chef, was on the ration-run on the airfield and a piece of shrapnel grazed his head, causing a superficial wound.

*

The attack upon Eindhoven aerodrome lasted some twenty-three minutes by most accounts, which makes it about 9.43 a.m. when it ended. Yet the Germans didn't have it totally all their own way. At 9.30 the CO of 414 RCAF Squadron, Squadron Leader Gordon Wonnacott DFC returned to the airfield from his early sortie.

Wonnacott had been on an artillery recce with another pilot, in the Heinsburg area but low cloud and intense German AA fire had affected their duty and split up the two men. Giving up, Wonnacott headed for home. Approaching base he saw smoke rising into the air and a considerable number of enemy aircraft milling about. He immediately waded into them, picking out a German fighter and firing from 450 yards, but he skidded to one side and had to break away. Pulling up he spotted a 109. One of his cannons had packed up so he fired with just his machine-guns from 100 yards, seeing strikes. Closing in again his next burst caused more strikes, then the German pilot jettisoned his cockpit canopy and baled out.

The Canadian was quickly onto another Messerschmitt, his fire causing the German pilot to take violent evasive action and then he pulled his 109 into a loop very near the ground. Staying with it, Wonnacott fired another short burst from 250 yards, flames starting to pour back but then three FW190s attacked him from behind. Wonnacott turned into these three, firing at number one, saw hits, then broke away to the left to avoid the other two 190s.

Now out of ammunition, and his one cannon still jammed, he broke off the action which had carried him north-east of Helmond, and returned to base. He claimed two 109s destroyed and the Focke Wulf as damaged. However, a 190 was found in the area of his combat with a dead pilot aboard, so Wonnacott was credited with three victories, a feat which resulted in the award of a bar to his DFC.

It was probably one of Wonnacott's victims that Colonel Rupert Preston saw as he left one of his Regiment HQs (leaving the window frame behind!!):

I considered the best thing I could do was to return to Group HQ and report the situation to Air Vice-Marshal Broadhurst. On the way back I saw about 200 yards away from the road, a Spitfire chasing a German fighter around a haystack. The German crash-landed about 100 yards from me. The pilot got out unhurt and surrendered to my driver. I put him in the back of my jeep and took him to HQ. I gather he was second in command of the raid. I handed him over to Group Captain Paul Davoud. The German spoke English very well and said that the war was over for them as far as he was concerned.

I then knocked on Broady's door and went into his office. He was on the telephone to Air Marshal Coningham in Brussels and the conversation I overheard went something like this: 'They're flying down just above the houses here!' Broadhurst replied, 'Don't worry, they're flying below my window here!', and at that moment several did go by.

I then told Broady what was going on but he said, 'Don't worry, we've got them on the radar, we'll get them on the way back.' Then I went back and saw all the wreckage.

Colonel R. Preston, RAF Regiment

I was in my office in Eindhoven and heard lots of activity. I looked out of the window to see a recce Spitfire chasing a 109, being chased by a 109, being chased by a recce Spitfire!! I could see that the airfield was being attacked and so rang the Group Control Centre to find out what was going on. Air Marshal Coningham rang me from Brussels where there was also an attack in progress on Evere airfield.

Some Typhoons at Eindhoven were caught with bombs on lining up for take-off, but at one of the forward airfields a wing of Canadian Spitfires were just about to take off as the Huns formed overhead – obviously not briefed to attack that airfield. They were brought into contact and caused great damage to the German fighters. Most of the rest of my Group had been sent off at daylight on armed recces. They were recalled but most had used up their ammo beating up trains, etc. The Tac and PR aircraft were recalled and of course had all their ammunition and it was a section of these I saw in action.

Air Vice-Marshal H. Broadhurst, AOC 83 Group

Yellow Section of 439 RCAF Squadron were on their way back from their weather recce to St Vith, led by Flying Officer Bob Laurence (RB233). They were warned by radio that large numbers of enemy aircraft were flying east from the direction of Eindhoven and to keep a sharp watch for them.

At 9.45 a.m., near Deurne, they saw fifteen to twenty FW190s flying at various heights from 500 to 1,000 feet. The four Typhoon pilots engaged them at once. Laurence, after some considerable manoeuvering, got onto the tail of one Focke Wulf. Opening fire he saw strikes on its right wing, a second burst obtaining hits on the wings and fuselage. The 190 was now down to 800 feet and began to rock and go down towards the ground, but then another 190 fastened onto Laurence's tail and he had to break to the left. As he glanced back he saw the 190 pilot take to his parachute.

Shaking off his attacker, Laurence went after another 190 he saw turning away from him, and was able to close in to 75-100 yards.

Two bursts produced hits and the cockpit canopy and bits and pieces flew back. Then the 190's nose dropped towards the ground. As it fell, it slowly rolled over onto its back and then it crashed into a brick building and burst into flames.

Flying Officer Hugh Fraser (RB281) also waded into the 190s which seemed to be beating up ground targets and being mixed up with one or two Spitfires. A dog-fight seemed to be raging at between 200 and 1,000 feet. Losing Laurence in the mêlée for a moment, he then saw him chasing a 190 with another on his tail. Fraser went after the attacking 190, his first burst knocking pieces from it. Then the 190 caught fire and went straight in on its back.

Fraser had now lost sight of Laurence and a passing 190 got in a burst at his own Typhoon and scored hits. He then saw a long-nosed Focke Wulf 190D in a shallow dive beneath him, flying towards Venlo. Fraser went after it, the 190 being only 100 feet up. Closing rapidly he fired several short bursts, the last from 50 yards. Pieces flew off the 190 and the German fighter went into the deck near a large windmill at an estimated 400 mph. The 190 blew up, Fraser having to break violently to avoid the debris.

Laurence and Fraser, and Flying Officer W. Anderson (RB198) landed at Volkel because of the damage at Eindhoven, but the fourth Typhoon failed to get back. This was flown by Flying Officer S. Angelini (MN589). Angelini had only flown fourteen operations with the squadron and this was his first show since 5th December, having been in England waiting for clear weather to fly a Typhoon back to Holland. His body was found on the 3rd in his aircraft, near Rips where he had been shot down. Stabsfeldwebel Schubert of JG6 claimed a Typhoon shot down north of Venlo.

One of Laurence's victims was reported to be one of the leaders of the German attack force, and the Canadian was awarded the DFC shortly afterwards.

The two Spitfires seen by Hugh Fraser in this action may have been from Gordon Wonnacott's 414 Squadron. Flying Officer L. Woloschuk and his No 2, Flight Lieutenant W.C. Sawers, had been on their way back from their Tac/R mission to Neus/Cologne when they were attacked by FW190s at 7,000 feet, west of Roermond. Bill Sawers saw the attack coming and yelled a warning to his leader. As Sawers attacked one 190, Wally Woloschuk saw another 190 get behind his No 2. Turning sharply, he got behind the Focke Wulf and opened fire at 600 yards hoping to cause the 190 pilot to break away. He succeeded and continued after the 190, closing in to 150 yards. More bursts set the German on fire and enveloped in black smoke and flames it went down. Sawers, warned off the danger behind him, fired a quick shot at his 190, and then broke away, seeing his leader's victim go down in flames.

Returning towards Eindhoven, Woloschuk saw some more enemy fighters, and attacked a straggling Me109, scoring hits before he lost it in cloud.

*

Also returning at this time was Squadron Leader Lennie Lambert and his flight from 168 Squadron.

After the strafing attack in the Bastogne Salient, four of us formed up and climbed through the cloud and above it we found the other two. It was then, as we climbed into radio range that we began to hear lots of garbled messages and gathered that a massive air attack was taking place. But we didn't really know what was going on until we met enemy aircraft – being led by a Mustang!

The reason we got involved was because I saw the Mustang, and having flown Mustangs quite a bit before, recognised it instantly and thought it was in trouble. Having been hit myself in the ground strafe, and having to fly my Typhoon (MN265) with my right leg straight out giving it full right rudder to keep the Tiffie flying straight, I decided all I could do to help was to try and create a diversion, and that's what we did. I just dived through the oncoming aircraft, but what I didn't know was that the Mustang was leading the enemy fighters.

There was no doubt about it, it was was a Mustang. In retrospect I suppose I should have recognised what was happening before I dived but I thought he was being chased and we had very little fuel and ammo. left anyway. We were told the following day that a Mustang had led the aircraft that had attacked Evere or Melsbroek and we had no reason to doubt it as this is what we had seen. After the war I understood the Germans themselves confirmed that one German pilot led quite a large force of fighters in a Mustang.

Squadron Leader L.H. Lambert, OC 168 Squadron

Flight Lieutenant John D. 'Joe' Stubbs DFC (JP515) also saw the Mustang flying without any markings, flying the same height and course as the Me109s, about 600 yards ahead of them. The 109s were making no attempt to close with the Mustang.

Squadron Leader Lambert was flying at about 6,500 feet with two other Typhoons covering Stubbs and his two wingmen who were at 6,000 feet. The enemy aircraft saw the Typhoons and began to climb steeply up-sun. The six Typhoons turned towards them and two 109s broke left and dived past Flight Lieutenant R.M. Stevens (MN999), No 3 to Lambert. Another 109 attacked from astern, and Lambert called a break to the left, the 109 climbing steeply ahead of him. Flight Lieutenant Stubbs came in behind the 109 ahead of Lambert and climbed to 10,000 feet where he came into range. Closing in, Joe Stubbs fired with short bursts from 600 yards. The Messerschmitt was hit and Lambert and Flying Officer W.G. Huddart (EK382) saw strikes but the 109 gradually pulled out of range.[1]

*

Other Typhoons were also returning to Eindhoven, Flight Lieutenant George Clubley DFC was leading his flight of 137 Squadron back from a successful train strafe south of Steinheim. They had also shot up a railway station between Wessel and Emmerich.

I had just arrived on 137 Squadron and was on my first trip with them on 1st January. There was nothing to indicate it was any different from any other except we sighted an Me262 at about 8,000 feet over the Rhine area. We turned towards him but he left us standing with the greatest of ease. We then found a He111

[1] F/O W.G. Huddart, an Australian, was reported missing 22nd January 1945.

which we attacked. Although I had done about 140 operational flights with the Typhoon, this was my first attempt at shooting at an enemy aircraft and I suspect that my accuracy left much to be desired. However, when I came around again, the Heinkel was on the ground – possibly I had hit him or more probably the pilot felt it was the safest place!

Flight Lieutenant G. Clubley, 137 Squadron

They first spotted the Heinkel near Minden, below them and to the right, flying eastwards at 100 feet. Clubley (PD611) and his No 2, Pilot Officer D.E.G. Martyn, a Canadian, (JT247), attacked from above and behind. Clubley opened fire from about 300 yards seeing strikes on its starboard engine, the Heinkel weaving 'energetically'. Martyn then attacked seeing more hits and then the German began to trail smoke from the damaged engine. Going down, the Heinkel made a well controlled forced landing in a field, but no one was seen to get out. Flying Officer Cole dived down and shot up the bomber, seeing hits on its tail.

Returning to Eindhoven the 137 boys saw columns of smoke rising from the base but they were diverted to Volkel. 168 Squadron was also diverted to Volkel. Lennie Lambert remembers:

When we finally reached Eindhoven there was a lot of fires burning and the runway had been hit, so we were diverted to Volkel. As I landed there I ran out of petrol as I turned off the runway.

*

Colonel Preston's RAF Regiment gunners, 2703, 2773 and 2817 Squadrons, fired 2,750 rounds at what they estimated to be a total force of about seventy German fighters. They claimed six destroyed.

Number 2703 Squadron was in action very quickly and several attacking fighters diverted their attacks to the gun positions rather than the dispersed aircraft. The Germans were flying so low that the Bofors gun crews had a difficult job trying to hit them. 2703 suffered some casualties in the attack. Corporal Wills and Leading Aircraftmen Thomas and Brown were wounded at their guns, while Leading Aircraftmen Saint (a driver) and Varley (MT) were caught by shrapnel while sheltering near B Flight HQ. Varley received special mention for his courage in sitting quite still, smoking a cigarette and drinking a cup of tea while the doctor attended to Saint before telling the doctor that he too was wounded in the back. As the doctor was then to discover, Varley was the most seriously wounded of the five men.

When later the squadron was given credit for five shared victories, it was able to show excellent proof of one of its victories. No 8 gun post had the cockpit canopy from one FW190 which it had shot off its victim!

Squadron Leader J.D.P. Watney's 2773 Squadron opened fire on the attackers with the exception of No 10 gun Detachment which was in the middle of a C & M (Care & Maintenance) inspection. With the other guns all blazing away, No 10 Detachment worked furiously to re-assemble their gun, completing it in time to loose off seven rounds and claim one Me109 damaged.

This squadron too suffered casualties. Leading Aircraftman Tranter (gunner) was shot through the arm and Leading Aircraftman Christie (cook) shot through the leg. One three-ton Bedford lorry was burnt out and several other vehicles damaged. The unit's new orderly room was hit and damaged. One amusing story came from No 9 Detachment. They were firing away when the No 4 man yelled, 'Stoppage! held.' The No 3 man, eye glued to the gun-sight, and traversing frantically, shouted back angrily, 'Fuck the stoppage – keep firing!'

The Bren gunners of 2806 Squadron fired at the attackers as they swept over the airfield at zero feet, seeing several hits. They had to cease fire when Spitfires came onto the scene. Leading Aircraftman Vassey, one of the squadron's drivers, was severely wounded while waiting to draw rations from the DID and died soon afterwards in hospital.

It transpired that a 109 had been shot down a short distance from our dispersal so we naturally went out to visit the scene later and I vividly recollect the typical 'German' smell associated with their aircraft and equipment. The locals had, presumably, already visited the scene of the crash as the pilot's wristwatch was missing. We did, however, collect his maps which were duly handed over to Intelligence and which had obviously been specially produced, since the tracks to the various airfields under attack had been actually printed on them. Perhaps this is an example of what we are pleased to call Teutonic thoroughness.

Flying Officer H.G. Pattinson, 182 Squadron

*

As the attack ended at Eindhoven and the noise abated, so the cost to the RAF began to be measured. Smoke from burning aeroplanes and vehicles drifted across the airfield. Fire engines and ambulances raced about, fighting the many fires and searching for the wounded and the dead among the debris.

Fortunately my wing, because it was well dispersed, came off best of all and although we had a lot of aircraft damaged we had very few completely destroyed. However, I see from looking at my log-book, that my own personal aircraft which had been hit by flak a few days before during an attack in the Ardennes and which I had air tested on 30th December, must have been badly damaged because I took over a new aircraft after the attack.

Wing Commander C.D. North-Lewis, Leader 124 Wing

Our losses were, I believe, two Ansons and two or three Austers. All we were left with was one Auster, and one Anson at Gilze Reijen, where I had left it the previous evening, returning from Paris to find Eindhoven closed by fog. We had to have the Anson back immediately for a run to England, so the one Auster was laid on to take me to Gilze to collect it. We arrived there to find it looking like a pepper-pot, the fabric badly damaged by our own ack-ack. However, a hurried patch job, back to Eindhoven and on to England.

Our only casualty was a cook from our Mess. He decided it would be safer in the nearby woods than in the Mess, a very solid building, but a cannon shell hit him in the leg!

Warrant Officer F.R. Newell, 83 Group Communication Squadron

Then there was silence and after all the noise it was quite

incredible. Going outside, I saw a petrol bowser, which had been parked alongside the hut, had been hit and holed in several places, petrol running out in little streams with tiny flickers of flame here and there. It constituted quite a danger so I hopped in and drove it to a safe distance. The breeze created by driving must have extinguished the flames as it didn't burn and all we lost was a few gallons of high octane fuel.

Our marquee had been hit and the odd parachute was damaged but nothing else. Our aircraft did suffer though – very badly – and as far as I can recollect we only had two fully serviceable out of twenty-four. My own aircraft XM-D was badly hit by a burst of cannon fire. The fuselage was holed, the instrument panel shattered and a round which had pierced the armour plate behind the seat went through my parachute and out through the cockpit floor.

Flying Officer H.G. Pattinson, 182 Squadron

Our own dispersal was relatively undamaged though, of course, we had lost Flight Sergeant Burrows. Apart from the shock to everyone who had been convinced that the Luftwaffe no longer existed, there were amusing incidents. We were one of the few squadrons which still had its Hurricane with which all Typhoon squadrons were equipped for initial training. One of the 'perks' of being a flight or squadron commander was that this aircraft could be used to fly to the UK on leave. As my home was in Orkney, I was looking forward to the perk. Needless to say a FW190 made a special attack on our lonely Hurricane and reduced it to wreckage. Also the wing equipment stores were attacked and our caravan destroyed. I suspect this van must have had elastic sides, otherwise it could not have held all the equipment which was claimed had to be written off or replaced!

Flight Lieutenant G. Clubley, 137 Squadron

The squadron diarist of 247 Squadron wrote quite eloquently of the attack:

Today the weather was perfect to welcome a New Year, clear viz and brilliant sunshine, crispness in the air and a typical copybook freshness of a year newly born. All pilots boarded transport and left early for the airfield as a long range job was in the air. Then, out of the blue came the whistle of bombs, the scream of diving planes, the chatter of machine-guns and the heavier thump of cannon and it seemed as though the floodgates of hell had suddenly swung back to release Old Nick's devilish horde. First came the jet bombers and after bombs away, the MEs and FWs. Wave after wave they came in, strafing the airfield from end to end – twenty-three minutes of hell that paralysed everyone, but in a very few minutes the regiment was pooping away, clawing down one after the other of the Teutonic horde, and were those gunner boys pleased to have at long last the much desired opportunity of showing the RAF that even the regiment had its place. But the Huns pressed on regardless coming in at fifty feet or less, and apparently concentrating on destroying aircraft. One 'screamer' squadron was caught on the end of the runway and suffered badly. Several were complete burn-outs, and the rest rendered unserviceable. Petrol dumps of 143 Wing was set on fire, a bomb-dump of 143 Wing was set on fire and 1,000 lb bombs exploded every few minutes. Individual kites in dispersal were set on fire, rockets ignited and flashed in all directions. The equipment section went up in a glorious mass of flames, Austers flapped their wings and joined in the conflagration, and slowly a pall of smoke formed above the airfield and blotted out the sun to turn the morning light into evening twilight.

247 Squadron, Form 540

About half an hour after the raid, all the RAF squadron commanders were sitting in Kit North-Lewis' caravan drinking a rather shaky coffee, when there was a God-awful explosion as our bomb dump blew up. Fortunately it was on the other side of the airfield.

Squadron Leader G.J. Gray, CO 182 Squadron

*

Jagdgeschwader 3 had been fairly successful in its attack upon Eindhoven. Heinz Bär had claimed two Typhoons on the ground in the initial attack, undoubtedly the first two aircraft of 438 Squadron. However, over the aerodrome and in action with 439 and 485 Squadrons, as well as 440 Squadron, over the field and afterwards, plus losses to ground defensive fire, JG3 lost a total of sixteen pilots, ten being killed, six being taken prisoner, while two other pilots returned home wounded.

*

After the raid, at the bottom end of the airfield where the Canadians were, thick black smoke columns were rising and explosions, including one big one that sent a mushroom cloud up to a great height, added to a very noisy morning.

Shortly after this, as I was watching, several large formations of USAAF medium bombers passed overhead towards the German positions. The lead plane broke away and started circling Eindhoven, then a British plane flew up towards it, firing a Very flare. The lead plane then re-joined its formation and resumed leading them towards the German lines. I've often wondered if the leader thought he was over his target!

Some days before the raid, a four-engined USAAF bomber, badly shot up, force landed on the airfield and an American ground crew came and worked hard for many days repairing it and even changed its engines, completing the job on New Year's Eve. After the raid I saw the American crew-chief standing with his men, scratching his head, looking at the burnt-out piece of twisted metal that was once their pride and joy. One of our 'Erks' stepped forward and said, 'Well, Chief, you really have something to repair now!'

Later, during a visit to the sick-bay for treatment to my knee, I saw the bodies of several German pilots lying outside with snow flakes slowly falling on them. They looked very young. Inside were more bodies covered by blankets, their boots were RAF and Army types. Many wounded were also there so I came out and dressed my own wound. It healed well but I still have the scar.

Leading Aircraftman D.C. Shepherd, 137 Squadron

One feat of personal heroism came from a Canadian Armourer in 39 Wing – Flight Sergeant R.G.C. Beatty. When the attack started he mounted a Bren gun on a partly broken down wall and proceeded to engage the enemy fighters as they came in. Despite the fact that he was practically unprotected he emptied several magazines into several Germans including a FW190 which flew straight at him at a height of about twenty-five feet but which fortunately did not fire. Beatty was thought to have scored hits on at least two fighters, one of which may have crashed.

Whatever the material damage inflicted upon Eindhoven and its wings and squadrons, the personal injuries sustained by the men on the ground were severe. The Canadian Wing's Medical Officer found himself swamped with wounded soon after the guns had stopped firing. He quickly cleared the few patients from his sick quarters to make room for the dozens of wounded and injured that arrived by trucks, ambulances, even a petrol bowser. Within minutes the ward and the corridors were literally covered with men with gaping wounds and bloodied uniforms. In one corner sat an airman, screaming as he held up two mangled hands. Another who had been having trouble with varicose veins looked down at a shattered leg and said, 'They sure fixed my veins for me.' He died the next day. Even as the bomb dump blew up to shower everyone with glass, the tending of the wounded continued.

In the afternoon the Mess was cleaned up, and the dead prepared for burial – including the bodies of four Luftwaffe pilots. There were also many small injuries, mostly sprains caused during hasty retreats from the airfield as the machine-guns and cannons began to sweep the field.

At the Unit's dispersal, 'planes so laboriously repaired were now in various states of destruction, very few being left unmarked. Some were burning fiercely, cannon shells exploding at intervals. Mercifully the only man wounded was a Corporal driver of a Coles crane, but later we learned that LAC Osborne who had been with me the previous evening, had been killed when the huge tyre of a Coles crane exploded after being pierced by a cannon shell. Sergeant Scott and LAC Brown were both wounded in the same incident!

Corporal E. W. J. Sadler, 403 R & S Unit

CHAPTER SIX

Ursel and St Denis Westrem

Following an early briefing by commanders of all three Gruppen of Oberst Herbert Ihelefeld's Jagdgeschwader 1, based at Twente, Drone and Rheine, the pilots felt better. Little had been said the previous evening but being confined to their bases, everyone guessed something big was in the offing. Once the plan of the operation was given to them, they also felt a little happier because for much of the outward flight would be flown over territory held by their own forces.

Flying across north-west Germany and across Holland they would reach the sea north off The Hague, turn south-west to follow the coast before turning inland towards their targets – the airfields of Maldegem, Ursel and St Denis Westrem. I and III Gruppen were assigned the first two, II Gruppe the third.

Led by two Ju88s, JG1, like JG6, was routed to Spakenburg at the southern tip of the Zuider Zee but would carry on westwards to the Dutch coast. However, the 'safest' part, over German-held territory, proved an early danger for, in the secrecy of the overall plan, German AA defences had not been fully alerted to expect large formations of low level Luftwaffe fighters flying over them. Being more used to seeing large armada of RAF or USAAF aeroplanes only, they not unnaturally adopted the usual role of 'shoot first and ...' Thus Hauptmann Hackbarth's I Gruppe came under friendly AA fire, losing two FW190s flown by Feldwebels Comtesse and Kilian, and a third later, south of Rotterdam, piloted by Feldwebel Heinz Böhmer.

Despite this frustration, and with a strong urge to break radio silence, the force of JG1 flew on, turned to fly down the coast and shortly after 9 a.m., turned in over the coast between Blankenburge and Knokke and headed for Bruges. Reaching this historic town, the main force headed east for the base at Maldegem while No 4 Staffel, led by Oberleutnant Meinhoff, broke away to attack Ursel.

The plan of attack against Maldegem was that I and III Gruppen would make five attacking runs over the air base, but now II Gruppe appeared on the scene and, in the confusion, several Focke Wulf pilots of I Gruppe tagged onto them and were led off towards St Denis Westrem.

However, the Me109G-14 pilots of III Gruppe reached Maldegem but had some difficulty in picking out ground targets, and so went in to see what they could hit. An estimated dozen Me109s (according to 349 Squadron) arrived over the airfield at 9.20 a.m. (135 Wing Diary states 8.45 a.m.!!). 349 Squadron recorded that the first run-in was a dummy pass at tree-top height, followed by at least three more passes, each time with guns blazing. Coming in out of the morning sun, very little damage was done to 349, as their Spitfire IXEs were all well dispersed and in fact only one of their Spitfires was destroyed. Coming in over the hangars, the Messerschmitt pilots were unable to pick out the Belgian squadron's aircraft, and when they did see them, it was too late to get their sights on.

Luckily for the Germans, the AA defences had been moved some days previously and the only defence the airfield could muster was Vickers guns, rifles, sten-guns and revolvers.

Not so fortunate were the New Zealanders of 485 (NZ) Squadron. According to their diarist the attack was made by six Me109Es! at 9.10 a.m. They, however lost a total of eleven of their Spitfire IXEs destroyed, plus two more so badly damaged as to be beyond repair, plus 135 Wing Leader's personal Spitfire.

Aircraft fitters were in the process of starting up the squadron's aircraft when the attack began and arguments among the airmen as to whether the low flying aircraft were Mustangs or Thunderbolts were apparently settled in the nearby ditches!

With flames and smoke from burning and exploding Spitfires rising from the airfield, the New Zealand pilots were directing revolver fire from windows and doorways of the billets under the direction of their CO, Squadron Leader J.G. Pattison, who was blazing away with a German Mauser rifle. The squadron 'battle dress' was a variety of pyjamas, polo-necked sweaters and underpants!

Had it not been for ice on the runway, the Spitfires would have been in the air some thirty minutes earlier and Maldegem would have had very few losses on the ground. As it was, 485 Squadron were left with just five serviceable Spitfires when the Messerschmitts left. III Gruppe, however, did not get away scot-free. Despite meagre defensive fire, two pilots were shot down over the airfield, both being captured.

*

Meantime, Oberleutnant Meinhoff arrived over Ursel having lost one of his Staffel of five men, Feldwebel Fritzsche, to Allied AA fire. At Ursel was No 424 Re-arming and Refuelling Unit. This unit had been formed at Merston in the autumn of 1944 and sailed to Ostend in November, still as part of Fighter Command. As the object was to use part of Fighter Command in an offensive role for two or three days at a time on the Continent, from bases in England, the single runway airfield at Ursel was used for these units to be serviced. It was situated mid-way between Bruges and Ghent. One of the airfield Controllers was Sergeant Peter Crowest.

> The reception and despatch of up to twelve squadrons of Spitfires on such a small airstrip set some exciting problems, especially as they always seemed to arrive at the same moment. Obviously with limited petrol capacity they couldn't be left circling for too long. The despatch of six squadrons from one end of the runway followed by the take-off of six squadrons from the other end was a traumatic experience for an airfield controller accustomed to the deliberate tempo of aircraft in Bomber Command or 2nd TAF.
>
> There was a choice of two positions for the airfield controller at Ursel. One was at the top of an open-topped tower made of logs positioned opposite the middle of the runway. The other was on the ground at the down-wind end of the runway and here there were some low concrete walls behind which one could shelter if under fire. Fortunately I was stationed at the latter position on the morning of 1st January.

We were positioned for duty at 9 a.m. and had barely time to judge the extent of our hangovers from the 'night before' when we heard and saw a squadron of low flying fighters approaching. An enquiry from my CO as to whether we were expecting Spitfires was answered when I said that they were not Spitfires but Focke Wulf 190s. Moments later I was firmly gripping the ground!

These three FW190s proceeded to shoot up the airfield. There were four or five sundry unserviceable aircraft on the ground and these were destroyed. Fortunately twelve squadrons of Spitfires had returned to England the day before!

We had no ground defence and the corporal in charge of the fire tender asked if he should engage the enemy with his sten-gun. I told him to remain under cover. So far as I recall, there were no personnel casualties at Ursel that morning.

Sergeant P. Crowest, 424 R & R U

Another airman of 424 R & R Unit was Leading Aircraftman Ernest Green who was a member of the MT Section.

1st January 1945 started off as a beautiful bright sunny day. December had been very cold with rain, snow and ice, also fog which closed most airfields round this part of the Continent. Ursel, I remember, was the only one to stay open, because we never gave up clearing the runway with snow ploughs and salt, flown in from England by Dakotas.

The RAF men were billeted in Ursel village about one mile from the airfield, in an old bakery owned by a young couple who had a baby daughter. There were eight airmen (all trades). Most days we were up at 6.30 a.m., washed, shaved and then breakfast in an old disused leather factory at the end of the village. We then took a truck up to the airfield to report to the MT Section. That morning I was told to get a small van and pick up a work party on the other side of the airfield and take them to the Control Tower, as nearby was a plane that had been damaged in a raid and had landed on our field for a few repairs, but before I could do this job, I was given a list of various vans etc, that required to have the petrol and mileage checked for the end of the month log-books. Also on the airfield was an American B17 Flying Fortress which had landed on the field after being shot up over Germany. This was having repairs carried out by American mechanics over several weeks and the job was nearly finished. The Fortress was standing near our oil storage dump and the Spitfire bomb dump. On most fine days there would have been several squadrons of Spitfires which flew in from RAF Manston at dawn. During daylight hours they would raid the rocket sites and other targets. They had flown off the day before.

I collected my mileage and petrol amounts and was about to take my repair party out to the plane, a Mosquito, when I remembered that I had forgotten to check another truck some way back, so I stopped my van, ran back, got the details, when in the distance I heard aircraft and thought it must be some of ours about to land. Suddenly there was a very loud explosion and when I looked to see where it came from the first thing I saw was the Mosquito near the Control Tower going up in flames and black smoke. More gunfire and then the B17 Fortress was in flames, also the oil drums. Everyone started to take cover in a ditch and elsewhere. I saw three or four FW190s, with the sun on them, and flying along as if they were on a weekend trip with not a care in the world. With all this going on an RAF Sergeant Armourer came out of his store hut with a machine-gun, got down in the ditch and had a go at the departing planes. What he was calling the Luftwaffe cannot be put in print! I can see him now with this machine-gun pointed up to the sky, expecting to hit one of the 190s.

Soon the fighters were gone and people got into fire parties to try and pull the oil drums away from the vicinity of the B17, but it was too late. The Fortress was a total wreck. When I found my party of repair men, we just looked at each other and knew that had I not forgotten to check the last truck we would all have been in the middle of that first attacking pass standing by the Mosquito. I heard afterwards that several of my mates thought I had gone up with the plane.

When things started to cool down it was found that several bullets had hit the ammunition store doors but had not exploded and were in fact dummies – probably made by forced labourers in Germany. When life on the airfield returned to normal people went around with tongue in cheek when aircraft noises were heard, saying, 'It's only one of ours!' and thank goodness that is how it remained at Ursel.

Leading Aircraftman E.H. Green, 424 R & R U

Two other aircraft destroyed on the ground were Lancaster bombers which had been damaged on operations and flopped down at Ursel. Oberleutnant Meinhoff and his two wingmen flew off but he was hit subsequently by ground fire over Breda on the way home and was killed.

*

Meanwhile II/JG1 arrived over St Denis Westrem, the home of No 131 (Polish) Wing and 85 Group's Communication Squadron. As mentioned in Chapter Two, the three Polish squadrons had left their base about an hour earlier – luckily for them but unluckily for the Germans, as we shall see.

On St Denis Westrem that cold January morning was one air force officer who was on his way back to England. L.A. Simmons, a former soldier in WW1 who had later served in the RAF, had re-joined the Air Force when WW2 began. Having arrived at St Denis the previous day, en-route for England, it was arranged that he should be flown out early the next day, 1st January, by the Communications Squadron. He was told to report to the Flight Office at 9.30 a.m. L.A. Simmons recorded the events which followed in a notebook of recollections:

New Year's Day broke bright and clear. There hadn't been any more snow falls during the night but what was left of the previous days snow was frozen hard. I drove myself in one of our jeeps ... and arrived at the field in good time. The sun was shining brightly and there wasn't a cloud in the sky. The sort of morning when one feels that it is good to be alive.

I reported to the Flight Office and was told the number of the aeroplane that was to take me. The machines belonging to the Communications Flight were parked in a batch some 200 yards

on the aerodrome from the Flight Office and for some reason my
driver hadn't departed, he said, 'Jump in, Sir, I'll drive you over,
why walk?'

There were quite a lot of machines standing there. Five
Ansons, a Mosquito, a Spitfire and a couple of Austers. My jeep
pulled up close to the tail of an Anson which happened to be the
one my number was on. The mechanics were brushing snow
from the wings and hot air was being applied to the engines from
a Commer Heater Van. It was now 9.30 – the time we were told
we should be taking off, but so far no sight of a pilot.

I got my bag out of the jeep but when I tried the door of the
Anson I found it jammed and it was five minutes before it could
be got open. Two or three of my fellow passengers had rolled up
while we were struggling with the door and when it was opened,
two got in before me. I tossed my bag in and was halfway in
myself when I happened to look over my shoulder and saw a
mass of aircraft coming towards the 'drome from the north and
while I yet looked, crowds of lights started coming from them –
and a second later, TAT, TAT, TAT, TAT, TAT, TAT, PUM, PUM,
PUM, PUM, which developed into the most appalling clatter you
ever did hear.

I found myself flat on my face on the ground between the jeep,
with my head burried under my hat. The Anson which I so
nearly got into was a mass of flames within two minutes and the
petrol tanks were due to go up. I glanced along the ground to my
left. The cannon tracers were hitting the ground and bouncing
off in graceful curves and there seemed to be hundreds of them,
in fact there were. It was a free-for-all for the Jerry pilots as there
was no ground defences at all! They flew round and attacked
and attacked again till their ammunition was used up.

When I looked under the jeep I found I wasn't alone. There
was at least five people under it and from what I could see they
all looked to be badly hit – torn trousers with bloody flesh
showing. I decided to make a dash for the edge of the 'drome. I
decided to make it in short dashes. Each time a FW190 dived, I
dived on my face and after three or four of these efforts I gained a
disused gun-pit, which was half full of oil drums.

*

Just a few moments before these events occurred, 302 Polish Squadron had begun to return from its dawn mission – its armed recce operation, during which targets had been dive-bombed. The squadron had lost one of its number when returning towards base, flying over the area which often saw V1 flying bomb activity. Flight Sergeant Stanislaw Celak (MH883) was hit by Allied AA fire but he successfully force-landed in a field.

The squadron, minus Celak, arrived back at St Denis Westrem at just the wrong moment and were in the process of landing when JG1 struck. Also in the air was Flying Officer Waclaw Chojnacki (MJ281 ZF-P) of 308 Squadron. He had flown out with his squadron, but in the dive-bomb attack on a ferry and buildings near Wounstrecht, Chojnacki found he was unable to release his two bombs. At 9.05 a.m., Flight Lieutenant Ignacy Olszewski, leading 308, ordered Chojnacki to try to jettison the bombs while he and the others circled north of the Maas. Not seeing him again, Olszewski called Chojnacki on the radio and ordered him home. He therefore left his companions and returned directly to base. He arrived over St Denis at 9.27 a.m. circling slowly before he began his final approach.

It was at this moment, with most of 302 Squadron landing, others about to land and Flying Officer Chojnacki on finals, that JG1 came in for their first strafing attack.

Seeing the German fighters, Chojnacki raised his undercarriage and immediatedly went into the attack, presumably with both bombs still on board! On the ground was one pilot who had not been flying that morning – Sergeant Strobel. Witnessing the start of the action over the airfield, Strobel later made this report:

> I was at 308 Squadron's dispersal when the enemy attacked the airfield. I escaped from there and hid in a roadside ditch. I saw a single Spitfire arriving over base at 2,000 feet in a port turn. Three FW190s were just coming in to strafe. The Spitfire, marked ZF-P, piloted by Flying Officer Chojnacki, noticed these enemy aircraft and while still on the turn fired on the rearmost from 800 yards. The enemy aircraft was hit in the tail and a large part of the tail flew off. The enemy pilot lost control and being low, hit a tree with its starboard wing, hit the top of a small

building on the airfield perimeter and came to rest inside a (Flying) Fortress standing on the ground. I then lost sight of the Spitfire in the smoke from the burning Fortress but saw it a moment later chasing another 190, but three other 190s on his tail. The Spitfire broke to starboard and I lost him again.

The gallant 27-year-old Chojnacki, who had been with 308 Squadron since February 1944, was himself shot down and killed a few moments later. As this happened the rest of the Polish pilots were either being engaged over other parts of Holland on their way back or about to join combat with the attacking JG1 pilots over their base airfield at St Denis. They were to have a field day.

CHAPTER SEVEN

The Poles in Action

Receiving Chojnacki's radio acknowledgement that he was returning to base, Olszewski too set course for St Denis. Nearing the River Schelde, Olszewski saw that a convoy of ships in the river were firing, the Polish leader turning the squadron in that direction. Just then Sergeant Stanislaw Breyner's voice came over the R/T – 'Enemy aircraft very low, below and in front of us!'

Breyner, at 4,000 feet, broke formation and dived after two aircraft flying low towards the sun which made it difficult for him to identify them. Closing to 100 yards he recognised them as FW190s, flying at 200 feet. He was just about to fire when the second 190 pilot saw the Spitfire. Both pulled up very sharply, then rolled and dived. One of the Focke Wulfs crashed straight into a building and the other into the ground before they could pull out of their panic dives.[1]

Flight Lieutenant Olszewski attacked several 190s, forcing three to turn and separate from the others. The remainder flew away to the north-east, pursued by Flight Lieutenant Bronislaw Mach with others of the squadron. Meantime, Flight Sergeant Zygmunt Soczynski tackled another 190, firing from 100 yards, seeing strikes on the tail and cockpit. Moments later the 190 rolled onto its port wing and crashed. These actions were in the Lokeron area, some distance to the east of Ghent and St Denis Westrem.

Chasing the other gaggle of 190s, Flight Lieutenant Mach closed in behind one, firing from 200 yards down to 100 yards. Hitting the German fighter, he watched it turn onto its back as the pilot baled

[1] Breyner died on 17th February 1945 following injuries received in a flying accident on 12th February.

out, coming down in the Schelde near Termonde, almost due north of Ghent.

Then, Flight Lieutenant Olszewski heard over the radio a conversation between the GCC and 317 Squadron that Antwerpe was under attack. Gathering five Spitfires from the action, Olszewski led them towards Ghent at 2,000 feet, but then saw smoke rising from the direction of St Denis. 'Look out!' he warned, 'Germans attacking our airfield. Those with enough petrol make for Ghent, those who haven't land at Maldegem.'

Closing in on the airfield, Olszewski expected to see the enemy aircraft withdraw but instead he saw them circling over the airfield and repeating their strafing attacks. Seemingly, the Luftwaffe pilots, not expecting opposition from the west, were unaware of the approaching Spitfire.

*

Moments before Olszewski's arrival, Flight Sergeant Josef Stanowski approached the field. Getting low on fuel he had broken away from the others and headed for home, reaching St Denis before the others to find German fighters shooting it up. He immediately closed in on a FW190 and hammered it with all his armament. The 190 caught fire at once and crashed in flames south of Ghent. Turning, he engaged another 190 flying east, fired from 100 yards. The 190's wheels flopped down as Stanowski fired again, seeing the 190 dive into the centre of the town and explode. Now right out of petrol, Stanowski had to make a force-landing northeast of the town.

Olszewski and his pilots waded into the mass of German fighters above the airfield; the Polish leader selected a Focke Wulf and opened fire. Hit by cannon fire the 190 flicked onto its back and crashed just east of Ghent. Flying Officer Tadeusz Szlenkier arrived over base at 3,000 feet and spotted a 190 attacking a Spitfire. He dived upon it as the 190 began to level out, then opened fire from 250 yards. The German fighter was well below 1,000 feet and Szlenkier's deadly fire smashed its right wing, sending the fighter over onto its back seconds before it hit the ground. Szlenkier's Spitfire (MK346 ZF-T) was then hit and shortly afterwards he was forced to crash-land.

On our return from the morning sortie we had very little fuel left. Nevertheless we had height advantage and therefore were in a superior position. Despite a numerical disadvantage of one to two, this enabled us to score heavily. I claimed one FW190A-8 that day. It fell near a small place called Rosdam which is some five kilometres west from Zwignaarde and two kilometres east of Deurle. A large part of the aircraft, including the engine and cockpit, got buried in the ground. This was due to the high momentum at impact and the softness of the soggy ground.

It was always a wonder to me that the German commander did not send a flight of his Focke Wulfs up to 15,000 or 20,000 feet, in order to protect his strafing, low level flying machines. If he had done so the story would have been different. One interesting aspect of our encounter with the Me109s and FW190s was that a few of these aircraft were flown by Latvian pilots serving with the Luftwaffe.

Flying Officer T.K. Szlenkier, 308 Squadron

Pilot Officer Andrzej Dromlewicz also went after a 190 which was attacking a Spitfire, forcing the enemy pilot to break to the right. Dromlewicz followed, closed in to 300 yards and continued to fire until his cannon ammo. gave out. Pulling up into a climb the 190 caught a burst from the Pole's machine-guns, which blasted pieces from its right wing. Rolling over, the 190's pilot took to his parachute.

This fight ended some distance to the west of Ghent and nearby Flight Lieutenant Mach gained his second victory. Following his first kill to the north near Termonde, Mach had headed for the battle over base and following a tussle with two 190s, one of which he had damaged, he began to chase another which had attacked him. This fight commenced at 2,000 feet but was soon down to zero feet as the German pilot tried to escape. His fire produced strikes on the 190 and its cockpit canopy flew off as Mach's guns fell silent. Shortly afterwards the 190 went down and crashed west of Terneuzen.

Mach's number three was Warrant Officer Stanislaw Bednarcyzk, who had seen his section leader's first victim go down and over base saw a 190 attempt an attack on Mach. Attacking this aircraft, he shot it down south-west of the airfield.

*

As these Spitfires chased, attacked and pursued these FW190s over and around the airfield amidst the smoke from the burning aircraft on the ground, 317 Squadron had also arrived on the scene.

The Squadron Commander, Squadron Leader Marian Chelmecki, at twenty-eight years old and holder of three Polish KWs a veteran Polish air fighter, had led his pilots in a successful attack that morning before receiving a radio call that some sixty German aircraft were assembling north of his position. As he flew back towards Ghent, GCC then notified him that Antwerpe and his own base were under attack.

Flying towards Antwerpe, Chelmecki then heard the voice of Olszewski that 308 Squadron were in action over St Denis. The pilots of 317 easily picked out their base from the clouds of black smoke that rose into the air, and then they saw the German fighters circling and diving. Not hesitating for a moment, Chelmecki led his men into the attack.

As the Polish squadron commander dived into the midst of the attacking enemy fighters, another Spitfire roared past him, firing into a FW190 which simply disintegrated in the air. The Spitfire was flown by Flight Lieutenant Czeslaw Mroczyk and as he pulled up, another 190 slid onto his tail. Chelmecki saw this and pulled in between the 190 and Mroczyk's machine, forcing the German pilot to pull into a sharp lefthand turn. Chelmecki climbed into the sun and seeing a 190 began a strafing run on the airfield from the direction of Ghent, dived at it. Opening fire with cannon and machine-guns from 400 yards, Chelmecki lost the 190 as it dived through the smoke from the burning American Fortress, flying in a righthand diving turn.

The Pole may have lost sight of his 190 but people on the ground saw what happened to it. Flight Lieutenant Jan Bendix, Senior Intelligence Officer with 302 Squadron was leaving his room when the enemy first attacked. Watching the attack develop he saw a FW190 strafing a line of Spitfires from the direction of Ghent. As it went through the smoke from the Fortress, it was clearly out of control. It then hit a small building and crashed in flames just beyond the nearby railway line. This was the second Focke Wulf to hit this particular building, the first being Waclaw Chojnacki's victim. As the second FW190 blew up, Bendix saw Chelmecki's Spitfire pull up into a climbing turn above the smoke.

Sergeant K. Hubert arrived over the base at 2,000 feet and attacked a red-nosed 190 which he saw 1,700 feet below him. One long burst sent the Focke Wulf crashing into the centre of Ghent. Climbing again, Sergeant Hubert saw three FW190s and attacked the rearmost, using the rest of his ammunition. Flames began to stream from the 190 but then he saw a Spitfire being attacked by another 190 and quickly made a pass at the German, forcing the pilot to break off his attack.

When Warrant Officer Stanislaw Piesik arrived over Ghent he saw two FWs passing the airfield after a strafing run, and he dived after them. As he fired into one, it went into a gentle turn to the left, while a second burst caused an explosion and a stream of smoke. Piesik then had tracer shells zip over his cockpit canopy and he quickly broke away, leaving his victim in flames and going down. As he levelled out, another 190 came in head-on and although Piesik's return fire was reduced as his cannon ammunition gave out, his machine guns scored hits on the 190's cowling.

Warrant Officer Zenobieuz Wdowczynski arrived over the base alone, having developed engine trouble earlier on the dawn mission. He heard of the battle over the radio and as he reached the airfield saw a 190 flying over Ghent at 1,000 feet. Despite his rough engine, the Polish pilot attacked the German fighter which went down and crashed north-east of Ghent. Then a 190 attacked his Spitfire. Wdowczynski pulled up sharply, stalled and went into a spin. Managing to pull out he made for the airfield but then his engine finally gave out and he had to crash-land.

As Flight Lieutenant Roman Hrycak came over the airfield he saw a FW190 diving down to attack the base's petrol dump. Chasing the German, he fired from 200 yards seeing hits on the cockpit. The 190 was right on the deck but then began to pull up sharply and the Polish pilot lost sight of it. However, three groundcrewman saw the 190 go down. Leading Aircraftman E. Zielinski was taking cover at 317's dispersal and saw the 190 go for the dump and be attacked by a Spitfire coded JH-H (Hrycak's

Spitfire). The 190 trailed smoke and went down. Corporal Z.
Kalecki was actually taking cover under a petrol bowser which he
had been refuelling at the dump when the 190s came in. This 190
actually fired at his bowser, but as it flashed overhead, Kalecki saw
the pursuing Spitfire firing and hitting the Focke Wulf. Leading
Aircraftman Bohdan Gronowski looked out of a window to see the
190 and the Spitfire. After the Spitfire's attack the 190 pulled up,
streamed smoke, rolled over and went down behind some
buildings.

In the air battle above the airfield, Flight Lieutenant Zbigniew
Zmigrodzki chased another 190 away to the east, his fire producing
black smoke from its engine. Seeing another 190 coming in on his
tail, he broke away, leaving his victim heading east leaving a trail of
smoke. Zmigrodzki then saw a Spitfire being chased by a 190, the
Spitfire too leaving a smoke trail as it made a gentle righthand turn.
Zmigrodzki attacked the 190 and saw some hits but the Spitfire was
finished, and it went down and hit the ground. It was piloted by
Flight Lieutenant Tadeusz Powierza, aged thirty, who had been
with 317 Squadron since August 1944, following service with 303
and 302 Squadrons. Holder of the Polish KW, Powierza was killed
in his machine (MK190 JH-P).

*

Flying Officer Wlodzimierz 'Jim' Link of 308 Squadron, who had
gone down with a cold and sore throat, thereby missing the dawn
show, was asleep in his bed when the attack began. He awoke to
find several of his comrades running and scurrying about dressed in
underwear and pyjamas, rapidly covered with greatcoats or Irvine
flying jackets. With nobody knowing what was behind the attack,
and expecting something big to happen next, Link was sent into the
local town to collect as many brother pilots who were off duty, as he
could find. With enemy aircraft still roaring overhead, trying to
steer the Adler car over icy roads, all thoughts of his cold were
quickly forgotten.

He only managed to locate three pilots and by the time he
returned to the aerodrome the attack was over and the field covered
in smoke and flames.

*

While the battle raged, L.A. Simmons, on the ground, had vacated his disused gun pit and made a final dash from there to the edge of the airfield. Here, he discovered he had been slightly injured by two splinters, one had hit him in the left forearm, and a second nicked his ear lobe. He also discovered that a number of his would-be passengers had been badly injured and he helped to dress their wounds. His diary continued:

> Just after I finished the last dash, there was four pretty hefty explosions and I thought for a moment we were to be treated to a bombing as well. Two tall columns of smoke were going up from Ghent itself which looked like bomb bursts. Several Spitfires of the Polish Wing (were engaged) and the smoke from the town came from two Focke Wulfs that had been shot down into the streets. The other two explosions had been fragmentation bombs. The view from where I was standing looked very grim. Thirty or forty machines were burning together with some transport.

Living near the airfield at St Denis Westrem was the de Meulemeester family. Staying with them was Charles de Penaranda, who was engaged to the de Meulemeesters' daughter. He recalls:

On this New Year's Day, the first free New Year for four years it was bitter cold. It had snowed and the ditches were frozen over. My future in-laws' house is situated on the territory of Zwijnaarde, a village a few miles south of Ghent, and about a mile away from the St Denis airfield. A few days before the last desperate attack launched by the Luftwaffe on 1st January, an American Flying Fortress had made a forced landing on the airfield.

My future in-laws, my fiancée and myself set out on foot about 9.30 a.m., to bring New Year's greetings to our family in a nearby village. Suddenly we heard and saw a plane flying very low, which was quite a customary thing, so we didn't pay much attention to it. We hadn't realised it was a German plane until a few seconds afterwards, a second plane swooped along and we heard the unmistakable stutter of machine-guns. We fell flat on our faces in the frozen ditches and could hear heavy firing coming from the direction of St Denis Westrem followed by a terrific crash not far from where we were lying.

All this lasted a few minutes – they seemed very long to us – and when eventually everything seemed to quieten down, we left our uncomfortable position. We could see a huge column of smoke rising from the airfield, several Allied fighters having been hit on the ground as well as the Flying Fortress, much to the delight of the American maintenance crew which had been assigned the job of repairing it which was now quite out of the question.

The heavy explosion that we heard was that of a German fighter that had crashed in a field quite close to where we had been cooling off in the ditches. The fighter had also hit an old willow tree and the pilot had been killed. The military authorities who later came to the spot were very surprised to disover an owl in the plane's engine. The poor thing had been brutally carried off when the fighter struck its tree. The Polish pilots based at St Denis intercepted the attackers on their way back from an early mission.

The Polish airmen are not forgotten here. At St Denis Westrem there is a 'Polish Wing' Street and every year a remembrance service is held in the church of St Denis Westrem for the Poles who were killed in action.

In this same church on that January morning were townspeople crowded for the 9 a.m. Mass. When the congregation heard the noise of the attack, they came out to see what was happening but rapidly dashed back inside when they realised what was occurring over the airfield.

*

As the air battle began to end, several Polish pilots were now desperately short of fuel and asked for permission to land. Squadron Leader Chelmecki flew over the runway to check if it was clear and undamaged, then gave permission to land. Flight Lieutenant Mroczyk landed across the runway with a damaged

Spitfire and no petrol, blocking the runway. Chelmecki, therefore, had to divert the other pilots to either Ursel or Courtrai. Sergeant Breyner didn't make either and as his fuel ran out he had to force-land near Brussels.

When the surviving JG1 pilots left St Denis behind them, they left the aerodrome covered in smoke and littered with burning aircraft. Nine Spitfires of 302 Squadron were destroyed on the ground and with the loss of Flight Sergeant Celak's earlier, it made ten for the day. 308 Squadron lost six Spitfires on the ground, one in combat with four others damaged, mainly in forced landings. 317 Squadron also lost six on the ground, a seventh in combat plus another damaged in the air.

The exact extent of the damage to other aircraft on the airfield, or the losses to the Communications Squadron is not certain. The American B17 was destroyed plus also a Stirling of 295 Squadron, and possibly a Spitfire of 316 Polish Squadron.

*

When the noise of aircraft died down, L.A. Simmons found there was quite a number of dead and wounded about him and later an ambulance arrived. One of the wounded was a Commander. Simmons recorded:

> I asked the Commander if he were in pain. He said he couldn't feel anything at all but what was worrying him was that his only suit of pyjamas was in his suitcase that he'd left standing by the Anson! Would I be so good as to go see if I could rescue it? I did and it was very nearly my undoing. I expect it was just about the maddest thing to do to attempt to walk among burning aircraft which were firing their guns all over the place, not to mention oxygen bottles exploding.
>
> I got to where I was able to see our late machine and could plainly see the suitcase burning merrily. On turning round to come back the one and only Mosquito fired a cannon – the shell roared past my right ear and into the ground a few yards away!
>
> It appears that one or both of the two men that had got into the Anson had been burned with the machine – I didn't feel very bright when I was told this. On our way out to the main road I

saw the wreckage of a German fighter – apparently this machine had dived in very low across the main road that borders the 'drome and had collided with the nose of a Stirling bomber that was parked together with a Liberator and two Fortresses. The 190, after hitting the Stirling at a tremendous speed, had hit the ground and gone skating across the frozen snow shedding bits of itself in all directions.

The troops watched one of the Polish Spitfires shoot down a Focke Wulf into the next street (in Ghent). The pilot – a fair haired boy of seventeen or eighteen parachuted into the canal but was pulled out unhurt.

So much for New Year's Day. I think I have to thank a jammed door of that Anson for my being alive. Also the pilot of the Anson for being late as we would have undoubtedly been shot down if we had taken off on time. We would have run into the whole bunch of them.

*

JG1 lost eighteen pilots killed, six taken prisoner with another pilot wounded, II Gruppe losing ten of those killed and one prisoner. One of those lost was Hauptmann Georg Hackbarth, the Gruppenkommandeur, who actually crashed on the airfield. Stabsfeldwebel Fritz Hofmann of the 3rd Staffel was shot down by flak and taken prisoner. Leutnant Swoboda's 5th Staffel lost five pilots. One Focke Wulf dived into a flower shop not far from Ghent railway station, another hit a roof in the town and ended up in a garden. The FW190A-8 that had come down by the de Meulemeesters' home had been flown by Feldwebel Harrys Klints of 2/JG1 a Latvian pilot in service with the Luftwaffe.

The Germans were unfortunate in being engaged by the returning Polish Wing. For their part, the ever aggressive Poles claimed a total of twenty destroyed two probably destroyed and five damaged for the loss of two pilots in combat. The Polish leader of the wing, Group Captain A. Gabszewicz DSO, DFC, VM, KW, received the following signal from the AOC 84 Group:

My very best congratulations to you and your squadrons on their great show this morning. In destroying twenty-one Huns you more than made up for your losses on the ground and taught the enemy a lesson he will not soon forget.

One British pilot landed at St Denis Westrem – the new CO of 257 Squadron who had only just been appointed to command, and who had been on leave in England, Squadron Leader Arthur Todd.

I do remember the attacks, since I was on my way back from the UK, having been on leave. All the bases had been attacked and I had to divert from my original flight plan to Deurne. I landed at the base of the Polish Spitfire Wing, who were airborne at the time of the attack and so escaped destruction on the ground. One thing I remember well was that the Luftwaffe changed all their radio frequencies so that we had no warning through the 'Y' service.

Squadron Leader A.G. Todd, CO 257 Squadron

CHAPTER EIGHT

Grimbergen and Evere

Oberstleutnant Josep 'Pips' Priller, one of the most distinguished German fighter pilots on the Western Front, was the CO of Jagdgeschwader 26, 'Schlageter'. His Staff Staffel and I Gruppe were based at Fürstenau and he was to lead them against Grimbergen airfield, just north of Brussels. He was reinforced by three flying instructors from a Special Staffel of JG104, who had flown in from Fürth, near Nuremberg on the 31st, plus seventeen aircraft from III/JG54 from Varrelbusch. All units were equipped with long-nosed FW190D-9s.

Priller's II and III Gruppen, commanded by two other highly experienced and successful air fighters, Major Anton Hackl and Hauptmann Walter Krupinski, flying D-9s and Me109s respectively. These two units would attack another of the Brussels airfields – Evere.

*

The German pilots were up early and with Priller, flying at the head of the Grimbergen force were on their airfield at 6 a.m. They too would fly to Spakenburg, led by two Ju88s, then turn to the south by the Hague where they would make for Brussels. The other two Gruppen would go for Evere.

Leaving the ground at 8.15 a.m., Priller's formation consisting of 67 FW190s, flew out at 100-150 feet. Between Utrecht and Rotterdam the force came under severe German AA fire which brought down Oberleutnant Franz Kunz, leader of the 2nd Staffel, followed by other casualties west of Rotterdam. As if this was not enough, the Allied gunners opened up on them as they crossed the Schelde Estuary, damaging Stabfeldwebel Steinkamp's 190, forcing him to bale out into captivity. Two other FWs went into the water and Corporal Dieter Krägeloh of 3/JG26 collected hits. He flew on but when engaged by Spitfires his propeller was shot away, forcing him to crash-land. He too was taken prisoner.

II and III/JG26 also suffered from ground fire on their route, two aircraft being shot down by German flak as they reached the Zuider Zee. Others were hit over the Schelde.

*

Pips Priller found Grimbergen without difficulty at 9.20 a.m., leading his men in in three waves as planned. But all they found was an empty airfield. All there was was just four American B17s, one Mustang fighter and a twin-engined aeroplane. The attack set all four bombers and the Mustang on fire, while the other pilots gave vent to their feelings by strafing the hangers, barracks and other buildings. Several trucks and petrol bowsers were also destroyed or damaged. One airman was killed and two others wounded.

On Grimbergen was Group Captain Aleksander Gabszewicz DSO, DFC, VM, KW. Despite his high rank he was a flying leader. He had been in action when the Germans invaded his native Poland on 1st September 1939, then fought in France, later escaping to England to fly with the RAF. He had flown all through the war and was still flying on operations when the war ended in May 1945.

Gabszewicz had flown to Grimbergen with his adjutant, from his base at St Denis Westrem, on 31st December. His wing was due to move into Grimbergen and the Group Captain wanted to see what the airfield had to offer. Shortly after nine o'clock he and his adjutant came out of their billet to drive to the Mess for breakfast. They heard aircraft in the air and wondered who was flying over Grimbergen so early. They thought it must be some Spitfires, then Gabszewicz yelled – 'They're bloody Focke Wulfs!'

Despite bullets whistling about them they drove to the Headquarters building where the Group Captain put a call through to St Denis only to find they too were under air attack. His wing leader at St Denis, and his second in command, Wing Commander Tadeusz Sawicz DFC, was able, however, to confirm that his squadrons were airborne.

Gabszewicz then organised troops to fire small arms at the attackers. Whether it was these men or the RAF Regiment is not certain, but all were cheered when one Focke Wulf bellied in onto the airfield, its pilot being taken into captivity.

One of the four B17s on the aerodrome had a crew of mechanics working on it. During the attack one mechanic ran passed the Group Captain yelling, 'Jeez, did you see that, did you see that? A bullet just passed between me and my body!'

Gabszewicz was very pleased to learn of his wing's success over its home base, and was pleased that he had told his pilots not to have a party on the night of the 31st but to wait until they moved to Grimbergen.

*

The RAF Regiment was in evidence at Grimbergen. Two flights of 2777 Squadron and one flight of 2719 had been tasked as airfield defence and the attacking aircraft were engaged. Bren guns mounted on recce cars and the Brens of the rifle flight of 2719 blazed away. Three German aircraft were shot down and two damaged. 2777 reported not only FW190s but Me109s in the attack and fire was held on the first pass but when the Germans came in again, so Flight Lieutenant L.W. Boulter, commanding No 3 Flight, ordered his men to open fire. During the action the regiment gunners clearly saw German aircraft circle and shoot up the field for about fifteen minutes, and saw too one aircraft crash on the airfield and one come down near Wolverthem. The pilot of the D-9 that came down on the airfield was Feldwebel G.Egli of JG54 who lied about his unit when captured.

The third fighter claimed was later found by Flying Officer Hunt; the pilot, on being captured, confirmed being hit by light flak as he came over a church on his approach to the airfield. 2777 Squadron was located by this church. Leutnant Theo Nibel of 10/ JG54, after strafing the twin-engined machine, went for one of the gun positions but suddenly his engine cut out and he crash-landed near Wemmel. He is said in one account to have been brought down by a bullet from a Belgian resistance fighter with a well aimed hit in his radiator, but in fact he hit a partridge which knocked a hole in the 190's radiator.

; G/Capt Jimmy Fenton DSO DFC
(Control Centre), AVM Harry
adhurst DSO DFC AFC, AOC 83
up, AM Arthur Coningham DSO MC
C, OC 2nd TAF 1944-45.

dle left: Generalmajor Dietrich Peltz,
man who masterminded Operation

Bodenplatte.

Bottom left: Oberst Gotthardt Handrick, commander of Jagddivision Nr.3.

Bottom right: Wing Commander J B Wray DFC, OC 122 Tempest Wing, Volkel, in front of his personal Tempest.

Top left: Major Karl Borris, commander of I/JG26, attacked Grimbergen.

Top centre: Unteroffizier Hans Kukla, 4th Staffel, JG26, attacked Grimbergen, finding the field un-operational.

Top right: Leutnant Konrad Dammeier, JG6.

Bottom: Pilots of 7/JG26; Ltn Andel, Uf Meihs, Ltn Gottfried Dietze, Uffz Walter Stumpf and Uffz Leopold Speer. Speer was killed on 1 January, flying a D-9, while Stumpf strafed ships on the Schelde on the way home.

left: Leutnant Hans Wulff, 8/JG6, ught down and taken prisoner.

right: LAC Dennis Brooks, No.6022 on Eindhoven.

ddle left: LAC Donald Macdonald, 121 g on Eindhoven. He took shelter in an ice-covered shell hole.

Bottom: Flight Lieutenant Dave Mercer of 268 Squadron, was one of the first airmen to meet the attacking German forces and shot down a Ju188 'pathfinder'.

Top left: Pilot Officer H 'Artie' Shaw, 56 Squadron.

Top right: Oberstleutnant Heinz Bär, leader of JG3, which attacked Eindhoven.

Bottom left: Squadron Leader Gerry Gray DFC, OC 182 Squadron. He arrived on Eindhoven airfield to see his Typhoon strafed by German fighters.

Bottom right: LAC Des Shepherd of 137 Squadron, watched as the Wing's Typhoo were strafed on the ground and saw two German fighters collide right above him.

left: Some of the men of No.403
U on Eindhoven. LAC George Davis
nding on the wing of the striped-down
oon, LAC Shepherd is sitting; Sgt
vick and LAC Reg Williams in front.

right: Flying Officer Pat Pattinson
2 Squadron, drove a damaged petrol
er to a safe spot despite flames

and leaking fuel.

Middle right: Flight Lieutenant George
Clubley DFC, shot down a He111 on
1 January, his first day with 137 Squadron.

Bottom: Wing Commander C D 'Kit'
North-Lewis DSO DFC, OC 124 Typhoon
Wing at Eindhoven.

Top: Burning Typhoons on
Eindhoven airfield.

Middle left: Burning Eindhoven,
1 January 1945.

Middle right: Burning B17 Fortress on

Ursel airfield. Soon afterwards the petr
drums began to explode.

Bottom: Shot down Me109 on Eindhove
airfield.

left: Sergeant Peter Crowest, Airfield
troller on Ursel.

right: LAC Ernest Green (right),
se forgetfullness probably saved his
his companions' lives.

Middle: Flying Officer Waclaw Chojnecki,
308 Polish Squadron, who died over his
base airfield, fighting the attackers.

Bottom: Flying Officer Tadeusz Szlenkier,
308 Polish Squadron, with the wreckage of
the FW190 he shot down on 1 January.

Top: Burning St Denis Westrem.

Middle right: A Polish airman poses by the wreckage of a 109, brought down over St Denis Westrem on 1 January.

Bottom left: This German fighter crashed through the roof of this house in Ghent. The marking suggests a III Gruppe machine (JG1?)

Bottom right: Oberstleutnant Herbert Ihlefeld led JG1's attack upon St Denis Westrem.

Not unnaturally the men of the 4th Rifle Flight of 2719 Squadron also claimed these victories, and final confirmation by 84 Group HQ gave shared credit to both squadrons which was something of a record for small arms fire in one attack action.

Two members of 2719 Squadron were wounded when their vehicle was strafed on the road between Gilze and Breda — Flight Lieutenant J.H. Dyson and Leading Aircraftman G. Crouch. Although wounded in the head and back by an explosive shell, Leading Aircraftman Crouch kept his vehicle on the road and later halted off the main road, thereby keeping the road clear for other traffic.

*

By contrast to Priller's frustrating discovery of an empty airfield at Grimbergen, his II and III Gruppen's attack on Evere was a very different matter.

At Evere was No 127 Wing — Canadian — comprising three Spitfire squadrons, 403, 416 and 421. The wing was commanded by Group Captain W.R. 'Iron Bill' MacBrien RCAF, its Wing Commander Flying being an Englishman, Wing Commander J.E. Johnson DSO, DFC, one of Fighter Command's most successful fighter pilots. On 1st January there were over forty Spitfires on the ground, on the eastern side of the airfield. On the western side was a collection of B17s, Austers and Ansons, a Beechcraft belonging to Prince Bernhard of the Netherlands, and a luxurious VIP Dakota.

Evere's single runway was covered with ice; a sharp frost during the night, followed by rain which had then frozen. Therefore, the usual dawn patrols were delayed until the runway could be gritted. Evere's control called for a weather recce, so two Spitfires of 403 RCAF Squadron took off with some care, just before 9 a.m., and radioed that provided pilots did not use their brakes harshly the runway was all right. This being the case, another section of 403 prepared to take off, while 416 Squadron was called to Readiness.

Although the Germans recorded their attack on Evere began on schedule at 9.20 a.m., the Canadians state it was 9.30 and that in fact the second pair from 403 Squadron were airborne at 9.28. As the Luftwaffe pilots came in they could see tightly packed rows of aircraft, Spitfires and four-engined bombers. As they headed towards these juicy targets the pilots let go their drop tanks. Gunther Bloemertz recorded:

> There lay the broad airfield ... right along our faintly glimmering sights. Hundreds of bombers and fighters were standing drawn up on all sides of the field. Our bursts smacked into the parade. At that moment a few Spitfires were taking off – they moved right into the deadly hail, overturned, crashed or burst into flames.

At the end of the runway it was 416 Squadron that were in the act of taking off, their throttles open following 403 Squadron's two-man section take-off. Leading 416 was Flight Lieutenant D.W.A. Harling DFC, a 23-year-old Canadian from Quebec. Only a few days previously he and some of his comrades had attended his sister's wedding in Brussels. (She was a Canadian nurse.)

As the first section of 416 Squadron rolled forward, the Germans struck, cannon shells slicing through the air among the moving Spitfires. Harling gunned his motor and roared down the runway and in seconds was airborne and whipping up his undercarriage. Behind him the next three Spitfires were all hit but the pilots all jumped out unhurt – Flight Lieutenant Leo Nault,[1] Warrant Officer Lou Jean and Pilot Officer Ken Williams. Major Hackl, Feldwebel Lutz-Wilhelm Burkhardt, Oberleutnant Adolf Glunz and Leutnant Sly of JG26 each claimed a scrambling Spitfire.

Dave Harling gained height as quickly as he could and within moments he was over the Belgian Capital. Here he engaged several Me109s, shot one down but was then shot down himself, crashed and was killed.

*

On the ground, Bill MacBrien and Johnnie Johnson, from a relatively safe position, watched as the German fighters came in, either singly or in pairs. The two men could do little more than

---

[1] A note in 416 Squadron's diary for 9th August 1944 welcomed Nault to his second operational tour. His first had been as an air gunner, and the ironic comment was '... so he should have a 'sharp' eye for the Hun!'

shout with rage as their Spitfires caught fire before their eyes.

There was a small caravan at the end of the runway which was in use as an office for the airfield controller – the duty controller calmly remaining at his post and directing those Spitfires still airborne. Another member of the wing, Flight Lieutenant Frank Minton, its Intelligence Officer, answered a ringing telephone in another operations caravan. The voice of a staff officer came through warning Minton that there were large formations of enemy fighters near Evere and that the wing Spitfires should be 'scrambled'. Not without a sense of humour, Minton replied. 'You're too late. If I stick this 'phone outside you'll hear their bloody cannons!'

*

In the air the attacking Germans were engaged by the two pilots of 403 Squadron who had left the ground just as the enemy appeared. Pilot Officer Steve Butte (RR256) and his Number Two, Flight Sergeant G.K. Lindsay (SM312), flying Spitfire XVIs, waded in.

Leutnant Gunther Bloemertz said in his book *Heaven Next Stop*:

The first fires were now blazing up among the parked aircraft. As we continued our undisturbed diving on to the rows of bombers, heavy blue-black clouds of smoke were rising from nearly forty aircraft.

Suddenly peacocks' eyes – British roundels – were racing towards us – Spitfires must have taken off from other airfields. It was hard to distinguish friend from foe. Everyone scattered. Groups and flights curved in to attack the attackers and a wild chase began, a turmoil without front lines. Tracer flashed in all directions and damaged aircraft were diving earthwards with dark smoke clouds or blazing comet tails astern of them, huge umbrellas of smoke billowing up to the sky from where they struck – several parachutes were dropping peacefully towards the earth.

Steve Butte's first realisation of the enemy's presence was when he saw a formation of aircraft to his left as he became airborne. They were flying in an opposite direction and were about 300 yards away. Immediately he identified them as Me109s and radioed to his wingman, ordering jet tanks to be dropped. His own tank failed to jettison but he still broke into the 109 formation, selected one and fired as he closed from 250 to 100 yards. It went down in flames and crashed. He then went after a Focke Wulf, seeing strikes from his fire. The 190 flew on in a straight line to crash behind a row of houses.

Turning back to the action, Butte selected another Messerschmitt, firing from 175 to 100 yards which blasted bits off the 109, then caused smoke to spew back. One piece of the German plane hit his belly tank. Smoke from the airfield caused him to lose his position, but as he cleared it, he saw the 109 practically on its back and in a steep dive well below 500 feet. He then attacked another 109 but his guns fell silent but he believed he damaged it and something else hit his jet. tank. All he could do then was to use his camera gun on one of two FW190s that he then tangled with before he cleared the danger area to await the 'All clear'.

Lindsay, meantime, after seeing his leader shoot down the first ME109, lost Butte, then fired quick bursts at two German fighters. Seeing then a 109 starting down towards the aerodrome, Lindsay attacked, seeing strikes but he was then attacked himself, losing his victim which was in a slow turn north of the 'drome at 200 feet. Shaking his attackers, Lindsay then went at a 190 but before he could fire he was attacked yet again.

Climbing clear he looked down to see a FW190 below, attacked and scored hits on its belly and long range fuel tank, which the German then jettisoned. The 190 broke to the left, followed by the Canadian still firing, and saw flames shoot back from its engine. Circling round, he watched as the Focke Wulf crashed in flames.

It was now that 403 Squadron's first recce pair of Spitfires returned to Evere. Flight Lieutenant R.L. Reeves and his Number Two Flying Officer Mackenzie Reeves (KH-A) had been flying in the Weert area. After flying for forty minutes control informed them of ten plus bandits in their area. Shortly afterwards they saw Grimbergen aerodrome just after it had been shot-up and to avoid friendly flak they dived away from the danger zone.

Climbing again to to 3,000 feet, they began to see smoke rising from the direction of Brussels. Approaching Evere, they saw a

FW190 climbing. Flight Lieutenant Reeves went after it and 'Mac' Reeves lost sight of his leader and the German. Mac Reeves then saw thirty or more 190s and 109s milling about over Evere and chasing one 190 scored hits which caused smoke to stream from it. The 190 then rolled over onto its back, hit the ground and blew up. Selecting another Focke Wulf, the Canadian hammered it from 150 yards, scoring hits on engine and wings. Smoke began to pour from it, then the 190 rolled over and the pilot baled out, floating down into the suburbs of Brussels.

In his action, Flight Lieutenant R.L. Reeves, had his engine pack up and he had to remain above the battle nursing his engine, being unable to engage any of the numerous hostile fighters below him.

*

The Regiment gunners on Evere, 2800 Squadron and two flights of 2742 Squadron, put up a barrage of fire from 40 mm shells from eleven guns (2800 Sqdn) together with 2742 Squadron's Bren guns. Squadron Leader C.V. Lewin, the CO of 2800, visited his guns during the action while Flight Lieutenant L.C. Moynihan actively directed the fire of the guns nearest his HQ. Sergeant Ross, of No 7 gun, claimed three hits on German fighters and both he and the squadron adjutant, Flying Officer Herbert, were later Mentioned in Despatches.

Acting Squadron Leader A. Raine's two flights of 2742 Squadron brought their Brens into action, firing from the windows of their billets, scoring several hits. In total the RAFR gunners claimed three fighters destroyed and ten damaged. One of 2800 Squadron's Thornycrofts was burnt out and another damaged, but no personnel casualties were reported.

*

Despite the number of Spitfires on Evere, the shooting of the Germans proved poor. According to the Wing Leader, Johnnie Johnson, their marksmanship was atrocious and the German attempts reminded him of a bunch of beginners of their first solo effort. As far as he was concerned the attack was tactically well planned but poor flying let them down.

Total losses for No 127 Wing were just eleven Spitfires on the ground, plus Dave Harling's Spitfire XVI in the air. Twelve other Spitfires were damaged. Eleven MT vehicles were hit but only one totally destroyed. There was only one fatality amongst those on the ground, Leading Aircraftman Robert Charles Medford (36) RCAF from Ontario died, with nine other airmen wounded. On the other side of the 'drome, smoke rose from burning transport aircraft and damaged B17s. Prince Bernhard's Beechcraft was also burning, as was the VIP Dakota.

The four Canadians in the air, Harling, Butte, Lindsay and Mac Reeves scored possibly eight victories despite overwhelming odds. Steve Butte was awarded the DFC in February, Mac Reeves was lost at the end of March in a strafing attack.

CHAPTER NINE

The Canadians at Heesch

The gallant defenders of Evere were not the only Canadians to manage to get among the raiding Luftwaffe fighters on 1st January. At Heesch, north of Volkel, No 126 Canadian Wing started the New Year in deadly fashion. There was five Spitfire squadrons here, 410, 402, 411, 412 and 442 RCAF.

At 9.14 a.m., 410 Squadron were at the end of the runway when an estimated forty-plus Me109s and FW190s swept across the airfield heading due south. A very hurried scramble resulted, the mad take-off causing the Canadians to separate in the air.

The German fighters were from JG6, who had missed in the main their assigned target at Volkel. As these pilots began to realise that their plan had gone awry they began to split up, the formation soon finding itself scattered over the flat, featureless Dutch countryside. Some found themselves involved over Eindhoven, but most stumbled upon Heesch ten miles to the north-west of Volkel.

Leading Yellow Section of 401 Squadron was Flying Officer G.D.A.T. Cameron (MJ448). Scrambling into the clear sunny morning sky, he pulled up his Spitfire IX just enough to get a shot at two Me109s. Firing at the right-hand 109 from 300 yards, he saw an explosion near the cockpit, then the machine nosed down towards the ground. Cameron was already after the other Messerschmitt, firing to score hits on the fuselage behind the cockpit, followed by flames. A third 109 flew to his right; Cameron chased this and, firing from 400 yards, scored more hits. Another burst caused glycol to stream back from the striken 109, but then the Canadian ran out of ammunition. However, the 109 was finished, Cameron watching the 109 until it crash-landed in a field just north of the aerodrome. Cameron had shot down three Me109s within minutes of becoming airborne – in ten minutes he was back on the ground!

When Flight Lieutenant John MacKay became airborne (MH240) he led his section clear of the airfield, and ground control vectored them to the Reichwald area. Here he found a Focke Wulf, flying on the deck towards the north-east. Going down behind the 190, the German pilot began to take violent evasive action as MacKay snapped off burst after burst at him. Finally the 190 settled into a straight line for a moment, allowing MacKay to get on target. The 190 exploded and crashed in flames.

Losing the rest of his men, MacKay headed back towards Heesch at zero feet. Near Nijmegen he was fired at from the ground but then he spotted two aircraft coming towards him from the east. As he broke into them he found it was a 190 being chased by a Tempest. As the two antagonists turned, the 190 reversed the action and began closing in on the Tempest's tail. MacKay engaged the 190 but his guns stopped firing – out of shells. Pressing his now toothless attack, he closed right into 30 yards and as the 190 pilot tried to avoid him, his wing struck an ice-covered lake, nosed in and blew up.

Pulling up from this victory he ran into a Me109 heading west. Closing in on the 109's tail he forced the German pilot down on the deck while taking hectic evasive action. Seconds later the panicked pilot hit the ground, bounced into some trees and smashed into pieces. MacKay's superb flying skill brought the 23-year-old Canadian from Winnipeg, two victories when out of ammunition – it also brought him an immediate award of the DFC.[1]

Flight Lieutenant W.E. Foster (ML141) flying Blue 3 to MacKay went after a FW190 south-east of Nijmegen and attacked. His guns scored hits on the fighter damaging it, but as his fuel was running low the Canadian had to let it go.

*

[1] The last victory was officially shared with two Tempests flown by Ness and Shaw of 56 Squadron, whose combat reports describe exactly the 109 crashing into the trees and breaking up.

The pilots of 411 RCAF Squadron had left the ground at 8.50 a.m. on a Fighter Reconnaissance Sweep to the Osnabrück-Münster area and so missed the attack by JG6. However, one pilot ran into enemy fighters near Twente – the pilot was Flight Lieutenant R.J. 'Dick' Audet.

Aged twenty-two, Dick Audet came from Alberta from French-Canadian stock. He had been in England since the end of 1942 but had had a variety of flying jobs, most far removed from war. Finally he joined 411 RCAF Squadron in September 1944 in Belgium but even then combat eluded him. However, on 29th December, he shot down no less than five German aircraft in his first real action. Now three days later, Audet was in action for the second time.

On the early morning mission he became separated from the others and was trying to reform with them south-west of Enschede when he was bounced by four British Typhoons. Luckily they missed him and by the time he'd sorted this out he had lost the other Spitfires completely. Therefore, probably thinking his luck was again back to square one, he turned back towards base. But then he spotted a FW190 at 5,000 feet, he being at 9,000 feet. The 190 was heading towards Enschede as he attacked. However, the German pilot had seen him and put his 190 into a gentle righthand turn. Audet turned too and fired, scoring hits which caused the 190 to roll over and spin down, with a brief show of flame, before hitting the ground.

Regaining height, Audet saw another 190 heading in the same direction as the first. Audet hauled after the 190 whose pilot seemed to be trying to out-run the Canadian, but omitted to drop his long range tank. Firing as he followed the 190 in a turn to the right, bits of fuselage and rudder was shot away and its engine seemed to stop. Audet overshot but curving round for a second attack he saw that the enemy pilot appeared to be looking for a place to land. Audet gave it another burst and almost immediately the 190 dived into the ground just east of Haarsdergen.

This made it seven victories for Audet in two combats. He went on to claim 11½ victories and win the DFC and bar before he was killed in action on 9th March 1945.

*

At three minutes to 9 o'clock the Spitfires of 442 RCAF Squadron became airborne for an early sweep to the Lingen-Münster area. When JG6 appeared over Heesch, base control called 442, recalling them to the aerodrome. They quickly obeyed and they too were able to engage large numbers of Luftwaffe fighters, in the Venlo area.

First back to Heesch, however, was Flight Lieutenant D.C. Gordon (MH728) who had aborted with a rough engine and low oil pressure. Having reached the airfield when down to 7,000 feet, he saw AA fire and instantly thought it must be a sneak attack by a German jet which did sometimes occur.

Reducing height to see if he could pick it up, he suddenly saw about fifty or more Focke Wulfs and Messerschmitts on the deck, flying south. Despite his rough engine, Don 'Chunky' Gordon picked out the nearest 190 and fired a deflection shot at it from 200 yards. The 190 flicked over to the left and went right into the ground where it exploded. Going after another 190 ahead and to his left, he closed in behind the German. His burst from 300 yards obtained strikes and smoke. The 190 flew on for about five seconds then nosed over into the ground and blew up.

Gordon was then hit from behind, either by flak or by a German fighter. Shell splinters peppered him in the back of the head, neck and shoulders, forcing him to crash-land in a field just south of the aerodrome. As he gingerly clambered out of his Spitfire, an enthusiastic Dutch women rushed up to him and slapped him heartily *on the back* and wished him a happy new year!

Hearing over the radio that Gordon was in action and then in trouble, Flight Lieutenant R.C. Smith (RR196), who was also aborting the mission with fuel tank trouble, headed south to see if he could spot him. It was then that he saw Eindhoven aerodrome under attack. Seeing some Focke Wulfs and Messerschmitts flying below, Smith circled, then picking one that was slightly on its own, he dived to the attack. He nipped in, fired, pulled up and then dived again to shoot at another 109. In this way he got in bursts at three 109s, then spotted a FW190 closing on on him from the left. Smith broke towards it as the German pilot fired, then Smith climbed and the 190 dived away. Smith rolled down behind yet another Me109, chasing it down to ground level, but oil spewed on his windscreen and he had to break off the pursuit.

Climbing to 800 feet as his forward vision cleared, he saw a 190 coming up from the deck on his left. Putting his Spitfire into a diving turn he attacked the Focke Wulf from head-on, both pilots pumping shells at each other from a range of 300 yards, but both missed. The German pilot broke to the left at the last moment, passing over Smith's cockpit with just feet to spare. Still amidst dozens of enemy fighters, the Canadian quickly found another 190 on the deck and gave chase. This German pilot seemed better than Smith had encountered so far and he could not get a bead on his Focke Wulf. Then when the German finally straightened out, Smith found he had run out of ammunition.

His fuel was also running low as he turned for home and at 7,000 feet his engine cut out but he glided into Heesch to make a successful dead-stick landing. Meanwhile, ground observers at Eindhoven and 83 Group HQ, had seen the Canadian in action above them, identified the squadron code letters on his Spitfire and radioed congratulations. They had seen him score strikes on one Me109 and caused the pilot of another to bale out. In all, Flight Lieutenant Smith had been in the middle of forty enemy fighters and made attacks on ten of them.

*

412 RCAF Squadron, commanded by Squadron Leader D.H. Dover, flying Spitfire IXs, were also preparing for an early sortie when JG6 came across the airfield. Dover led his men off after the Germans, control vectoring them into the Venlo region.

Ten miles north-west of Venlo, Flight Lieutenant B.E. Macpherson (PT186) saw some of the Volkel Tempests scrapping with FW190s, on the deck, at 9.55 a.m. Picking out a lone FW190 flying eastwards at 500 feet, he went down after it. The 190 began to climb for some cloud cover, but Macpherson fired from astern just as the 190 reached them. Hits and flame appeared about the 190's cockpit and it levelled out. Firing again, the Canadian scored more hits but then flak forced him to turn away. Looking back he saw a parachute appear and the 190 crash.

Flying Officer V. Smith (PT357) got involved in a dog-fight with a Focke Wulf but managed to shake it off. He then saw another beneath him and turned down on it. The German pilot flew in a straight line, allowing Smith to get in a good shot at him which slammed into the cockpit and wing roots. The pilot was obviously hit, for the 190 nosed straight on and smashed to pieces in a wood and exploded in flames.

North-east of Helmond, Flight Lieutenant J.P. Doak engaged a FW190, his fire causing smoke to stream out of the German fighter. It flew on for a few seconds, then flicked over and hit the ground.

*

While all these actions were in progress, the main force of 442 Squadron was now in the Lingen area on their dawn sweep when the call came. The radio warning that German aircraft were over base had the Canadians turning for home. Flight Lieutenant N.A. Keen DFC (MJ425) led them back but they ran into enemy fighters north-west of Venlo, they waded in. Keen chased one at low level, both fighters contour-chasing over the Dutch countryside. Strikes sparkled on the Focke Wulf which Keen was after, which then appeared to partially explode just before it hit the ground.

Flight Lieutenant D.M. Pieri (NH489) flying number four in Yellow Section, also got in amongst the 190s and with his section leader dived at six of them but then lost his leader in the mêlée. He damaged one 190 but then was engaged by another. Losing this one he saw a Spitfire (Flying Officer L.H. Wilson – MH369) being chased by a 190. Don Pieri curved after it and fired. The Focke Wulf pulled up then dived into an open field and exploded.

Seeing another 190 on the deck, Pieri attacked and scored hits on the cockpit and wing root. It too rose up then spun into the ground and blew up. Pieri's engine now began to play up so he turned for base but saw another 190 at ground level flying north-east. Attacking this one too, he blasted pieces from it but then its oil coated the Canadian's windscreen and he lost sight of the German.

Further to the north, Flight Lieutenant J.B. Lumsden DFC (PV148) and his Red Section saw an Me262 jet at about 1,800 feet just below some cloud. It was heading east towards Wessel, passing right in front of the Canadians. Lumsden broke in behind it and scored a hit on its tail as it went into cloud. Going through the cloud he ran right into a FW190. Making a straight head-on attack the two aircraft roared passed each other. Lumsden hauling round after it, closed in and fired. He saw his fire burst on the 190 and score hits on it before it flew into the sun. Flying Officer J.A. Cousineau (MJ463), flying as Lumsden's wingman, also fired at this 190, hitting its engine cowling, but he too lost it as the German pilot climbed into the sun and cloud.

Another Messerschmitt 262 was found by Flight Lieutenant R.K. Trumley (BL423) and his section – or rather it found them! It came at the four Spitfires head-on. As it fired the Canadians all fired back and although none of them saw any hits, as the 262 went by them it began to stream smoke. With the Canadians hard after it, firing, the jet still easily outpaced them and flew off. All four Canadians reported this Me262 to be adorned with '... definite American markings on its sides with crosses on wings and swastika, in the American style.'

These successes in combat were not gained without loss. Flying Officer D.A. Brigden (MK240) was shot down in the Venlo area. His Spitfire crashed into a field, Brigden being killed instantly. Flying Officer L.H. Wilson's Spitfire was hot up by cannon fire, but he got down unhurt.

*

With most of the Canadians airborne when the Luftwaffe struck, they found little in the way of targets on the ground. They did manage to put a fair sized hole in the roof of 411's dispersal hut but that was about all. As well as having to contend with the Canadians in the air, the RAF Regiment was also active at Heesch.

Numbers 2734 and 2819 Squadrons fired a total of 344 rounds, their gunners being 'in their glory'. These two squadrons claimed a total of seven German fighters destroyed and two damaged, two of the former crashing on the airfield.

For JG6 it was a disaster. Their whole attack had gone wrong from the start of their final turn towards the assigned target. Lost, spread out and totally un-coordinated despite the pains-taking briefing by its leaders, even down to the aid of a table-top model, it became a shambles. JG6 lost not only its Kommandeur, Oberstleutnant Johann Kogler, but Hauptmann Ewald Trost, CO of I Gruppe (both taken prisoner) and three Staffel leaders.

The Canadians of 126 Wing had had a successful morning, yet for them the day was far from over.

CHAPTER TEN

Melsbroek

Spakenburg was also the turning point for Jagdgeschwader 27. Its Kommandeur was Major Ludwig Franzisket, holder of the Knight's Cross, and who had some forty victories flying against the Allies since 1939. His I Gruppe was led by Hauptmann Eberhard Schade, II Gruppe by Hauptmann Gerhard Hoyer (who was to die on 21st January 1945), III Gruppe by Hauptmann Emile Clade who was to end the war with twenty-seven victories, and IV Gruppe by Hauptmann Heinz Dudeck. It was equipped with Me109G-10 and K4 aircraft.

A total of seventy fighters took off from just west of Osnabrück, JG27 being reinforced by FW190s of IV Gruppe JG54. Flying low and led by Ju88s, this force too suffered from German flak. Two aeroplanes were shot down before reaching Utrecht and a third went down as they reached the front line. This latter was Leutnant Heinrich Weisse, Staffelkapitän of 2/JG27 who died as his 109 crashed into the banks of the Waal. As they approached their target area, some fighters from III Gruppe broke away when they spotted Gilze Reijen airfield but the rest carried on towards Brussels and Melsbroek.

*

Melsbroek was the home of No 34 (Photo-Reconnaissance) Wing and No 139 Bomber Wing from 2 Group, Bomber Command. The latter wing comprised three Mitchell squadrons, 98, 180 and 320. All three squadrons were fortunate in having a dawn raid against a road centre at Dasburg. They had left Melsbroek at 8.30 a.m. escorted by Spitfires from Woensdrecht. However, there were some Mitchells dotted about the airfield.

No 34 Wing comprised 16 Squadron flying PR Spitfire XIs, 69 Squadron with night low-level recce: Wellington XIIIs, and 140 Squadron with Mosquito XVIs for both day and night recconnaissance operations.

There was, of course, a good deal happening at Melsbroek on the morning of 1st January. Few people remained asleep following the take-off roars of 35 Mitchell bombers. Wing Commander Mike Shaw was up early despite the party to celebrate not only the New Year but his award of the DSO. As the day dawned the realisation also dawned on him that he had agreed to air test the now repaired Short Stirling bomber. He was not looking forward to it but at least it would keep him out of his office for an hour or so.

Flight Lieutenant Hugh Tudor, a member of 140 Squadron, was also up and breakfasting with fellow pilot Flight Lieutenant Ian Ewing.

I'd been with 140 Squadron for about six months and a great friend of mine was an Australian – Ian Ewing. On 1st January morning, early, we were going back to UK to collect my father, a former RFC pilot in the First World War and who was back in the RAF. It had been arranged that he would come over to Melsbroek to spend a few days with us on an operational squadron. There was room for three people in a Mosquito, so that was the plan.

Ian and I had breakfast in the Mess and were just getting into a jeep to travel to the airfield, which was on the other side of the road from the Officer's Mess, when Ian, who was a pipe smoker, said he'd forgotten his pipe. He went back for it which delayed us for about ten to fifteen minutes. While he was getting it, a crowd of the squadron boys were standing around. It was a lovely clear morning, and one of the boys said, 'Christ! look at those three Hurricanes.' These were aircraft, low flying, coming across the airfield, and I yelled, 'Hurricanes be buggered – they're 109s.'
Flight Lieutenant H.M.H. Tudor, 140 Squadron

The morning following our party, we came out of the Mess after breakfast when we saw these low flying aeroplanes beating up the place. We thought who on earth was doing that, thinking they were RAF until we saw black crosses on them, and so we thought we'd better take cover, and dived into the nearest air raid shelter until things died down a bit.

Wing Commander M.J.A. Shaw, CO 69 Squadron

On 1st January I was due to be first off, but the airfield at first light was very frozen and, although I had been briefed for a flight around the Ruhr to look at the airfields, it was necessary for our airfield staff to inspect the runways and taxi-ways again since they did not think them fit for taxi-ing and take-off. Whilst waiting in the Operations Room, we were attacked by a large number of Me109s and FW190s.

Flight Lieutenant E.R. Dutt, 16 Squadron

As the attack began, Hugh Tudor and Ian Ewing dashed back into the Mess and to the rooms of some of the squadron crews who were still in bed.

It would be difficult to forget 1st January 1945. I had been flying the night before and was in bed when the attack started. Hugh Tudor and Ian Ewing were scheduled to take one of our Mosquitos back to UK and they awoke me and my navigator, Bill Harper, to warn us of the attack. Our first reaction was that they were fooling but the sound of cannon fire was enough to get us to the door of our billet and our first sight was that of a fighter at low level with its tailwheel down – an Me109. We put on flying boots and greatcoats over our pyjamas, and with our tin-hats and Smith & Wesson .38 pistols, went out onto the sport field next to our billet.

Squadron Leader R.D. Walton, 140 Squadron

Coming in low from the west, the fighter pilots of JG27 found a number of different aircraft types on the airfield. As well as Wellingtons, Spitfires and Mosquitos of the resident RAF Wings, there were some American B17 Flying Fortresses, and P47 Thunderbolt fighters, as well as an assortment of light aircraft – and of course one Short Stirling.

Royal Air Force Regiment gunners manned the defences. 2701

Squadron had six of its guns out of action for anti-flying bomb patrols, but the rest were on the airfield. They fired 197 rounds, claiming four German fighters destroyed and four damaged. Their No 4 gun was subjected to frequent and vicious attacks by the attackers but kept up a steady return fire, claiming two of the four destroyed. 2717 Squadron had only its No 2 Flight on Melsbroek and engaged the fighters with Bren guns only. 2871 Squadron also helped in the defence and when a house adjoining the unit's HQ site was set on fire, it was put out by Regiment personnel.

Flight Lieutenant E.R. Dutt, 16 Squadron
They strafed the aircraft on the airfield; 69 Squadron, I believe, lost fourteen Wellingtons which were parked in a row. We lost two Spitfires destroyed on the ground, the Dutch Mitchell Wing lost a few Mitchells, and a number of damaged Fortresses and Liberators parked on the airfield were also destroyed. The enemy aircraft were diving through the camp area at ground level shooting us up with cannon and machine-gun fire, and although I believe one Me109 at least was shot down by the perimeter gunners, there was little else we could do.

Squadron Leader R.D. Walton, 140 Squadron
The accommodation area was on the other side of the road from the airfield and as the Luftwaffe fighters were concentrating on the aircraft rather than on buildings, we had a grandstand view of the operation. We all pooped off ineffectual shots at the aircraft with our .38s, at the ones that flew over us. One chap, I think it was Squadron Leader 'Chunky' Chown, the Wing Engineering Officer, was blasting away with a double barrelled shot gun. At least it relieved our feelings!

It was inconceivable at that stage of the war, when we believed we had complete air superiority, that enemy aircraft could do a number of strafing runs along the lines of our aircraft (which were not dispersed), and doing stall-turns at the end of each run to line up for the next. 69 Squadron Wellington, and my Flight, B Flight, of 140 Squadron, were night PRU and therefore all on the ground. Just under half of the aircraft from both wings were sitting ducks for the attack.

As a major airfield, Melsbroek was also a forward emergency field. We had a USAAF B17 sitting there which had made an emergency landing the day before with its hydraulics shot away, which made for a spectacular landing at high speed, the crew popping parachutes out of its hatches to stop it after touchdown.

I think that 140 Squadron lost six Mosquitos, mostly from B Flight (we had only one aircraft which could have operated that night if required – but thankfully it was not); 16 Squadron lost six Spitfires (three destroyed and three damaged – NLRF) and 69 Squadron 14 Wellingtons. The only serviceable Wimpy had had brake failure the previous night and was left at the far side of the airfield.

Flight Lieutenant H.M.H. Tudor, 140 Squadron
When the strafing started, the 109s were attacking the airfield, going back up in climbing turns, then diving down back on the airfield. Smoke started to build up from the airfield as aircraft were shot-up, then the Germans disappeared.

As far as myself was concerned, Ian Ewing and I went across to the airfield when the attack ended. A number of our aircraft had been shot-up. My own aircraft, in which my helmet was hanging over the control column, and the parachute in the seat, had been riddled. The Mosquito was a write-off (NS567). The helmet had two bullet holes through it, the parachute pack shredded. There is no doubt in my mind that had Ian not forgotten his pipe, if we hadn't been in the aeroplane we'd have been pretty close to getting in it, and of course, our dispersal was in the middle of the airfield, with tents for our crew room, etc. It was really a lucky escape for us both.

Wing Commander M.J.A. Shaw, CO 69 Squadron
I knew that the ground crews would be preparing the aircraft for night flying tests etc, for Ops that night and as soon as it was safe to do so, I drove over to the airfield from the Mess and found things in complete chaos. Aeroplanes were burning all around and there were, unfortunately, some casualties from among our airmen. I had little to do except look at this dreadful shambles of burning Wimpies and others, Spitfires, Mosquitos etc.

One consolation was that 139 Wing – Mitchells – which shared the airfield with us, were on ops. They always lined their Mitchells up on the disused runway in a lovely straight line. Luckily they had taken off shortly before the Germans arrived, or there really would have been more of a shambles.

I then went to my office which was in the domestic side of the camp where the Mess was. I went in and was amazed to find that there was a bullet hole through the window and the bullet was embedded in the wall on the other side of my desk which I extracted. Had I been sitting at my desk it would have gone right through my head.

And the Stirling I was due to air test: it was destroyed by the Germans. In retrospect I breathed a sigh of relief that I didn't have to fly it.

*

Another unit at Melsbroek was the 'Sparrow Flight'. This was the Handley Page Harrow flight of 271 Squadron which was based at Down Ampney in England. 271 Squadron was mainly a Dakota transport squadron and in fact on 1st January twelve of its Dakota IIIs flew from there to airfields on the Continent with both freight and passengers. None, however, was involved in the German attack. But its Harrows were already standing on Melsbroek airfield when they came in to attack, seven Harrows being strafed and destroyed. One of the flight's ground crew, Leading Aircraftman Jack Hyams, aged twenty-one, from Willesden, Middlesex, was killed.

*

Evere airfield was quite near Melsbroek and received its attack at the same time. Both Ray Dutt and Ron Walton could see this attack from Melsbroek.

Wing Commander Johnnie Johnson had a Spitfire Wing across the road on Evere airfield which adjoined ours, and they tried to scramble some of their aircraft. Two of them were destroyed as they were trying to take-off along the runway.

Flight Lieutenant E.R. Dutt, 16 Squadron

We could see Evere airfield, a few miles along the road to Brussels, was also under attack, as was an airstrip to the north where the Polish Wing was based.

Altogether there were about twenty casualties at Melsbroek, of which six died, mostly ground crews who were servicing the aircraft at the time. We were fortunate that the attack was concentrated on the airfield itself and not on the separate accommodation area where casualties in personnel would have been much higher. But at that time in the war, aircraft were the most profitable targets.

Squadron Leader R.D. Walton, 140 Squadron

*

JG27s I and II Gruppen had attacked in straight runs along Melsbroek's north-south runway, followed by IV/JG54's FW190s. Hauptmann Heinz Dudeck led IV/JG27 in from the south-east, from out of the sun. Dudeck's first pass put him in line to blast a four-engined aircraft, then he shot up a twin-engined machine. In total he and his men made four or five runs amid the rising smoke, and as they broke away, ground defensive fire was on the increase.

As IV/JG27 flew off to the north-east towards Harmatport they were engaged by RAF fighters and others of JG27 also ran into opposing fighters. Dudeck's own aircraft ran into trouble. Whether hit by the RAF, ground fire, or had just plain engine failure is obscure but suddenly his motor was dead. He was at 500 metres so he had little choice than to bale out, but his parachute snagged on his machine's tail and tore. He came to earth rather more quickly as a result but landed in a tree. He was taken prisoner.

JG27 lost fourteen pilots killed, missing or prisoners, plus another wounded. Eight of these went down in air fights or to flak on the flight back towards the German lines.

*

Apart from the losses in aircraft, the RAF lost a number of personnel during the attack. Five ground crewmen of 6069 Servicing Echelon were either killed or died soon afterwards as a result of wounds. Twenty-five others were injured. When the attack began most were out at dispersal points working on the

Wellingtons and the nearest cover was too far away to be of value.

Number 16 Squadron and its 6016 SE suffered no losses in men but three of its Spitfires were burnt out and three more destroyed. 140 Squadron lost six Mosquitos.

Of the Mitchell Wing, 98 Squadron had one aircraft written off plus two damaged, 180 Squadron had three write-offs and three damaged, 320 Squadron had two destroyed. Hugh Tudor distinctly remembers one Mitchell being taxied into a blister hangar at the height of the attack.

Following their raid on Dasburg, the Mitchells were diverted to Epinoy following a radio call telling them not to return to Melsbroek. They finally returned to their home base in the early afternoon.

CHAPTER ELEVEN

Deurne

The target for the fighter pilots of Jagdgeschwader 77 on this first morning of January 1945 was the aerodrome at Antwerpe-Deurne. Based in northern Germany on airfields just to the west of Osnabrück, JG77 had nearly 200 miles to fly to arrive at its assigned target.

Like most of the Western Front fighter units, JG77 had suffered heavy casualties over the autumn and winter of 1944. Indeed, its Kommandeur, Major Johannes Wiese, Knight's Cross with Oak Leaves, was shot down and badly wounded on Christmas Eve having claimed 133 victories. His place was taken by Major Erich Leie, Knight's Cross, on 29th December. Leie had over 100 kills, having been in action since 1940.

Although its bases were located nearer as the crow flies to Antwerpe than 200 miles, the plan was to fly in a wide sweep, in order to approach Deurne from the direction of Rotterdam. Like every other unit, they would fly low in order to gain full measure of surprise. So much secrecy in fact, that Deurne might easily have been semi-alert, for at around 4.30 a.m. a sneak raid by a German bomber resulted in the destruction of a Dakota aircraft!

There were two RAF wings on Deurne, 145 and 146, the former with four Spitfire squadrons, the latter with five Typhoon squadrons. The wing leader of the Spitfires was Wing Commander W.V. Crawford-Compton DSO, DFC, about to leave for a job at 11 Fighter Group HQ; the Typhoon wing leader was Wing Commander Denys Gillam DSO, DFC, AFC.

*

Over 100 JG77 aircraft took off into a clear morning sky, flying to

Lippe, then on to Borken. Fifteen minutes past Borken the Messerschmitts turned south-west and headed for Rotterdam. Nearing the front-line, German naval gunners opened up on the German formations.

As the German pilots reached the eastern side of the Ooster Schelde, some of I Gruppe spotted the airfield of Woensdrecht (also known as Bergen op Zoom) away to the left, and went in to strafe it. They found the airfield empty – most of its Spitfires were flying.

No 132 Wing was based at Woensdrecht, comprising 66, 127, RAF Squadrons, 322 Dutch Squadron, and two Norwegian squadrons, 331 and 332. Of the Dutch squadron, only the ground party had arrived, the aircraft and pilots were not due to arrive for a day or so. The two Norwegian squadrons were not flying but 66 and 127 Squadrons had taken off at 9.10 a.m., just minutes before the attack, to mount an escort for Melsbroek's Mitchells attacking Dasburg. 66 was led by Squadron Leader R. Easby (SM202), 127 by Squadron Leader S.F. Sampson DFC (RR242).

> We were flying a fighter sweep over the Ardennes battle area in support of a bomb raid soon after dawn but heard of the activity over the radio. We saw nothing of interest on our mission and as some of us later began to run short of fuel, I led two chaps to Grimbergen where we refuelled. Although Grimbergen had been attacked, there was no visible signs of damage there. Shortly afterwards we returned to Woensdrecht.
>
> *Flight Lieutenant H.R. Lea, 127 Squadron*

Shortly after the German fighters passed Woensdrecht, where the men on the ground had only seen about six fighters fly over the airfield, 127 Squadron scrambled three aircraft, led by Flight Lieutenant A.R. Covington (RK859), with orders to cover the Antwerpe area, but they saw no signs of enemy aircraft. Major J. Tvedte, CO of 332 Squadron, led his squadron off to defend the airfield but the Germans left it alone.

*

Meanwhile, the main German formation reached Antwerpe, its pilots seeing the vast dock areas and the cathedral spires and towers. II Gruppe, however, had trouble locating the aerodrome and began circling aimlessly to the north-east of the city. However, III Gruppe crossed the Schelde and had no sooner done so when they came under fire from the airfield defences.

It was full daylight with clear, slightly hazy sky, when the roar of engines was heard and to our great surprise we saw a huge fleet of German fighters arrive, crossing the airfield from the embankment side. This enormous fleet seemed to be in complete disorder being a mixed bag of Me109s and FW190s flying like a great gaggle at heights from 150 to some 300 feet. There was some firing from the attackers but the embankment and perhaps the mixed gaggle, saved the Typhoon wing from large scale destruction. 257 Squadron lost two aircraft and I think the total Typhoon loss was around six or eight aircraft. The Spitfire wing on the distant side came under attack but I do not know of any casualties.

Flight Lieutenant S. J. Eaton, 257 Squadron

I was acting CO at the time, as Martin Rumbold was away visiting a friend in Lille and I remember getting the lads to bed early as we were on first thing next morning. We were billeted in small houses near the 'drome and had a rotten Mess and not much to drink except plenty of advocaat!

We were called by the duty 'erk' but it wasn't very early as it was winter time. However, I was down at dispersal for the early morning show – Army support east of Dordrecht – when the attack began. I well remember standing on a bank with my pilots and yelling at the Germans, 'Weave you stupid bastards!' They were flying straight and level and being shot at by the ground forces. We couldn't take off at the time because of the ice on the runway. I later wrote in my log-book: 'Runway frozen – watched eight 190s and twelve 109s fly over 'drome. They strafed a few aircraft but put up a very poor show. AA got 9, Mustangs 2.'

Flight Lieutenant R. E. G. Sheward, 263 Squadron

The way the Germans mounted their attack was certainly amateurish from the RAF's standpoint. In 193 Squadron's diary it

was described: 'They stooged across slow, like a Sunday picnic ...'
329 French Squadron recorded: 'The Me's seemed to be playing
possum with the gunners coming down to 200-300 feet.' It was also
frustrating for the French pilots of 341 Squadron because the ice
prevented a scramble and '... our pilots had to watch six Me109s
flying across the airfield at zero feet ...'

The night before we had an enormous squadron party in
Antwerpe, so 'come the dawn' there were a few hangovers about.
I was a flight lieutenant in charge of A Flight of 193 Squadron
which at the time was commanded by Squadron Leader Derek
Erasmus, a Rhodesian from 266 Squadron.

As I remember 1st January, we were briefed to do a show on
the Vianen Bridge south of Utrecht but could not take off
because of ice on the runway. We occupied one side of the
airfield and the other was used by the Dakotas of Transport
Command for some leave flights etc, to the UK. Also on that side
was the first heavy AA company overseas, manned by ATS. I
think they must have had hangovers as well as they didn't really
manage to fire a shot.

We were all at dispersal when the German Air Force arrived.
As I recall it was about a couple of dozen Me109s in two or three
waves, flying at about 50-100 feet. The Dakotas, because of their
size, must have attracted them because most of the damage was
inflicted there. We managed to get one aircraft off but they had
gone before we could do anything.

Flight Lieutenant J.G. Simpson, 193 Squadron

The previous night we had a very heavy snow-fall and all
personnel were turned out at dawn to clear the runway. This was
just about completed when the German raid took place. They
damaged a DC3 and a Fortress which were parked in front of the
hangers, but did little damage to any of the fighter squadrons,
who were well dispersed.

Wing Commander D.E. Gillam, Leader 146 Wing

The diarist of 197 Squadron also confirms the view given by many
eye-witnesses of the attack on the airfields: 'Judging by the way

they withdrew at peculiar heights and speeds, some of their pilots were none too experienced.' And he continued: 'Despite eloquent and pointed advice given to the AA gunners by the pilots from the perimeter track, only two (EA) were shot down locally.'

This latter point was also commented upon by 257 Squadron:

... all pilots were forced to sit on the deck and swear at the ack-ack gunners. However, on the whole the enemy aircraft put up a very poor show and Group Captain D. Gillam DSO, DFC, AFC was heard to remark: 'If any of my boys put on a show like that I'd tear them off a strip!'

Also on Deurne that morning was Leading Aircraftman Charles Southgate:

On New Year's Day I was with a mobile signals unit at Deurne attached to 145 Wing. The unit was a ground/air – ground/ground mobile VHF Point Relay, operating independently under the Station Signals Officer, usually at the edge of the airstrip.

I recall the flap that morning, with the RAF Regiment coming out well and shooting down a few enemy aircraft. We didn't suffer too much damage although there were awful rumours about other wings elsewhere being badly damaged. The winter that year was pretty severe but Deurne was a good strip. I'm sure our squadrons would have wreaked more damage if we hadn't been caught with our 'pants down'.

Leading Aircraftman C.R. Southgate, Mobile Signals Unit

I was an instrument repairer with 6341 Servicing Echelon, attached to 341 (Free French) Squadron on 145 Wing. I remember I was working on one of our Spitfires when someone remarked on the unusual looking planes passing across the other side of the airfield. I looked up and said, 'They're Thunderbolts', when they opened fire at some grounded aircraft; I think there were some American planes which were also using the airfield.

To my recollection there were only about six German aircraft involved, FW190s. They made several passes over the airfield but

I did not hear of any damage to aircraft or casualties on our wing. Their attack, such as it was, was over in a few minutes but one lone FW190 later flew directly over my head at very low altitude as I was working on an aircraft, and fired a burst of cannon or machine-gun fire at the flying control tower.

As it happened, at that time all airmen were required to carry their personal firearms with them at all times, because of the German push in the Ardennes which had Antwerpe as one of its targets. (Normally we left our rifles and sten guns in the billets.) Consequently several of the troops had a shot at the enemy planes, probably causing greater risk to us than the Germans. A notice very quickly appeared in Daily Routine Orders forbidding the use of small-arms against enemy aircraft!!

Leading Aircraftman J.B. Hopley, 341 Squadron

*

RAF losses on Deurne were few. 193 Squadron reported that the enemy only damaged or destroyed 'a few kites'. 197 Squadron recorded that only three wing aircraft lost/damaged although 257 Squadron stated that fourteen aircraft were hit, two being from 257 Squadron. 266 Squadron lost one Typhoon – apparently '... the most 'clapped-out' on the squadron.'

The RAF Regiment on Deurne, 2880 Squadron, recorded that eight RAF aircraft received damage on the ground, while 84 Group HQ noted seven casualties – one Typhoon Category A, two Typhoons Category B, while five others were Category AC.

Regiment gunners engaged twelve Me109s and four FW190s at 9.25 a.m., three guns firing sixteen rounds as the German fighters came in from out of the sun. At 9.40 the squadron recorded that twelve Me109s and two Me110s (sic) made a low level attack on the airfield installations with cannon and machine-gun fire. One Me109 was damaged and it was noted that the enemy fighters carried red, yellow and black stripes on their fuselages. At ten o'clock two Me109s and a FW190 strafed the airfield, these carrying black and white bands on their fuselages. The squadron had one casualty when Corporal Ford was hit in the mouth by a piece of shrapnel.

Regiment gunners at Woensdrecht were also in action, when elements of JG77 flew over the base earlier. 2816 Squadron saw the German fighters circle the airfield but they made no direct attack upon it. 2872 Squadron, however, spotted eight FW190s flying at zero feet to the southwest at 9.25 a.m. Sixteen minutes later its No 4 gun position fired at a FW190 and claimed its destruction while the No 5 position hit a German fighter which crashed four miles to the north of them. No 9 gun claimed another damaged. At 9.45 No 1 gun claimed a hit on one Me109; the fighter was seen to stream smoke and begin to lose height, five miles to the east, a parachute or piece of the aircraft being seen to drop away from it.

Meanwhile, No 2 Flight of 2816 Squadron, detached to Deurne, had two of its guards on duty engage a low flying fighter with machine-gun and rifle fire. At one of Deurne's airfield gates, the occupants of a jeep attempted to crash through, totally ignoring the red lamp and guard challenges. The Regiment guards were forced to fire at the jeep, wounding one of the occupants.

*

As for JG77 and their part in Bodenplatte, it was hardly worth the effort. After flying 200 miles they inflicted minimal damage – those of them who actually made any sort of attack – and it cost them six pilots killed, four taken captive and of course ten aircraft lost. Two of the latter came down in the Antwerpe area and two other casualties occurred on the return flight. Of the hundred or so fighters deployed, no more than thirty are believed to have actually made an attack. The two RAF wings based at Deurne could not know just how lucky they had been.

CHAPTER TWELVE

The Central Thrust

The central thrust of Operation Bodenplatte became the responsibility of JG2, JG4 and JG11 – assigned to attack mainly American bases.

JG2 – the famous Richthofen Geschwader – had all three of its Gruppen briefed for their part in the plan, aimed at the aerodrome of St Trond. St Trond, like many other bases attacked on this day, was no stranger to German pilots. For years it had been the home of many of the Luftwaffe's most successful night fighter pilots, not the least of whom was Major Heinz-Wolfgang Schnaufer, Knight's Cross holder with Oak Leaves, Swords and Diamond, in recognition of over 100 night victories. He became known as the 'Ghost of St Trond' to Allied flyers. It was now the home of two Thunderbolt Groups, the 48th and 404th of the American 9th Tactical Air Force.

Following a somewhat hurried and brief briefing, the Richthofen pilots took-off at 8 a.m. with orders to form up and meet the pilots of Oberst Alfred Druschel's SG (Schlachtgeschwader) 4. Druschel, just short of his twenty-eighth birthday, held the Knight's Cross with Oak Leaves and Swords and had been a pre-war pilot. Flying since the beginning of the war he had flown some 800 missions as an assault pilot and was promoted to Oberst on 1st January 1945. His SG4 was equipped with FW190 F-8s, some carrying rockets.

Kommandeur of JG2 was Oberstleutnant Kurt Bühligen, just twenty-eight, another experienced pilot with the Knight's Cross, Oak Leaves and Swords. He had over 100 victories all achieved with JG2 since 1940. His I and III Gruppen had long-nosed FW190 D-9s, II Gruppe having Me109Gs.

Forming up, the main formation turned west between Giessen and Frankfurt but within minutes one FW190 of III Gruppe began to pour out smoke and go down. Anxiously the other pilots willed the pilot to bale out, radio silence stopping them from yelling at the pilot to do so. Then the 190's engine burst into flames and Feldwebel Fritz Altpeter of 11 Staffel crashed to his death near Dierdorf.

The Richthofen pilots carried on towards the High Eifel, then north-west to the River Meuse to join up with SG4 from the Cologne area between Liége and Aachen. However, SG4 came under heavy ground fire from Aachen, the first German city captured by the Allies. Four FW190s were shot down including that of Alfred Druschel. His 190 crashed somewhere south of the city, but his remains were never found. Shortly afterwards JG2 ran into heavy AA fire which caused a number of casualties.

As they eventually reached their target airfield, the German pilots were met by a hail of ground fire as the defences had already been alerted to the approach of their aircraft. Virtually every Staffel lost aircraft; II Gruppe lost its leader, Hauptmann Georg Schroder, over the target; others were shot down on the return flights via Venlo.

American losses on the ground were minimal but the attacking force lost twenty-three pilots killed or missing, ten taken prisoner and four wounded – a loss of almost a third of its strength. Sixteen were lost from I Gruppe alone.

*

JG4, meanwhile, had been heading for the airfield at LeCulot, led in by a Ju88. At LeCulot the Luftwaffe pilots expected to find, according to the latest reconnaissance photos, up to 100 American P47 Thunderbolts, plus some medium and heavy bombers.

Following the briefing by JG4's Kommandeur, Major Gerhard Michalski, Knight's Cross and Oak Leaves, who had shot down twenty-six RAF fighters over Malta as part of his seventy victories, the Focke Wulfs and Messerschmitts began to leave the ground at 8.10 a.m. Once in the air the fighters did not properly form up but carried on independently until they reached Bingen. In better formation but still split up they headed on towards the Moselle.

Nearing Prüm in the Eifel at 8.40, the sun began to break through. The pilots should now have been able to make out LeCulot, situated north of the Wavre, ten miles from Brussels, but LeCulot was not attacked at all that day.

Most probably, those who found an airfield to attack, found St Trond, whose defences were alert as already recorded. Others may have stumbled on Ophoven, or Asch. Many others just stooged around and finally decided that their only offensive contribution was to shoot-up American ground positions around Bastogne. It was a total and costly failure for JG4. Gefreiter Walter Wagner of 5 Staffel II/JG4, force-landed at St Trond with only slight damage to his FW190 A-8, and only when taken into captivity did he learn that he was not at LeCulot. Many of his companions fared far worse. Most seemed scattered all over the area, being shot at from various ground positions as well as from St Trond, Ophoven, Asch, ground defences from both German and Allied lines in the Ardennes, and even some got caught up in JG27's attack on Melsbroek.

In all JG4 lost seventeen pilots killed, missing and wounded, plus a further six taken prisoner of war – a 42% casualty rate. All for virtually nothing in return. By that evening II Gruppe of JG4 had less than ten serviceable aircraft available.

*

If JG2 and JG4's missions were disastrous failures, then JG11's attack was a catastrophe! Commanded by the veteran air fighter and leader, the one eyed Oberstleutnant Günther Specht, holder of the Knight's Cross and who had been in action since 1939 and a Gruppen Kommandeur in JG11 since 1943, leader of the whole Geschwader since April 1944, their target was Asch.

Asch was an airfield housing USAAF squadrons, the American residents being the men of the 352nd and 366th Fighter Groups equipped with P51 Mustangs and P47 Thunderbolts respectively.

*

The adjutant of III/JG11, Oberleutnant Fiedler, had known of Bodenplatte since before the commencement of the Ardennes offensive. He had been amongst those select Staffel leaders briefed

: Crashed FWl90 at St Denis Westrem, ost certainly from JG1.

dle left: Flight Lieutenant Bronislaw :h, Flying Officer Tadeuz Szlenkier Pilot Officer Andrzej Dromlewicz. three shot down German fighters on nuary.

Middle right: Unteroffizier Gerhard Behrens of 8/JG1, killed in action.

Bottom: Leutenant Theo Nibel's FW190D-9, 10/JG54, Grimbergen airfield. His D-9 (Black 12) was the first one to fall into Allied hands.

Top left: Flying Officer Ray Dutt, 16 Squadron.

Top right: Wing Commander Mike Shaw DSO, CO of 69 Squadron. Bodenplatte saved him from test flying a repaired Stirling, much to his relief.

Bottom left: Squadron Leader Ron Walton and his navigator Bill Harper. The attack awoke them from their slumbers.

Bottom right: Ron Walton, Hugh Tudor and FO Ian Ewing of 140 Squadron. Ewing's pipe saved him and Tudor from being out on the airfield when the attack started.

Top left: A burning Spitfire of 16 Squadron.

Top right: The burnt out remains of a 69 Squadron Wellington.

Middle left: Oberstleutnant Kurt Buhlingen, leader of JG2, went for St Trond.

Above: LAC John Hopley, of No.6341 SE on Deurne, was working on a Spitfire when the attack came.

Left: Flight Lieutenant Ronnie Sheward of 263 Squadron on Deurne. He yelled advice to the attacking German pilots!

Top left: Hptm Horst-Günther von Fassong, Grüppenkommandeur III/JG11, was killed in the Asch attack, last seen being chased by P47s.

Top right: RAF Regiment Squadrons had several Flights equipped with Bren Guns to defend 2nd TAF's airfields.

Middle left: Major Günther Specht, Geschwader Kommodore JG11, killed flying against Asch.

Middle right: An RAF Regiment's 40 mm Bofors Gun.

Bottom: Me109, as if crushed by a giant' hand, lies on the Dutch countryside.

...eft: Flight Lieutenant Jerry Eaton ...7 Squadron.

...right: Flight Lieutenant Jimmy ...son of 193 Squadron.

...m left: Hauptmann Julius Meimberg, ...penkommandeur of II/JG53, went for

Metz-Frescaty airfield.

Bottom centre: Oberstleutnant Josef 'Pips' Priller, CO of JG26.

Bottom right: Pilot Officer Ron Pottinger - shot down and taken prisoner on 1 January 1945.

Top left: Oberleutnant Adolf Glunz, JG26, shot down a Spitfire over Evere.

Top right: Major Anton Häckl, leader of II/JG26, got another.

Bottom left: Hauptmann Walter Krupir leader of III/JG26, had to abort his att on Evere due to German AA damage.

Bottom right: Major Ludwig Franziske Kommandeur JG27, attacked Melsbro

Top left: Hauptmann Emile Clade, led …G27.

Top right: A FWl90 D-9 that did not return …by the side of a road in Belgium.

…dle: Flight Lieutenant H P Gibbons of 168 Squadron, shot down and killed over Eindhoven.

Bottom: Typhoons 5V-A (MN869) and 5V-S (RB257) 439 Squadron, on Eindhoven airfield. Note 20 mm cannon hole in the tail of the right-hand Tiffie.

Top left: Smashed Spitfire XI of 400 Squadron, Eindhoven.

Top right: Burning Mosquito XVI of 140 Squadron, Melsbroek.

Middle: Avro Lancaster, believed to be Ursel airfield.

Bottom: Dakota ablaze on Evere airfie

on II Jagdkorp's plan. His III Gruppe CO was yet another veteran air fighter with over 100 kills, Hauptmann Horst-Günther von Fassong, Knight's Cross.

All three Gruppen took off from their bases south of Frankfurt – Focke Wulfs and Messerschmitts – shortly before 8.30 a.m., led by the now familiar two Ju88, or in this case, Ju188s. Nearing Aachen, flak began to explode about them – the first casualty being Oberleutnant Fiedler's FW190. Hit in the head by a shell splinter he lost consciousness, coming too as British soldiers pulled him from his wrecked fighter plane.

Flying north along the Meuse, over the snow covered landscape, the fighter aircraft's low level slipstream shook the snow from the trees. Asch was now just minutes away.

*

No 125 Wing HQ was at Ophoven, situated just by the strip as Asch. 41 Squadron was on the first show of the day, Squadron Leader D.I. Benham DFC, AFC (RM791), having led his men down to the Rhine, north of Coblenz at 8.35. On this armed recce fifteen railway trucks were strafed and damaged by Benham's Red Section while Flight Lieutenant R.P. Harding and Flying Officer N.P. Gibbs attacked a large three-ton transport vessel on the river. As they completed these attacks they received a radio call that the Germans were over their home base. Three pilots had aborted this mission, but even these were lucky, all three having landed back at Ophoven at 8.55 a.m., still way ahead of the attack.

The pilots of 130 Squadron arrived at Ophoven from Diest on 31st December, their diarist recording that '... there should be more flying from now on ...!' The Belgian pilots of 350 Squadron had also arrived at Ophoven the day before, flying in from Evere. The squadron ground crews were loading their lorries at Evere in preparation for the road journey to Ophoven when German fighters came in from the direction of Brussels.

Meantime, at Ophoven, three of 350's Spitfires took off at nine o'clock to patrol in the Malmédy area, led by Flying Officer A. Van Wersch (RM729). 350's CO, temporarily, was Flight Lieutenant Jean Lavigne, Squadron Leader L. Collignon having been shot down by flak on Christmas Eve, suffering a broken leg.

The ground crews of 610 Squadron were also on the move from Evere and were attacked whilst travelling through Melsbroek, having just missed the opening of the attack on Evere. At 8.50 a.m., 610 Squadron mounted a four-man patrol, flying towards Maeseych.

*

On nearby Asch, the Americans too were up early. Despite heavy ground mist, eight Thunderbolts of the 391st Fighter Squadron, 366th Fighter Group, prepared for a dawn mission. Led by Captain Eber E. Simpson, they took off at 8.42 a.m. carrying 500 lb bombs – one P47 carrying rockets. They headed out into the Ardennes battle zone.

Controlled by their 'Marmite' control, they reached the battle line at 9 a.m. and were sent down to bomb and strafe German Mark IV tanks in Ondenval. They claimed five destroyed and five probably destroyed, a truck destroyed and the town left burning. Flak was light but one P47 was hit, the American pilot successfully belly landing south of Liège to return by road. Then, on the squadron's return flight, south of Malmédy, they ran into two Me109s, flying alone. Lieutenants John F. Bathurst and Donald G. Holt claimed them as destroyed.

At 9.16 a.m., a further eight Thunderbolts of the 366th Group, this time from the 390th Squadron, took off under the leadership of Captain Lowell B. Smith. Gaining height, the American pilots began to form up. Only a few miles away now, JG11 were approaching fast.

*

The Mustang Group commanded by Colonel Jim Mayden, was also ready to go. Deputy CO of the 352nd Group was Lieutenant Colonel John C. Meyer. Despite an order the previous evening assigning the Group for an escort detail on the 1st, which meant no early morning patrols could be flown, the pilots were far from happy. An escort mission deep into Germany meant no chance of a fight over the Ardennes.

Nevertheless, it was agreed that if weather permitted, the Group would put on a dawn sweep, provided they would be ready to fly the escort mission on time. A call for 7 a.m. was arranged, but at 7 o'clock the weather report was not good, and a fog covered the field at Asch. After breakfast, Meyer tried to get Headquarters to agree a patrol, but the answer was – No! Following more haggling with HQ it was finally agreed that Meyer could fly a twelve-man patrol if he could guarantee thirty-six fighters for the escort mission. Meyer agreed and quickly got Major William T. Halton to prepare his 487th Squadron for the early show. Meyer had used the argument that enemy air activity in the area was a threat to the Americans on the ground. He had no way of knowing how prophetic his argument was to be.

The twelve pilots assigned the patrol were in the briefing room at 9.05 a.m. Meyer would lead one Section, Bill Halton the second and Captain William T. Whisner the third. The patrol would go to the St Vith area, but it would have to be back in time to give cover to the escort Mustangs when they took off.

Climbing into their fighters, the American pilots taxied out towards the runway. It was still misty but clear enough for take-off. John Meyer reached the end of the runway which ran west-east, and turned his gun switch to fire, then switched on the gun sight. With twenty-two air to air kills already, Meyer was always ready for anything. Overhead he could see the eight Thunderbolts of the 390th circling – it was time to go!

Meyer gunned his motor and his Mustang began to gather speed. As it did so he began to see exploding AA shells. Speeding down the runway he radioed Marmite Control, but they had nothing on their screens, and nothing to report.

Above him, however, the Thunderbolt boys did have something to report. They could see fifty plus FW190s and Me109s streaming in to attack the airfield. The Germans were on the deck and coming in from the north-east. Jettisoning bombs and rockets, the 390th pilots waded in, covering the 487th's take-off.

Meyer, now fully alert, could see aircraft ahead of him, coming in fast and low. JG11 were on target. The closing speed was terrific. Dead ahead of him was a Focke Wulf 190 – others nearby. Still well below combat speed, Meyer was a sitting target. The 190 came in but the German obviously not expecting and certainly not seeing the scrambling Mustang, picked a parked C47 Dakota as his target.

The German pilot, Gefreiter Bohn, totally failed to see the Mustang but Meyer fired instinctively, was on target, and the 190 blew apart. The wreckage crashed just beyong the C47.

Bill 'Whiz' Whisner, leading Red Section, saw the air activity as he was taxy-ing out. He heard Meyer's enquiry of the Controller, and as Whisner became airborne, the Controller began to warn the Mustang pilots that bandits were over the strip. As Whisner climbed he could see the Thunderbolts mixing it with German fighters, then he ran into about thirty FW190s as he reached 1,500 feet. He aimed at one and pressed the gun button. Nothing! In the panic scramble he had forgotten to turn on his gun switch. Quickly correcting this oversight, he gave the 190 two bursts then watched the 190 hit the ground and explode. Then bullets began to strike his P51. Whisner broke to the right then pulled up sharply with a 190 just fifty yards behind him, pumping shells in his direction. Then another P51 came in behind the 190 and the German broke away.

Whisner could see several 20 mm hits in each of his wings, another had damaged his oil tank and the left aileron was not working. Despite losing oil he headed into a dog-fight, shot at another 190 and saw his fire hit home. The German pilot attempted to bale out but another burst from the American sent the 190 into the ground where it exploded. He was immediately after a Messerschmitt and began a scrap with it lasting several minutes but it ended when the German pilot took to his parachute.

Over the radio Whisner heard that the Germans were still strafing the airfield, so turned in that direction, seeing an Me109 strafing the north-east end of the field. Whisner went after it, but the German saw the Mustang coming and turned to meet it. Both pilots came at each other head-on, and on the second pass Whisner scored hits on the nose and wings of the 109. It went down, crashed and burned on the east side of the airfield. Four kills for Bill Whisner made him one of the 487th's top scorers of the day.

This is how Bill Whisner recorded his actions in his personal combat report later that day:

I was leading Red Flight. As we were taxiing out to the strip I saw some air activity east of the airfield. The squadron consisting of three four-ship flights, was taking off singly. As I started down the strip, Colonel Meyer called the Controller and inquired about bandits in the vic. As I pulled my wheels up, the Controller reported that there were bandits east of the field. We didn't take time to form up, but set course, wide open, straight for the bandits. There were a few P47s mixing it up with the bandits as I arrived. I ran into about thirty 190s at 1,500 feet. There were many 109s above them. I picked out a 190 and pressed the trigger. Nothing happened. I reached down and turned on my gun switch and gave him a couple of good bursts.

As I watched him hit the ground and explode, I felt myself being hit. I broke sharply to the right, and up. A 190 was about 50 yards behind me, firing away. As I was turning with him, another 51 attacked him and he broke off his attack on me. I then saw that I had several 20 mm holes in each wing, and another hit in my oil tank. My left aileron control was also out, I was losing oil, but my pressure and temperature were steady. Being over friendly territory I could see no reason for landing immediately so turned towards a big dogfight and shortly had another 190 in my sights. After hitting him several times, he attempted to bale out, but I gave him a burst as he raised up, and he went in with his plane, which exploded and burned. There were several 109s in the vic so I engaged one of them. We fought for five or ten minutes, and I finally managed to get behind him. I hit him good and the pilot baled out at 200 feet. I clobbered him as he baled out and he tumbled into the ground.

At this time I saw fifteen or twenty fires from crashed planes. Bandits were reported strafing the field, so I headed for the strip. I saw a 109 strafe the NE end of the strip. I started after him, and he turned into me. We made two head-on passes, and on the second I hit him in the nose and wings. He crashed and burned east of the strip. I chased several more bandits but they evaded in the clouds. I had oil on my windshield and canopy so came back to the strip and landed.

All of the EA were very aggressive, and extremely good pilots. I am very happy that we were able to shoot down twenty-three with a loss of none. We were outnumbered 5 to 1 with full fuselage tanks. The P47s on this field did a fine job, and helped us considerably. The co-operation among our fighters was extremely good and we did the job as a team.

Claim: two Me109s destroyed, two FW190s destroyed.

William T. Whisner, 0798190
Captain, Air Corps,
352nd Fighter Group.

Captain Henry M. Stewart II got three. He was the wingman to the squadron commander, Major Halton, following him off, then went up after two FW190s. They were flying east towards the front line. Halton fired at them as Stewart covered his leader but 'friendly' ground fire forced him to break away. He immediately ran into a 109 but lost it in a turn, then found another Messerschmitt, chasing it through cloud until he lost flying speed and had to break off yet again.

Coming back over Asch he got onto another 109, went to fire only to discover that he had knocked the gun switches off with his knee. Putting them back on he fired, scored a few strikes but then Bill Whisner came in and shot it down.

Once again over the airfield he saw two P51s chasing a 109 which broke violently. Cutting his throttle, Stewart slid in behind the German and fired, sending the 109 into the ground from 100 feet. Pulling up he saw another Me109 on the deck and dived. This too he shot down, despite intense ground fire slicing the air about him. A few moments later he got his third 109.

Lieutenant Alden P. Rigby shot a FW190 off of the tail of his leader, Lieutenant Ray Littge, the German going straight in from 500 feet after taking hits in the wings and cockpit. Going down after another 190 his gun-sight went out but firing a long burst until he saw hits on its wing roots, he got on target. The 190 began to leave a smoke trail, winged over and crashed into some trees.

Turning back over the airfield, Rigby saw a Me109 and a Thunderbolt in a fight, but when the T-bolt mushed out in a turn, he got in a long burst which smashed the German's cooling system. Streaming glycol the 109 crashed into a field. Deciding to land as he was running short of ammunition, the American then spotted two Mustangs scrapping with a 109. Just then the 109 broke in his direction, and Rigby fired the rest of his ammunition into it, whereupon the 109 dived into the ground. He claimed four victories (two shared) but only received credit for three.

Lieutenant Dean M. Huston saw a FW190 climbing up behind Lieutenant Sanford Moats who was himself attacking a 190. Yelling to Moats to break left, Moats did so as Huston came up underneath the German to fire a three-second burst. Flames shot out of the 190 which then dived into the ground. Moats himself shot down four that morning, commenting later that, 'I found all the enemy were very aggressive and the pilot of the last 109 was absolutely hot! We were handicapped by full fuselage tanks and ground fire ...' In his last scrap with the 'hot' 109 pilot, Moats was so low that he was only just able to recover and pull out above some trees. He was saved by Captain Stewart who got the 109.

Flying on the wing of Bill Whisner was Lieutenant Walker G. Diamond:

I was flying Red two as Captain Whisner's wing-man. We took off in string and were engaged immediately after take off. I had not joined Captain Whisner when he became engaged and I lost him before I could get close enough to stay with him. I got in trail with the first FW190 I saw and closed in on him firing. I saw scattered strikes on the fuselage and wing. We were very low and he crashed into some trees just as I overshot him.

I got on another 190's tail and fired at him in a turn and level. I saw strikes on the wings but he did not crash. I was then out of ammunition and broke away.

I claim one FW190 destroyed and one FW190 damaged.

Walker G. Diamond, 0829950
1st Lt, Air Corps,
352nd Fighter Group.

Colonel Meyer's wingman was Alex F. Sears:

I was flying White Two on Colonel Meyer's wing. We had just taken off when we were bounced by forty or fifty Me109s and FW190s. One Me109 came at me head-on and we made several passes at each other, both of us firing. On the third pass I got some strikes on his engine and shot part of the tail section away.

He started burning and went into a lazy spiral and crashed. I claim one Me109 Destroyed.

Alex F. Sears, 0699024
1st Lt, Air Corps,
352nd Fighter Group.

Following his first spectacular victory, John Meyer had continued to climb away from the air strip. He latched onto the tail of another FW190 but was caught in the German's slipstream. At that moment Meyer spotted a Messerschmitt in his mirror, its guns already winking at him. Fortunately another Mustang swept in and knocked the 109 from his tail. Meanwhile, the FW190 ahead of him rolled over onto its back, and although lost momentarily as he again checked his tail, Meyer spotted it again in a dive for the ground. Meyer felt certain that it would hit them but the Luftwaffe pilot just managed to pull out of his dive, clipping some of the top branches as he did so, before starting to streak away.

Meyer was after the retreating German in a moment, but then saw that in fact the 190 was heading in towards the airstrip, and seconds later both friend and enemy came under ground fire from the defenders. Undeterred, Meyer stayed with the Focke Wulf and fired as it appeared in his sights. Shells slammed into the Focke Wulf and the pilot dropped, looking for a likely spot on which to belly land. He made a desperate attempt to get his crippled fighter down but bounced as he hit the ground, flipped over and over, then broke up. Meyer had brought his score to twenty-four air kills.[1]

*

The air battle between JG11 and the Mustangs and Thunderbolts lasted for half an hour, resulting in the Americans claiming thirty-five victories, twenty-three for the Mustangs, twelve for the Thunderbolts – the latter Group only receiving credit for seven. Of these, Lieutenant Melvyn R. Paisley got three, while the leader that

[1] John Meyer was now credited with twenty-four air and thirteen ground kills – the highest for an American pilot in Europe. He was badly injured in a car crash on 9th January 1945, which ended his WW2 flying. However, he later flew in the Korean War, adding two Mig kills to his tally. Later still he became an Air Force General.

morning, Lowell Smith got one. Of the twelve Mustang pilots, eleven scored kills.

Americans on the ground had a perfect view of the battle that raged above them. Now and again a Focke Wulf or Messerschmitt broke free to dive and strafe the airfield, sending men on the ground into fox-holes or behind any kind of cover. Once an attacking fighter passed over, the men would re-emerge to watch the show. When a German aeroplane was shot down it was attended by a rousing cheer from the spectators. For the majority of those on the ground, it was the first dog-fight they had actually witnessed. Ground gunners of the 784th AAA claimed a further four German fighters. After the fight there was a vast semi-circle of burning aeroplanes that could be clearly seen from above the airfield.

Four Mustangs were also shot down but all four pilots baled out and got back safely. One Thunderbolt pilot also escaped by parachute and two other P47s were damaged in the battle. Most important, however, was that very little damage was done to the 100 or so aircraft on Asch airfield, so well did the two squadrons defend the base. The 352nd Group only recorded one Mustang damaged on the ground through ground strafing.

For JG11 it was a death blow. Their losses totalled twenty-one pilots killed or missing and four taken prisoner. These included the Geschwader Kommandeur, Günther Specht, and the CO of III Gruppe, Hauptmann von Fassong, who was last seen with two Thunderbolts on his tail.

*

One victory went to the RAF. The four-man patrol from 610 Squadron who had left for a patrol at 8.50, included Flight Lieutenant A.F.O. Gaze DFC and bar, an Australian with $7\frac{1}{2}$ victories. North of Liége they ran into intense 'friendly' AA fire from a now alerted ground defence force. In the evasive action, Tony Gaze became separated and so decided to return to Ophoven.

When at about one mile east of Asch, flying at 2,000 feet, he caught sight of eight FW190s heading north-east on the deck. Gaze dived down and, approached from dead astern, closing in on the rearmost. At 800 yards he was seen, the German pilot surging forward. Despite renewed ground fire the Australian closed into a range of 600 yards, fired a two-second burst, but missed, his shells bursting on the ground ahead of the 190. A second burst also missed, but avoiding yet more ground fire, Gaze fired for a third time as the 190 rose over a clump of trees. Hits splattered and sparkled on the 190's fuselage and belly, its flaps dropped and as Gaze flew over the German fighter, it nosed forward and hit the ground.

Tony Gaze watched for only a second and still followed by American ground fire he swiftly headed back towards Asch.[1]

*

The Americans had few casualties on the ground but the RAF suffered some losses on Ophoven. 350 Squadron had seven Spitfires destroyed or damaged. 41 and 610 Squadrons got off scot-free although 41 recorded that a fuel dump was set on fire. Three Spitfires of 130 Squadron were damaged and a Corporal of the unit's servicing echelon was wounded by an exploding cannon shell. Prompt action by two pilots, Sergeant P.E.H. Standish and Flight Sergeant P.H.J. Clay, saved the airman's life.

Flight Sergeant Philip Clay, at great personal risk, then taxied two Spitfires to a place of safety during the attack despite exploding ammunition from burning aircraft shooting all over the place. He then directed the crew of a fire tender in their fire-fighting operation and by his efforts over 200 gallons of high octane petrol was saved. Clay received the BEM for these exploits, was promoted to warrant officer and went on to win the DFC later in 1945.[2] Standish was commissioned with effect from 1st January but became tour-expired in February.

[1] Tony Gaze's brother Pilot Officer I.S.O. Gaze joined 610 Squadron with him in early 1941, but was killed in action on 23rd March 1941.

[2] Clay was shot down on 19th April 1945 after destroying a FW190. Taken prisoner he was released by advancing US troops on 2nd May and returned to the squadron.

CHAPTER THIRTEEN

The Southern Thrust

Although the main German attack was directed against the airfield in Holland and Belgium, an additional attack was directed across the border in France. Jagdgeschwader 53, situated on its bases around Stuttgart, was assigned to hit the airfield at Metz-Frescaty – Y34.

Metz-Frescaty was the home of the American 365th Fighter Group, comprising the 386th, 387th and 388th Fighter Squadrons. With effect from the 1st January 1945, the 365th passed from Administrative and operational control of the XIX Tactical Air Command, to that of the IX TAC. Its strength was thirty-eight officers and 100 enlisted men.

JG53 was commanded by 29-year-old Oberstleutnant Helmut Bennemann, holder of the Knight's Cross and with nearly ninety combat victories to his name. His pilots, briefed and ready, took off at dawn to fly almost due east with the rising sun behind them. Its II and IV Gruppen, were led by Hauptmann Julius Meimberg who had received his Knight's Cross in October 1944 (he had fifty victories), and Hauptmann Müer. These two units formed up over Karlsruhe to await III Gruppe, led by Hauptmann Luckenbach. This Gruppe's task was to knock-out the anti-aircraft defences at Metz while the other two Gruppen hit the parked aircraft.

However, the III Gruppe failed to make rendezvous. Coming in from Kirrlach, Luckenbach's pilots ran into some P47s on patrol who broke up their Messerschmitts. Having jettisoned their external tanks in the scrap, the Me109 pilots had to return home.

Despite the non-appearance of the III Gruppe (who had two pilots wounded in the action) the other two Gruppen headed in for Metz.

*

The morning at Metz dawned clear and bright. Lieutenant Colonel John R. Murphy, deputy commander of the 365th Group, stood in the watery sunlight outside the operations tent and guessed that the Group could fly at least six missions on such a promising day. Being Americans they in the Group were very keen to support their comrades on the ground in the Ardennes.

The Group had only just moved into Metz from A-84 in Mons, Belgium, and everyone was still getting settled in. Most of them were looking forward to the prospect of better flying weather than they had experienced in Belgium!

At 8.28 a.m., Major Arlo C. Henry Jr lead eleven P47s of the 387th Fighter Squadron on an armed recce to St Ingbert-Neunkirchen-Nohfelden-Dilberg. The Thunderbolts each carried two 500 lb bombs under their wings. They reached St Ingbert at ten minutes to nine o'clock, attacking rail transport. Five railways cars were destroyed and the line was cut. Shortly afterwards they attacked and destroyed a further five rail cars. The P47s began landing back at 9.13 a.m.

When they were doing so, the 388th Squadron, headed by Captain Jerry G. Mast, was taking off for Hombourg. As they neared Solgne they received a radio call that German aircraft were over Metz. They jettisoned their bombs and headed back.

On the ground at Metz the 389th Squadron was preparing for a 9.30 take-off, its aircraft standing on the knoll at the south-west corner of the airfield. Within minutes of the 387th getting down, distant AA bursts began to stain the morning sky. Ground crews and pilots stood watching, thinking they must be RAF Spitfires. The sound of this gunfire drifted across the airfield and those whose curiosity was aroused looked northward and saw six aircraft begin a low swoop towards them. As the airfields own AA guns began to open fire, personnel in the Group's HQ building leaped vainly for depressions in the ground, for ditches, fox-holes or any kind of shelter because at the time there was a distinct lack of slit-trenches – a condition which was corrected with some gusto and haste before the sun finally set that day! On the first pass one Messerschmitt zoomed south beyond the field where the pilot baled out to be captured by MPs.

More Me109s came in low, attacking on the deck in threes or

fours in all directions. Corporal Irving Wasserman of the 387th, whose 21st birthday fell on this day, was driving a BST pulling two trailers, each loaded with a dozen 500 lb bombs. Seeing bullets kicking up the snow ahead of him he quickly dived off the truck and jumped into a fox-hole near the bomb dump. Later he found a German shell case on the driving seat of his truck.

Staff Sergeant George Wasson started to walk across the airfield shortly before the 109s arrived, when someone threw a long cigarette butt down. Being a heavy smoker whose daily ration soon went, he picked the butt up and began to dry it out. Standing nearby, Staff Sergeant John Lehnert offered Wasson a Camel cigarette, which Wasson accepted, then they stood talking for several minutes.

Then someone yelled, 'Hey, look at those P51s buzzing the field.'

'P51s my ass,' yelled someone else, 'they're Germans!'

As Wasson and two others dived into a nearby shell-hole, Wasson was thinking that if it hadn't been for the cigarette he would have been right out in the middle of the airfield. (Who said smoking can damage your health!)

In the 388th domestic area, Sergeant Don Hutchins was happily sitting in an outside latrine reading the Stars and Stripes paper, when the attack began. With his trousers well and truly down he dived into the latrine pit! For quite some time afterwards his pals would sniff questioningly whenever he came near! The CO of the 386th Squadron, Major George R. Brooking, was caught in a similar situation in the officers' toilets. Hearing gunfire, he looked out of the ten flap to find himself staring right down the throats of sixteen Me109s as they came in. Pulling up the collar of his flight jacket, he dived out of the latrine and into the snow with his trousers round his knees! Quickly realising that this was all pretty ridiculous, he got up, hitched his pants, then fell and crawled to a nearby gun emplacement where he assisted the gunners in tracking the German fighters, one of which they shot down.

*

There was usually two 'alert' aircraft standing at the end of the runway but on this morning there was only one and in that sat Captain Tom Stanton.

The other alert pilot was First Lieutenant Samuel B. Lutz, and he was warming himself in front of a small fire with some engineers. As the 109s came in he and some others took shelter behind a streamroller where he had a grandstand view of the raid. He even began to loose off with his .45 automatic.

One Messerschmitt came in and strafed the lone alert P47. Lutz looked up and it seemed so close that he could have touched the German pilot as he flew over. At the very moment he looked up, Lutz saw the Luftwaffe pilot hit in the right eye by a .50 calibre bullet. The Messerschmitt nosed into the ground, broke up and disintegrated. The pilot was thrown out and his body went rolling and bounding along the runway. Even before the body stopped, Lutz saw two AA gunners jump out and claim the pilot's flying boots for souvenirs!

Another Messerschmitt crashed close to the 387th Squadron's HQ, the machine smashing into pieces. The Luftwaffe pilot was decapitated and both of his legs were hacked off above the knees. These were not the best sights for operational pilots to see. The next day, or the next week, it could be the same for one of them.

Stáff Sergeant Robert A. Gabarine was standing on the wing of a Thunderbolt on which he was working. Hearing the gunfire, he turned to see the 109s coming in and then a bullet went through the P47's propeller. The bullet creased his skull and knocked him unconscious to the ground. Another 386th man who was wounded was Staff Sergeant Kirby Garner who was sitting in a P47 awaiting his pilot's arrival. Jumping clear he began to waddle (he was wearing heavy sheepskin clothing) for cover. Bullets began to stitch the ground behind him and then he was hit in the arm. During the attack, Corporal Lee Weldon (388th) was seriously wounded. Second Lieutenant Carl Riggs of the 388th was slightly injured when one Me109 crashed near him, and the disintegrating aeroplane cartwheeled over his hiding place.

*

Two acts of heroism were carried out by Staff Sergeant John C. Lawless and Sergeant Olin S. Holcomb of the 386th Squadron. One of their Thunderbolts was hit and set on fire. It carried two

500 lb bombs and next to it stood another bombed-up P47. The two men grabbed fire extinguishers and despite attacking Me109s, they succeeded in putting out the fire. Both men were awarded the Soldiers Medal.

The Soldiers Medal also went to Staff Sergeant Gordon Hurt, a crew chief. A petrol bowser near his aircraft was set on fire. Helped by two other men, he started the P47 and taxied it away from the burning bowser to a place of safety.

When Corporal Lee Welden of the 388th was wounded in the thigh, he was working in the cockpit of a bombed-up Thunderbolt. The aircraft caught fire but because of his injury he was unable to extricate himself. Fortunately for him, Corporal Emanuel Catanuto was nearby and saw his plight. Jumping onto the wing of the 'Jug' and despite smoke and flames, Catanuto pulled Walden from the cockpit. Rolling off the wing, he ran, dragging the Corporal by his uninjured leg. They covered about thirty yards before the Thunderbolt blew up. Catanuto received the Soldiers Medal to add to his Bronze Star and Silver Star, the latter won only two weeks previously while on detached service with the 45th Infantry Division. Radioing for air support for American tanks, he then attacked a gun position with a tommy-gun, killing seven Germans. He later won the Purple Heart when he transferred from the Air Corps to the Infantry.

*

First Lieutenant Lavern Alcorn had been 'spare' pilot on the 388th's early mission. As nobody had dropped out, he had left the formation and headed back to Metz. As he approached the runway, flying along 'fat, dumb and happy' he was suddenly bracketed by exploding AA shells. He immediately went into violent evasive action and it was later recorded that some crazy American pilot was flying aerobatics during the attack! Looking down, Alcorn could now see the smoke and burning planes, so he jettisoned his two five hundred pounders, and turned in the direction of the now retreating German aircraft but found none.

In action on the airfield, the defence gunners scored a number of successes against the attacking Messerschmitts as already related.

One German fighter – a ball of flame – swept past Group HQ, burning petrol setting a communications truck on fire. It finally crashed in a wood a hundred yards from the building. The pilot was seen to be struggling to get out but his parachute had no chance to open. Miraculously the crashing aeroplane did not cause any injuries although the wood in which it fell was full of men who had taken shelter there. In total, the gunners claimed nine Me109s shot down, despite the complaint by the heavy AA crews that the 109s were flying so low that they could not train their guns on them properly.

After the raid, Major Brooking was at Headquarters when one of the captured Luftwaffe pilots was brought it. He was very cocky and when someone wanted to take his photograph, he insisted in first combing his hair and shining his boots.

Whilst Brooking was talking to the German flyer, the man walked over to the office window, arrogantly pointing to the burning Thunderbolts out on the airfield.

'What do you think of that?' said the German, throwing his head back and smiling. Major Brooking felt like knocking him down, but instead turned and walked out of the room.

Replacement aircraft soon began to be flown in while theGerman was still being interrogated on the base. Major Brooking went to see him, took him to a window and pointed to the new Thunderbolts.

'What do you think of that?' asked Brooking. The German nodded thoughtfully.

'That is what is beating us,' the German agreed sadly.

*

Losses at Metz were thirty Thunderbolts, twenty-two being totally destroyed with eight with AC category damage. Three more were slightly damaged. Hardest hit was the 386th Squadron with twelve destroyed and seven badly damaged. Next was the 387th with nine plus one damaged. The 388th had one destroyed and three damaged.

The Group's returning aircraft arrived too late to intervene. As they came back over their field, all they could see was burning aircraft and trucks. While smoke billowed skywards almost blocking out the New Year sun.

JG53's two attacking Gruppen each lost seven pilots, each losing five killed and two taken prisoner. Both units also had one pilot wounded.

CHAPTER FOURTEEN

'Get 'em back into the air'

The raid had lasted less than forty-five minutes, in some cases a good deal less. As the Me109, FW190 and Me262 pilots headed back towards Germany, to be engaged either by anti-aircraft gunners or Allied fighter pilots, the airfields seemed suddenly silent. Silent, except for the roar and crackle of burning aeroplanes, blazing petrol dumps, exploding ammunition, flaming trucks and the moans and cries of the wounded and dying.

On those airfields more seriously hit, RAF personnel fought the flames, cared for the wounded, covered up the dead, and watched the sky in case of further assaults.

The cost had to be counted but there were other priorities. Aircraft in air, returning from early raids or from combat, had to be re-armed, refuelled or diverted to other less seriously damaged airfields. At 83 Group HQ, Air Vice-Marshal Harry Broadhurst could look out at damaged Eindhoven, see his burning aeroplanes and know that he had to get his men back into the air. At that moment he had no clear idea how badly his Group or other Groups in 2nd TAF had been hit, but this experienced pilot and commander knew it was important to show the Germans that 2nd TAF was far from down and out. Air Marshal Coningham agreed – orders went out. Coningham was also on the telephone to Broadhurst after the dust had settled. Both men knew it would have been Dietrich Peltz that had organised the attacks and Coningham said as much to Broady. After all, as Coningham smilingly reminded his AOC, this was not the first time that Peltz had 'got him'.

The German leader was Dietrich Peltz and he had caught me in similar circumstances at night in Sicily. Also in the Desert when I was SASO to 'Mary' Coningham. On that occasion I was absent from my Headquarters.

Air Vice Marshal H. Broadhurst, AOC 83 Group

When Broadhurst's base had been attacked during the Desert Campaign, he had flown to a meeting in Cairo and was in fact on the return flight in a Spitfire. Coming from the flesh-pots, he had loaded his cockpit with lots of goodies, mostly fresh fruit and vegetables. Nearing his base he could see smoke rising and as he came overhead could see some of his men looking up at him. Enemy aircraft were still buzzing about and these men on the ground eagerly awaited the sight of Broadhurst getting amongst them and hopefully shooting a few of them down. However, Broadhurst with a cockpit full of produce was in no position to take on enemy aircraft in a dog-fight. Those watchers saw the inglorious sight of their base CO – the great ace from the skies over Northern France – being chased around at low level by some Italian fighters, fruit and vegetables bounding around his head as he skimmed around sand hills in full flight.

Following Peltz's attack on Broadhurst's bases in Sicily later in the war, Tedder was requesting information on losses, from his HQ in Tunisia. Broadhurst managed to stall him until enough tails, wings and fuselages could be gathered together to make an aircraft so that he could report to Tedder that it was not as bad as it really had been!

Now by the late morning of 1st January 1945, the order was to get aircraft up and out over Germany.

Immediately the attack was over Group Headquarters told me to get as many aircraft airborne as possible, using all our wing call-signs so as to give the impression to the Germans that the damage inflicted had not been so severe as it actually was.

Wing Commander C.D. North-Lewis, Leader 124 Wing

*

Naturally those bases least damaged were able to get aeroplanes off almost immediately. From Volkel Squadron Leader R.L. 'Bob'

Spurdle DFC led nine Tempests of his 80 Squadron off at 10.30 a.m.
to fly an armed recce over the Paderborn-Bielefeld area. An hour
later when north-west of Münster, flying at 9,000 feet and heading
back towards base, Flying Officer J.W. Garland, a Canadian,
spotted an aircraft flying north-east on the deck passing towards his
right. Calling to Spurdle that he was going down to take a look,
John Garland rolled over and dived after the suspect aircraft. As he
levelled out on the deck he saw a second aircraft about three
quarters of a mile ahead of the first. He also saw that both aircraft
were German FW190s – long-nosed D-9s. Garland closed in to 200
yards behind the rearmost 190, fired a quick burst, blasting pieces
from it. A second burst hit its fuselage, wing roots and set its belly
tank on fire. As the 190 lost speed, Garland overshot it, seeing it
catch fire, go down and crash into a wood.

Closing in on the leading 190 which was also making a turn to
the left, Garland loosed off two bursts of fire. The 190 nosed down
into a field, caught fire, bounced several times, then lost its wings as
it smashed through some trees.[1]

*

The Canadians of 421 RCAF Squadron at Evere sent out eight
Spitfire XVIs led by Squadron Leader J.D. Browne DFC (SM293).
Two Spits aborted but the others found some ground targets,
shooting up a train, some lorries and finally strafing a factory for
good measure.

The Typhoons on Deurne, delayed by the ice on the runway,
were finally ready for offensive operations by late morning. First off
was 197 Squadron at 11.25 led by Flight Lieutenant R.C. Curwen.
Their target was the village of Meeuwen which they completely
demolished.

Flight Lieutenant J.G. 'Simmy' Simpson led A Flight of 193
Squadron away from Deurne at 11.30 to attack the bridge at
Vianen. One pilot aborted with engine trouble but fourteen bombs
went down towards the bridge but scored no hits. (193 eventually

---

[1] John Garland won the DFC and went to 3 Squadron as a flight
commander. He was taken prisoner on 8th February 1945. He was later a
Colonel in the RCAF.

destroyed the bridge on the 5th.)

Finally at 11.40 a.m. Flight Lieutenant Jerry Eaton led 257 Squadron's first show of 1945.

My log-book says the operation was a low level bombing sortie against a bridge near Beesch on the Utrecht road. Several direct hits were reported as was some light and heavy AA fire.

Flight Lieutenant S.J. Eaton, 257 Squadron

A large hole was blasted through the bridge but the flak hit and damaged one Typhoon, flown by Warrant Officer K.E. Button.

Flight Lieutenant Ronnie Sheward, also known as 'Bentos' by the boys in 263 Squadron (after Fray Bentos meat products since he had lived in the Argentine before the war), led eight aircraft off to attack barges east of Dordrecht. The Typhoon pilots located their targets and fifty-six direct rocket hits were claimed on more than twenty barges, many being left smoking and two in flames. Sheward got seven hits out of eight, and noted in his diary – 'Boys shooting well'.

Squadron Leader J.H. Deall (RB219) led seven Typhoons of his 266 Squadron also against barges, scoring hits on these as well as a warehouse.

*

Volkel's Typhoon Wing had also been ordered out, 175 Squadron sending out machines to Münster-Rheine region. They attacked a marshalling yard with rockets and cannon fire, meeting intense flak. Flying Officer T.T. Hall, an Australian, was hit in the port tank but got back safely. Pilot Officer W.R. Speedy, another Australian (MN358), developed a rough engine but he too made it home. On his way back, Hall spotted a German staff car near Ahaus and strafed it.

On their initial flight out, these four Typhoons had passed over two RAF Lancaster bombers when twenty miles north-east of Nijmegen. One was trailing what appeared to be a parachute. These were two of the force of Lancasters ordered out from England to attack the infamous Dortmund-Ems Canal. This force from Bomber Command had, it will be remembered, left their bases at around dawn. They had flown across the North Sea, seen nothing of the attacks on the airfields and reached their target area between 11.12 and 11.21 a.m.

The crew of Lancaster PA169 of 467 Squadron, flown by 29-year-old Australian from Adelaide, Flying Officer Maurice George Bache, had an eventful trip. His crew was Sergeant E. Wilson (Engineer), Flight Sergeant S.H. Nelson (Bomb aimer), Flying Officer L.E. Patison (Navigator), Flight Sergeant C.J. Dredger (Wireless Operator), Flight Sergeant L.G. Court (Mid-Upper Gunner) and Flight Sergeant J.M. Jay (Rear Gunner).

On approach to the target they could see heavy flak opening up on the formation ahead, south-west of Landbergen. Their Lancaster was then hit in the left wing and bomb bay but Bache flew in and bombed the target. No sooner had this been accomplished than they were hit again, this time in the No 1 fuel tank, causing a severe petrol loss. The engineer balanced the cross-feed but it did not last for more than a minute, so they switched back to No 2 tank.

The bomber was then hit again, the left side of the port inner engine being ripped open which then caught fire. Bache quickly ordered this engine closed down and the flames went out. Then the port outer engine was hit but it did not catch fire but power was lost and it later cut out, twenty miles south of the Rhine. The bomber gradually lost height and Bache found it difficult to control. A cable was attached to the right rudder and passed down into the bomb aimer's position for him to pull and help keep pressure on the right rudder. As they struggled to leave the target area, Bache saw another Lancaster hit in its bomb bay and start to spiral down against the incoming bomber stream, on fire.

Bache's Lancaster was losing height and he warned his crew that they might have to use their parachutes. Another Lancaster overtook them, flying on three engines with what to them, appeared to be a fair turn of speed! As they neared the River Maas they saw a Lancaster being engaged by ground fire and Bache and his crew knew that they too would have to fly through this flak belt and be unable to take any kind of evasive action. Still losing height the crew were warned that when they got down to 3,500 feet they would have to bale out; then fifteen miles short of the River Rhine

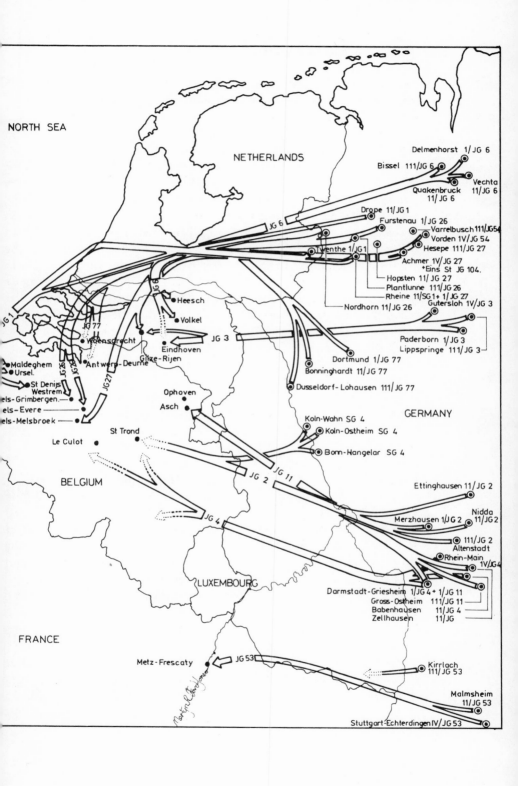

the port outer engine finally gave out. It would not feather and the propeller continued to windmill, while Bache had to reduce power on his starboard outer to prevent a swing to the left.

As they crossed the Maas the Lancaster was down to 3,500 feet and the crew took up crash positions, then the bomber was hit yet again. Damage was caused to the front turret, bombing panel, floor of the cockpit, roof and right wing. Bache ordered his crew to leave, which they did. The Australian was now alone in the crippled Lancaster and had to face the task of trying to get out. With his left foot hard on the right rudder pedal, he lowered his seat and held full right aileron with his left hand as he stepped across the engineer's position. The Lancaster began to roll, throwing him to the floor. Grabbing the hand rail in the bomb-aimer's compartment he hauled himself forward in the now girating aircraft, towards the open hatch. For a moment the slipstream held him against the rim but he finally pulled himself clear and immediately pulled his rip-cord. Only seconds later he hit the top of a pine tree, which snapped off and Bache fell heavily to the ground.

All his crew landed safely except the flight engineer and wireless operator who both had fractured ankles. Bache was awarded an immediate DSO.

*

Number 9 Squadron was the other unit to suffer serious casualties on the Dortmund-Ems Raid. Lancaster NG223 flown by Flying Officer B.W. Reaks was shot down, the crew being reported missing. Lancaster PD377 (WS-U) piloted by Flying Officer R.F.H. Denton from New Zealand was, like Bache's, hit over the target just after releasing its bombs. The crew, on its fifth mission, was Sergeant W.N. Hartshorne (engineer), Flight Sergeant E. Kneebone (navigator), Flying Officer F.H. Goebel (bomb aimer), Flight Sergeant G. Thompson (wireless operator), Sergeant E.J. Potts and Sergeant J.T. Price (mid-upper and rear gunners respectively).

A direct him from German AA fire smashed into the Lancaster and started a large fire in the fuselage, a second hit removing a large part of the cockpit perspex and set the port inner engine on fire. Losing height, Harry Denton, stunned momentarily, set course for friendly territory and then Denton discovered that two of his crew's parachutes had been torn open and were useless.

By the time the Lancaster reached the Rhine it was down to 4,000 feet, and Denton was suffering from frostbite. Meanwhile, back in the fuselage, the flak had opened a large hole in the bottom of the fuselage, set the machine on fire and trapped the two gunners. George Thompson could see the damage and knew that his two comrades were in deadly peril. He eased himself past the gaping hole and got to Potts' dorsal turret and extricated the unconscious gunner. The gunner's clothing was on fire and Thompson's clothing too was now burning but lifting Potts across his shoulders, Thompson then ferried him back over the hole. Safely over it, Thompson then beat out Potts' burning clothes with his bare hands. Despite his own injuries caused by the flames, Thompson then went back down the fuselage to get the rear gunner.

Unable to get out himself because of the fire, Hayden Price heard Thompson knocking on the doors of his rear turret. He opened them and Thompson helped the gunner out and got him too back over the hole to safety. Thompson, his face and hands in a terrible state, then went forward to tell his pilot that both gunners were out of danger.

As the Lancaster neared the Rhine it was hit yet again, knocking out the starboard inner engine. However, Denton crossed into Allied territory and later made a successful crash-landing, about a mile from the Headquarters of No 2734 RAF Regiment Squadron at Heesch. Ernie Potts later died from his burns and unhappily the brave George Thompson, also badly burned, succumbed to his injuries on 23rd January. He was awarded a posthumous Victoria Cross.

*

A little earlier, the Mosquitos of 8 Group had bombed their assigned targets. 128 Squadron had attacked railway tunnels near Coblenz in south-west Germany. 692 Squadron's aircraft also attacked tunnels in the same region. Flight Lieutenant G.T. Nairn (in PF414) with Sergeant D. Lunn, was shot down by light flak.

This crew had survived a crash-landing at Graveley in October 1944 and had gone on to complete forty operations.

*

On the airfields in Belgium and Holland, the squadrons began to receive back its aircraft following the late morning operations. They were quickly refuelled and rearmed for further sorties, now that the order to get aircraft into the air had been given.

CHAPTER FIFTEEN

The Day Continues

The next round of Allied air operations came at about mid-day. 74 Tiger Squadron and 345 (Free French) Squadron escorted American B26 Marauders bombing targets south of Trier, hitting the escape roads from the 'Rundstedt Pocket' south of Malmédy. 74 was led by Flight Lieutenant D.C. Usher DFC, DFM (NH469), 345 by Captaine Lemaire (PV143).

From Heesch 411 RCAF Squadron flew a fighter sweep over Münster and Osnabrück, led by Squadron Leader J.N. Newell. They saw nothing. Squadron Leader Dean Dover's 'Falcons' – 412 RCAF Squadron, took off at twelve noon. In the air, control informed Dover, flying as Crystal Red One, of enemy aircraft near Venlo. Still fearing a further attack by the Luftwaffe, the RAF were keen to be on top of any such development.

Halfway to Venlo, Dean Dover spotted a FW190 on the deck flying north-east. Dover (MK306) went after it, closing to 100 yards to fire a two-second burst. Strikes sparkled along its fuselage and on its tailplane, then Dover ordered his wingman to have a go.

Flying Officer Eric Kelly (PT352) fired a three-second burst from 300 down to 75 yards, saw strikes and flame stream back. It then dived into a wood and exploded. Meanwhile, Flight Lieutenant W.J. Banks DFC (ML277) had spotted a twin-engined aircraft going east, also on the deck. Wilfred Banks' first burst scored hits on the machine's port engine, and then a stream of smoke came from it. It was a Ju88, and a second burst brought flames and then the 88 crashed into a field where it blew up. Also on this patrol, the Canadians shot up a train south of Hamm.

Canadians of 416 Squadron from Evere also put up a patrol to the Bruhl-Mayen area, but it proved uneventful.

*

At Melsbroek Flight Lieutenant Ray Dutt finally got off on his reconnaissance mission at 12.15 p.m. In Spitfire PL854, he headed towards the enemy airfields in the Ruhr canal region around Dortmund.

> After the attack had ceased our runway was declared fit for take-off and I departed on my sortie round the Ruhr, during which I was intercepted by some FW190s in the Dortmund area. I think they may either have been returning from a sortie or were perhaps just forming up, since after a few minutes of engagement, I was able to break off and continue with my sortie.
>
> *Flight Lieutenant E.R. Dutt, 16 Squadron*

Hawker Tempests of 486 New Zealand Squadron went out on an armed recce shortly after mid-day although two had to abort with engine trouble. Flying over the Paderborn area, fifty plus enemy fighters were seen north of Münster at 12.35 p.m. The Tempest pilots tried to close but when still some miles off the Germans saw them and dived to zero feet and were lost. The Tempests shot-up a railway signal box instead.

*

The Typhoons went out in the early afternoon. Despite Eindhoven being badly hit, 124 Typhoon Wing put up two raids around one o'clock. Six Typhoons of 181 Squadron, led by Flight Lieutenant L.B. Boucher, attacked trains around Euskirchen. 247 Squadron also sent out six Typhoons to the same area led by Flight Lieutenant B.T. Tatham (MN585). No trains were found but the pilots fired their rockets at several trucks that were found.

No 198 Squadron from Gilze Reijen, led by Squadron Leader N.J. Durrant (JR505 TP-B), were also ordered to Euskirchen. They too found trucks near some woods, attacking them with rockets and cannon. Later 183 Squadron sent its Typhoons into the Ardennes. Led by Flight Lieutenant A.R. Cocks (EK498), they attacked and destroyed German lorries and shot-up troops.[1] On their return

---

[1] Flight Lieutenant Cocks was shot down on 8th February 1945 but seen to bale out.

flight Flying Officer Don Webber (EK497) was killed in one of those unfortunate accidents that happen in the madness of war. Approaching the circuit at Y29 – Asch – with his wheels down, he was attacked by an over zealous American Mustang pilot and killed.

No 610 Squadron at nearby Ophoven had sent up a four-man patrol led by Flight Lieutenant J.B. Sheppard to cover the Malmédy area, and they were warned that Me109s were over their base. Fearful of a repeat of the morning's attack, they returned hurriedly only to discover that the 109s were in fact 183's Typhoons, and that one had already been shot down by a Mustang.

Another pilot from Gilze died uselessly shortly afterwards: Flight Lieutenant P.J. Garland in a Spitfire XIV (RM803) of 2 Squadron. Three pilots of this squadron flew a Tac/R mission in the early afternoon. On their return at 3 p.m., Garland bounced badly on landing, stalled, crashed onto his back and was killed.

Deurne's Typhoons were also sent out. Squadron Leader C.D. 'Rastus' Erasmus led eight aircraft of his 193 bomb-carrying Tiffies against a busy crossroad junction. The roads were cut 'quite nicely' although one Typhoon was hit and damaged. Flying Officer Charlie Hall caught a 20 mm shell which exploded in his starboard main tank, but he and the others got home safely.[1]

Flight Lieutenant R.C. Curwen attacked targets around Aalborg with aircraft of 197 Squadron, while Squadron Leader J.H. Deall led his 266 Squadron to leave a factory burning at Keizersveer with cannon and rockets.[2] When these Tiffies were on their way home, Flying Officer A.R.S. Proctor of 263 Squadron was heading in the direction of Hedel, on the north side of the River Maas. The Germans had located an observation post in the spire of a church there which was causing considerable embarrassment to the Army. Proctor led eight Typhoons in to the attack and they scored sixteen

---

[1] Squadron Leader Erasmus was killed during a low level attack on a bridge on 9th March. Hit by AA fire he went straight in after releasing his bombs.

[2] Curwen was awarded the DFC and given command of 197 Squadron shortly afterwards.

direct rocket hits on the spire. A 'thank you' signal was later received from the Army.

At 2 p.m. 168 Squadron from Eindhoven sent out six Typhoons under Flight Lieutenant Johnny Stubbs, into the St Vith area, attacking some stationary road transport without loss, despite accurate return fire from the ground. This was Stubbs' last operation for he was killed the following day, as a direct result of Bodenplatte.

> Joe was doing an air test on one of the Typhoons that had been hit and damaged on the 1st. It was a very cold, frosty morning and I walked outside to dispersal to see him off and when he was halfway down the runway, which had been very badly cratered but repaired by the Dutch working all through the night, disaster struck. He had just started to become airborne when the Typhoon started wobbling all over the place. I could see something was wrong but couldn't see quite what. In fact his ammo. bays hadn't been fastened down properly and they lifted and destroyed the lift of the wings and he couldn't get properly airborne. He went off the runway, over cratered, frozen, mud patches and hit another Typhoon which had got a full load of rockets on board. When I got to the scene in my jeep, he had skidded along the ground and was well on fire. The cockpit was melting around him and all I could do was to lay on the ground as the exploding rockets from the other aircraft zoomed over my head. He was a marvellous, rough, tough Australian – so nice – we were both great friends.
>
> *Squadron Leader L.H. Lambert, OC 168 Squadron*

*

There was another last operational flight for a Tempest pilot in 3 Squadron on the afternoon of the 1st. It will be remembered that Pilot Officer Ron Pottinger had found on his return from leave that he was tour-expired and had only been put down as spare pilot for the dawn show. However, with the turmoil of the morning raids, his tour-expired state was temporarily forgotten and his name went down for a mission. Ron made no comment, he would fly. It was not a matter even of saying, OK, just one more op. His name went.

own and so he flew.

The patrol itself was uneventful but unluckily it ran into some ground fire over the Dülmen area and Ron's Tempest was hit in the engine. He was forced to take to his parachute, coming down to and near Haltern.

Whilst returning from this patrol at about 8,000 feet we ran into some heavy and accurate AA fire and my plane was hit. With oil everywhere and an engine temperature at danger point I baled out and landed in a wood alongside a railway line, eventually ending up in the town jail at a place I later was told was Dülman.

Pilot Officer R.W. Pottinger, 3 Squadron

Stripping off his parachute harness Ron was quickly spotted by some young German children and eventually picked up by a German patrol. He was taken to a nearby railway signal box and locked in a room below it. He was then taken into Dülmen. A few days later he was moved to Essen where he was questioned several times about the attack on Volkel and asked how much damage had been inflicted. Whether they believed him or not when he said very little damage had been caused, can only be guessed at, but finally he was sent to Barth via Berlin, being housed in a cattle truck during some heavy air raids on the city. Then, instead of going to Barth because of the advances of the Allied Armies, he ended up in a POW camp at Lukenwald.

*

The Canadians of 401 Squadron at Heesch, having had an exciting and rewarding encounter with German aircraft in the morning tustle, had another scrap in the afternoon.

Shortly after 2.30, Flight Lieutenant J.C. 'Jake' Lee (ML141) was on a patrol into enemy territory, and as if to turn the tables on the Germans, he led his Section into the circuit of Rheine aerodrome. He was just east of Münster when Red Leader ordered Lee's Yellow Section down onto two trains seen coming out of the town of Rheine. As he dived he saw a Messerschmitt 262 jet directly below him so he left the trains to give chase. The jet led the

Canadians into a cover patrol of about a dozen Me109s and FW190s over Rheine airfield. Lee went after one of the 109s, saw strikes from his fire on the cockpit and wings seconds before the German rolled over and nosed-dived straight into the ground. He then attacked a second 109, saw strikes all along its port side, then it flipped away in a smoking spiral.

Lee's wingman, Flying Officer D.F. Church (MK888) hit a Focke Wulf who broke away right over the airfield. Losing sight of it, Church latched onto another 109 he saw flying away from the airfield, fired from 400, then 300 yards. Black smoke poured from its engine, then the pilot baled out.

Yellow Three, Pilot Officer D.M. Horseburgh (EN569) attacked another Me109 and his fire caused one of its wheels to flop down. It then rolled onto its 'back and crashed. Meanwhile, Flight Lieutenant John Mackay (MK791) added to his morning successes by chasing either the original Me262 or another one and with his Number Three, Flight Sergeant A.K. Woodill (MJ671) claimed it as damaged before, a) Mackay's cannons packed up, and, b) the jet pulled away to the left and lost them!

These successes brought 401's tally for the first day of 1945 to nine destroyed, one probably destroyed and three damaged.

*

No 412 RCAF Squadron also added to their day's total on their third operation of 1st January. At 3.15 p.m., Squadron Leader Dean Dover led a patrol to Osnabrück and eight miles west of Gütersloh, when, flying at 12,000 feet and on a south-easterly heading, he spotted two aircraft flying on the deck. Diving down he got behind one of them, seeing that they were Me109s. Dover opened fire from 400 yards, seeing a hit on its left wing. The 109 began to turn as Dover closed right in to fifty yards, to give it a two-second burst. Strikes appeared all over the 109's wings and fuselage, then it flicked over onto its back, hit the ground and exploded.

Dover's wingman, Flight Lieutenant J.A. Swan, attacked the other Messerschmitt, hitting it on both wing roots. The 109 flicked violently to the left and crashed into the ground. These two kills were not gained without loss. From out of nowhere a FW190 dived on Flight Lieutenant J.P. Doak's Spitfire (MJ877) and set it on fire. Doak was seen to crash in flames.

*

Most of the final sorties of 1st January were undertaken by the Eindhoven Typhoons. 137 Squadron sent out four under Flying Officer K.G. Brain (PD611) to Uden. Pilot Officer E.C. Jarvis led a section of 181 Squadron and blasted the railway line between Wessel and Dorsten with rockets. 247 Squadron sent out a section under Flight Lieutenant E.A. Magee (MN585) and not finding any worthwhile targets, jettisoned their rockets into a factory at Veen. Pilot Officer F.R.F. Skelly of 438 RCAF Squadron, who had been shot up that morning, led six Typhoons out on an armed recce to attack targets of opportunity. Flight Lieutenant John Carr led four 439 RCAF Squadron aircraft on another A/R but were bounced by American Thunderbolts, luckily the Americans recognised that they were Typhoons and left them alone.

The Americans too had not been idle since the dawn raids. The P47s of the 366th Fighter Group at Asch had been particularly active. At 10.43 a.m., seven aircraft of the 389th Squadron, led by First Lieutenant James I. Taylor, dive-bombed targets of opportunity around Lascheid. One Tiger tank and four lorries were damaged.

Half an hour later eight aircraft of the 390th Squadron led by First Lieutenant Cecil C. Brotton Jr were sent out to Scheid, bombed some trucks – unsuccessfully – and because of light flak which was both intense and accurate, no attempt at strafing them was made. Eight Thunderbolts of the 391st Squadron, led by First Lieutenant W.R. Johnson, had more success on the 11.33 a.m. mission against tanks in the battle zone; ten of some thirty seen were attacked and damaged. The 391st also flew the first operation after lunch, Major Sheldon S. Brinson leading eight aircraft in a free-for-all over Herscheid. Their 500 lb bombs and .50 machine-guns destroyed eight out of fifteen lorries, and outside of the town they blasted five more, also damaging four light tanks. Further on, a field gun and another light tank were hit and knocked out. Later they strafed German soldiers they found marching along a road.

First Lieutenant Clair T. Cullinan with eight P47s of the 390th

Squadron bombed and strafed targets of opportunity around Lanzerath, damaging four trucks and knocking out two tanks and a building. Several more unidentified vehicles were also claimed.

Two aircraft each from the 389th and 390th Squadrons escorted six A-26 Invaders against Mont Le Bau near Namur mid-afternoon. Despite a good run over the target the A-26s did not bomb or strafe and flak shot down one of them, the pilot taking to his parachute. The P47s, however, did strafe the target area.

While these operations were in progress, the American 8th Air Force were over Europe from its bases in England. Mustang fighters from the 4th Fighter Group provided withdrawal support for the B17 Fortresses attacking targets around Derben, Stendal and Gethin, Germany. Two fighter formations led by Major Fred Glover and Major Pierce McKennon made rendezvous with the bombers north-east of Heligoland at 11.25 a.m., having taken off at around 9.30. The 336th Fighter Squadron bounced a group of Me109s over Ulzen at 12.30 and shot down four. Shortly afterwards a Me262 jet was also destroyed. The Luftwaffe continued to bleed.

*

In the late afternoon, Deurne's Spitfires flew uneventful patrols over the front and so did Spitfires from Woensdrecht. Then to complete a busy day a V1 rocket fell on the eastern end of Deurne airfield and made a huge crater.

CHAPTER SIXTEEN

Review

I remember that night working on the Flights until early morning, in freezing temperatures, repairing bullet damage to fuselage and mainplanes. I suppose we were getting ready for the next day, and, more attacks which did not materialise – thank God, but I now know that the Luftwaffe had shot its bolt that day.

Leading Aircraftman D.N. Macdonald, 125 Wing

It had been an action-packed day. Although badly mauled, the units of the RAF and USAAF on the receiving end of Bodenplatte had carried out their first orders after the attack – Get Back Into The Air! Some squadrons had been badly hit, others not so badly, but most had sustained some hurt. The first task was to replace lost equipment.

Within a couple of hours (of the attack) a transport aircraft arrived for some of our pilots to return to the UK to collect replacement aeroplanes – I think from Tangmere. I stayed to re-organise the squadron. About the only aircraft of my squadron that wasn't damaged was the squadron's 'Hurricane Hack' which did a regular run to Tangmere to fill up its long range tanks with beer – generously given free by a Chichester Brewery!

Whilst the boys were in England, the bus in which they were travelling, was 'hit' by a passing branch of a tree, and to the amazement of the other passengers, our 'brave lads' were under their seats like lightning!

I see from my log-book that we did an armed recce of the Münster area on 5th January, so it didn't take us long to recover.

Squadron Leader G.J. Gray, OC 182 Squadron

Within 48 hours we were back to full strength again – not operational as the new aircraft had to be fitted with one or two things, but we were up to full strength, which was a magnificent effort all round.

Wing Commander M.J.A. Shaw, OC 69 Squadron

One group of Typhoon pilots arrived in England and quickly took the opportunity for a quick trip to London. They arrived in a variety of uniforms, unshaven and generally dishevelled. Arriving at the top of an underground escalator they ran into a London policeman. Seeing their appearance the policeman began to rebuke them, asking what their CO would think if he saw them in that state.

'Why not ask him?' said one pilot. 'He's just coming up the escalator now.' One look at the equally scruffy-looking squadron commander left the policeman at a complete loss!

A refitting party was soon organised and were flown to England by Dakota. A very quiet evening was spent in the Mess, most of us having some degree of twitch.

182 Squadron's Form 540

Other squadrons too quickly began to re-equip. For example, that afternoon eight pilots of 440 RCAF Squadron left for England to pick up replacement Typhoons, as did the CO and three pilots of 400 RCAF Squadron.

As the German prisoner remarked at Metz, 'That is what is beating us.' The Allies could quickly replace its losses – the Luftwaffe could not and could not afford the crippling blow it had been dealt. Yet far greater than the loss in aircraft was the loss in pilots. 151 fighter pilots died or were posted as missing with another sixty-three taken prisoner – 214, including eighteen Staffel, Gruppen or Geschwader commanders. It was a body blow. As we now know, it was a blow from which the Luftwaffe, already reeling from severe losses in recent weeks, was not to recover.

It had been suggested that although the massive attack had finally been planned to coincide with the Ardennes offensive, the weather of course, preventing this, that the Germans, unable to deviate from a plan of action once conceived, launched Bodenplatte when clearly any advantage gained would be outweighed by possible losses. This could be said to be hindsight, but the Luftwaffe commanders must have known that despite some experienced air leadership, the rank and file of the fighter arm at that stage of the war was far from experienced enough to carry out a successful ground attack mission on such a large scale as that attempted. Nevertheless, if it had come off, with a far smaller casualty rate, then the early weeks of 1945 might have been quite different, although the end of the war would not have come any later.

> The Luftwaffe was always in with a good chance coming in low. Our radar on the Continent was not up to the standard of that in England, and with all the trees, low hills, etc, a force could get to us undetected.
>
> *Wing Commander J.B. Wray, OC 122 Wing*

As has been made clear already, if the Luftwaffe had struck just thirty minutes earlier it would have caught far more Allied aircraft on the ground, causing considerable mayhem. Yet planning or luck could in no way compensate for the lack of experience. The bottom of the Luftwaffe's barrel was, by late 1944, being well and truly scraped. There was little chance of the 'know-how' of the remaining unit leaders being imparted to the younger pilots on how a ground attack should be made. In many ways Bodenplatte was always doomed to a tragic failure.

Squadron Leader R.D. Walton, 140 Squadron
> The attack, which lasted about twenty minutes, was very spectacular and (at Melsbroek) very successful from the German point of view. When the attack was completed the enemy indulged in the odd slow roll before, incredibly, forming up in a fairly loose formation and flying east. The obvious withdrawal would have been at low level and individually. Thus they presented a superb target for the gunners in the 'Diver' area – concentrated gun positions which were sited to combat the V1 attacks on Antwerpe.

Flight Lieutenant H.M.H. Tudor, 140 Squadron

What was interesting to me was that they left in a gaggle at about a thousand or two thousand feet, which suggested they were pretty inexperienced, for if they had gone back home on the deck they would have been far safer.

Extracts from an 83 Group Report

In all cases the (German) aircraft approached at a tree-top level. In practice, however, this operation which would have been a major one for any airforce, seems to have been too much for the relatively inexperienced pilots to carry out as planned ...

Further evidence of the inadequacy of pilots and their tasks, is seen over the targets; erratic flying and shooting, a head-on collision, aircraft attacking with their jet. tanks still on, poor evasive action, were all seen.

Air Vice Marshal H. Broadbent, AOC, 83 Group

This sort of attack was always possible and could cause great damage. The risk is enormous but if you are in the ascendency and can afford the losses – as the Germans could in 1940 – it could be a winner. But against the Allies in 1945 it was a dead loss. I had repaired or replaced my losses within twenty-four hours or so, whereas Peltz had shot his bolt. He never tried it again and from there on our Air Superiority was as complete as one could ever expect to have it.

It was a little unfortunate that Ultra had supplied the intelligence but the assessors of the information had related it to ground attack training for the Ardennes offensive, but that is a story in itself.

It brought home to me with great force and not for the first time, that in a battle of this nature there is nothing the AOC can do about it. He is absolutely dependent on the Organisation, training and morale of his chaps, particularly the junior commanders and controllers.

A low level attack under radar cover and virtually without warning, leaves no time for the senior commander to do anything but depend on the reaction at the sharp end and I think my chaps reacted splendidly.

Just remember that we had been on the offensive all the way from UK – the Beachhead and through France and Belgium, and into Holland when suddenly the Germans took the offensive and concentrated in time and space and without any warning. Their losses were crippling and this time we could count what was shot down by picking up the wreckage and not by claims in the air!

Wing Commander C.D. North-Lewis, Leader 124 Wing
Fortunately, the attack was not repeated and within a relatively short time the wing was back to strength. Thirteen days after the attack we moved to Helmond which was closer to our area of operations and which we occupied on our own.

Looking back it is clear that we had become over complacent and were taken completely by surprise by the German attack. However, it is amazing that the Germans had up until this time made no effort whatsoever to deny us the complete freedom that we had enjoyed throughout the whole campaign. There is no doubt that had they made an attempt to deny us mastery of the air by attacking our airfields they could have made life very difficult for us. That they did not do so showed that the German Air Command had little idea of the principles of air warfare.

*

At this distance in time it is not possible to discover the exact losses on both sides on this January day. It is understood by one senior RAF commander that some files and papers on the losses suffered by the RAF were sent to Air Marshal Coningham on his order, and were not seen again.

Many figures have been quoted but one can never now be certain how the figures were compiled or what factors were taken into account in reaching such totals.

In a report by 83 Group at the time, figures of 127 operational aircraft destroyed and 133 damaged was recorded in the British area. Casualties to personnel totalled forty killed with 145 wounded. Eleven of the dead were pilots, six being killed in the air. Eight RAF aircraft were shot down in air combat during the raids.

In another report on the attack dated 3rd January 1945, RAF losses were shown as 120 operational aircraft destroyed and seventy-three damaged, plus twenty-four non-operational aircraft destroyed with a further eleven damaged. These were broken down as follows:

2nd TAF Operational Aircraft   – 73   destroyed,   73 damaged.
2nd TAF Non-operational Aircraft — 12 destroyed, 11 damaged.
USAAF Operational Aircraft   — 22 destroyed, 30 damaged.
USAAF Non-operational Aircraft   — 3 destroyed.

Other Commands on TAF Airfields:
   Operational   —25   some only
   Non-operational   —9   damaged.

SHAEF recorded losses of 122 operational aircraft on the ground, plus eight in the air. SHAEF HQ also noted 168 RAF aircraft written off.

The Americans of the IXth TAC recorded the loss of two aircraft to enemy aircraft, one lost to flak, plus eleven damaged – nine to flak and two to enemy aircraft. However, it is known that actual losses in air combat were four P51 Mustangs and one P47 Thunderbolt. Aircraft of the 8th Air Force spread over various airfields in the battle area were also listed as follows:

Destroyed on the ground – 16 B17 Flying Fortesses.
                               14 B24 Liberators.
                               8 P51 Mustangs.
                               2 P47 Thunderbolts.

SHAEF HQ recorded twenty-four four-engined American bombers destroyed at Melsbroek.

*

Luftwaffe losses were also quoted variously. 83 Group recorded a possible 460 claims! This was broken down as 160 shot down in the air, 300 by anti-aircraft fire – including American claims. A subsequent 83 Group report recorded ninety aircraft shot down by

84 Group, and the USAAF, plus thirty by 83 Group and the RAF Regiment. At that time, Army AA claims were still incomplete.

In a report on the attack dated 3rd January 1945, total claims were recorded as ninety-seven in the air by Allied aircraft, and 129 shot down by AA fire: total 226. This was broken down as:

In Allied Occupied Territory:

2nd TAF	45
9th AF	5
AA Army	44
RAF Regt	43
9th AF, Army area	40
HMSs, Scheldt	2

Outside Allied Occupied Territory:

2nd TAF	12
9th AF	35

SHAEF recorded later ninety-seven enemy aircraft destroyed in the air plus 129 by ground fire (forty-three by the RAF Regiment). It also recorded 125 destroyed, eighty-four by fighters and forty-one by AA fire. The American 9th Air Force claimed thirty-seven destroyed, while the ground gunners at Metz claimed mine.

*

In his excellent book *Six Months to Oblivion*, Werner Gerbig lists Luftwaffe pilot losses as 151 killed or missing, sixty-three taken prisoner and another eighteen wounded. This means that at least 214 Luftwaffe aircraft were lost plus whatever aircraft got back and either crashed, or force landed at bases or locations in Germany, or had later to be written off due to battle damage. Werner Gerbig says that this could total around 300 aircraft in total, or approximately 30% of the fighter force committed to the operation, which he lists as being 875 single-engined fighters.

If, therefore, the Allied aircraft lost on 1st January can be said to be about 150, and the Germans 300, Bodenplatte cost the attackers a two to one loss ratio. This in itself was a disaster but the real disaster was the loss it could not afford – 214 operational fighter pilots!

... as the hurried reports flew around the control room, I began to work out the list of dead and missing. Maybe I was doing this because I didn't want to think. The high-ups wanted to know how large the replacement would have to be. This unsentimental consideration was a perfectly sound one, for it was not the names but simply the numbers of the dead which reached the brain at the top with its calculating mechanism. This apparatus couldn't take the names into account, betokening as they did an incommunicable sorrow, the final loss of personalities, human beings whom wives, children, parents and friends mourned.

When I glanced up from my labours I saw only cheerful faces, blood-smeared or stiff with sweat as they might be – the faces of those who had won through. No – the dead were not with us. They were lying among glowing ashes, mutilated and charred, somewhere else. Someone mentioned a strange name to me.

'Who's that?'

'He stayed behind over Brussels. Quite a young chap,' several of the fellows who had come here the day previously told me. So I knew the seventeen year old, too, had not returned.

Gunther Bloemertz, JG26

Addendum

Since the original edition was published in 1982 a number of additional facts have emerged about 1 January 1945. In particular the list of Typhoon losses has been researched in detail by Chris Thomas and is included in the appendices. It makes interesting reading.

In addition, the following information concerning the attackers is offered too.

I Gruppe of KG(J)51 operated 21 Me262 jets, leading the raid on Eindhoven, the largest number of jets known to have been employed in a single operation by this unit. Ground gunners claimed one shot down and a second damaged, but this has not been confirmed. The 262s made a strafing run, followed by the piston aircraft.

Eindhoven

Heinz Bär led his fighters in from out of the rising sun, east to west, while others came in from north to south. Leutnant Muller's IV/JG3 comprised 28 FE190A-8s from Gütersloh, and attacked in fours from around 60 feet.

Unteroffizier Gerhard Schmidt of 3/JG3 was shot down by a Spitfire (probably 414 RCAF Sqdn) and bellied in to become a prisoner. Oberfeldwebel Friedrich Hameister of 4/JG3 was acting Staffelfuhrer despite this being his first operation as a fighter pilot. He had been 10 years in the Luftwaffe as an air gunner and engineer in the Spanish Civil War and later over England with KG4 and KG76. Becoming a bomber pilot he flew Ju88s with II/KG54. He joined JG3 on Boxing Day 1944. After setting a DC3 on fire, his Me109 G-14 was attacked from the rear, also hit by AA fire and he too force landed and was taken prisoner, his life as a fighter pilot over.

Ursel

JG1 comprised fifty fighters, 20 FW190 A-8s of I and II Gruppen and 30 Me109 G-14s of III Gruppe. II Gruppe went for Ursel, led by Hans Gottfried Meinhoff, a former recce pilot who had only recently been made CO of the 4th Staffel. They claimed one C47, one Mosquito and one other aircraft, plus a hangar destroyed.

On the return trip, Meinhoff was hit by AA fire and crashed to his death near Breda. Leutnant Hans Berger of I/JG1 claimed one Spitfire shot down.

Grimbergen

Pips Priller led JG26 in from the north-west – into the rising sun – as ordered! In consequence, his men were badly dazzled and came in in ragged formation. He only saw four 4-engined aircraft and a couple of fighters, one being a P51 Mustang, some trucks and bowsers. Climbing away from the field, he saw a large white diagonal cross on the tracking on the northern strip, denoting the airfield was non-operational. So much, he thought, for the Intelligence people's knowledge!

Karl Borris led I/JG26, finding an almost empty airfield and having been ordered not to use his radio, could not warn his 40+ pilots not to waste ammunition on B.60. Added to this, he had no idea how the 17 pilots of III/JG54 – attached to his force just for this attack – would react to this confusing situation.

One of his pilots, Feldwebel Karl-Heinz Hartmann, of 4/JG26, was flying his first mission, for despite joining the Luftwaffe in 1938, he had been retained as a flying instructor. Finally sent to a front-line unit, he arrived at Christmas 1944. Hit by ground fire, he baled out, his parachute opening one second before he hit the ground. He was taken prisoner – his war over. Fahnrich Hans-Joachim Werner of 3/JG26, along with others, strafed a B17 and a B24 but he too was hit by ground fire, baled out and landed at the edge of the airfield.

Feldwebel Gunther Egli of 11/JG54, was hit by German ground fire over Rotterdam and had to jettison his long-range tank. Going into strafe Grimbergen, his D-9 was hit again by Allied fire, and he crash landed near B.60's boundary, and was taken prisoner by some Poles. He gave his unit as being JG104, the fighter school he'd attended at Furth, so as not to give his captors his real unit. Ever since then, historians have concluded that some instructors from this school had taken part in Bodenplatte (including me in the original edition!).

So intense had been the fire from ground defences, that no fewer than eight FW190 D-9s of I/JG26 returned with flak damage – those flown by Oberleutnant Alfred Heckman (CO 3rd Staffel), Leutnant Karl-Heinz Ossenkop, Feldwebels Wolfgang Franz, Walter Kerber and Haeger, Unteroffiziers Gunther Kaehler, Gerhard Reichow and Karl Zeidler. Some of these were hit by German flak in the Scheldt area, and at least one was forced to abort the mission.

The German attackers claimed the half a dozen aircraft they had found at Grimbergen, but it appears only one B17, a Dakota and a fighter were actually destroyed. JG26 also claimed 12 trucks, two bowsers and two hangars, with others damaged.

Evere

II/JG26 released their long-range tanks as they came in, led by Hackl's D-9s which hit 416 Squadron's Spitfires. Feldwebel Harold Wuelfken of 1/JG26, became separated from his unit and instead of going for Grimbergen, dived on Evere with II Gruppe. He claimed two Spitfires on the ground.

Hauptmann Walter Krupinski's Me109 had been hit by German ground fire while crossing the front line but he had carried on; however, a clip holding the left engine cover had been shot away, the panel folding upwards. The airflow forced the machine to port but he found he could still fly it. By the time he was approaching B.56, his feet were starting to go numb with the strain on the rudder bar to keep himself straight. However, this veteran, also unable to fire his guns, now decided to abort, ordering Unteroffizier Georg Genth of the 12th Staffel to accompany him.

Unteroffizier Johannes Haertlein, in a G-14 of 7/JG27, also became separated from the Melsbroek attack force, so attacked Evere. Hit by ground fire on the way home, he baled out near Thielen in Belgium, to become a prisoner.

Adolf Glunz, CO of 6/JG26, made nine strafing runs over Evere, some against an aircraft hangar, after destroying a Spitfire in the air. He had spotted a twin-engined machine just inside the hangar and attacked. As he approached, flying low, he noticed the hangar was full of aircraft. As he came round for a second run, he saw the machine burning, the flames spreading to the hangar itself. Upon his return he claimed the destruction of five aircraft by fire, with two more damaged. Hackl made seven strafing runs.

Six 'Sparrow' aircraft – casevac Harrows of 271 Squadron – were set on fire, and Prince Bernhardt of the Netherlands had his personal Beechcraft burnt out. A VIP DC3 was also burnt.

Melsbroek

II/JG27 had been ordered to attack north to south, but Hauptmann Hans-Heinz Dudeck led the four Staffeln in at tree-top height from south to east – with the sun at their backs. IV/JG54 also attacked. Unteroffizier Gerhard Ohlenschlager of 15/JG54 was shot down by ground fire and taken prisoner. Fahnrich Otto Thiesen, of 2/JG27, was also brought down by ground fire, was badly burnt and taken prisoner.

Major Franzisket's pilots reported finding several American aircraft in one corner of B.58, claiming at least a dozen 4-engined aircraft left burning. Air Marshal Coningham's personal Mosquito was kept on B.58 and this too was destroyed.

JG54, from Vorden, flying in company with JG27, made straight strafing passes along the airfield's north-south runway, systematically destroying aircraft, for the loss of four fighters, one pilot being captured. On the return journey several pilots became lost or disorientated and went down to ground fire from both sides.

On the way back, Hauptmann Willi Heilmann, leader of the 9th Staffel, ordered Leutnant Hans Dortenmann's 12th Staffel to 5,000 feet as high cover but they were attacked by Spitfires over Hasselt. Heilmann climbed to help. One 190 was lost but three Spitfires claimed shot down.

A Report on the attack by Supreme Headquarters Allied Expeditionary Force

Accurate figures on enemy losses are difficult to tie-up, but those given so far by HQ 2nd TAF are: 97 enemy aircraft destroyed in the air, 129 destroyed by AA (43 by the Royal Air force Regt).

Our losses, 122 operational aircraft destroyed on the ground, six aircraft and eight pilots lost in the air.

Since the beginning of the battle of France Allied fighter-bomber operations have steadily increased in intensity to the point of being a decisive factor in tactical warfare. It is not unnatural, therefore, that repeated attempts should be made to deprive us. For two months the German Air Force tactical single engined fighter force on the Western Front were steadily built up to a strength of approximately 1,000 aircraft. On the few occasions it has operated all-out, noticeably for a few days immediately before and after Christmas where as many as 800-1,000 sorties were flown daily. This air effort had no great influence on the battle, certainly no serious interference was caused to the Allied fighter-bomber offensive, and alternative methods of attack were sought and put into practice on New Year's Day. It coincided with the German land offensive in the South.

Shortly after dawn exceptionally heavy grounds strafing attacks were made against Allied airfields. The attack was well planned and security excellent. Radio silence was kept throughout and all formations approached low enough to avoid radar detection. To facilitate this, Ju88 night-fighters were employed in numbers to act as pilot aircraft to which single engined fighters could form and rely on navigation to the target. All available forces were pressed into service. Over the targets the organisation broke down to some extent, shooting and flying was reported as erratic in some respects and one head-on collision occurred. The shortage of experienced section leaders is no doubt responsible and the position according to pilots shot down during the operation, had been aggravated by recent losses of Staffel and Group Commanders.

In view of losses it is illogical to suppose that other such costly attempts will be made. The High Command, however, has now given abundant proof that logic is no longer necessarily the feature of German Air Force operational policy, then there is no guarantee that similar attempts will not be made.

The AOC in C, 2nd TAF has stated that the attack caused but will not cause any reduction in air effort. By now this must be painfully clear to the enemy. Last week he failed to check our fighter-bombers in the air over the battle area. This week he failed to neutralize their effort by attacking them on the ground. It remains to be seen how long it will be before he admits his incapacity to interfere with the Allied air offensive at all.

An extract from a Report by Air Marshal Arthur Coningham on 2nd TAF, 1944-45

197. The air battle of New Year's Day 1945. During the winter period I was forced by the weather and the difficulty of transporting the heavy tonnages of all weather material, to concentrate the 2nd TAF on a smaller number of airfields, from which they could operate continuously. This led to congestion on most of the airfields available.

The enemy appreciating his increasing danger from the air took advantage of this and carried out a well timed, simultaneous attack on a maximum number of British and a few American airfields, by means of his fighting force which, owing to careful husbanding of his resources throughout the winter, had reached considerable proportions. Although good weather prevailed and initial surprise was achieved by the enemy, this operation became a victory for the Allied Air Forces. Not only did the enemy lose over 200 first line aircraft and pilots against British and American losses of about 122 operational aircraft destroyed mostly on the ground, so that only six British pilots were killed, he also lost support of his most experienced fighter leaders, putting a most serious effect on all his future air operations. The most competent German authority, General Galland, has since described this day's operation by the German Air Force as 'The final dagger thrust into the back of the Luftwaffe.'

Royal Air Force Wings and Squadrons

83 GROUP

121 Wing – Volkel   W/Cdr W. Pitt-Brown DFC
174 Squadron   Typhoon 1B   S/Ldr D.T.N. Kelly
175 Squadron   Typhoon 1B   S/Ldr R.W. Campbell
184 Squadron   Typhoon 1B   S/Ldr W. Smith DFC

122 Wing – Volkel   W/Cdr J.B. Wray DFC
3 Squadron   Tempest V   S/Ldr K.F. Thiele DSO, DFC*
56 Squadron   Tempest V   S/Ldr D.V.C. Cotes-Preedy GM, DFC
80 Squadron   Tempest V   S/Ldr R.L. Spurdle DFC
274 Squadron   Tempest V   S/Ldr A.H. Baird DFC
486 Squadron   Tempest V   S/Ldr A.E. Umbers DFC

124 Wing – Eindhoven   W/Cdr C.D. North-Lewis, DFC
137 Squadron   Typhoon 1B   S/Ldr R.G.V. Barraclough
181 Squadron   Typhoon 1B   S/Ldr D.R. Crawford
182 Squadron   Typhoon 1B   S/Ldr G.J. Gray DFC*
247 Squadron   Typhoon 1B   S/Ldr J.H. Bryant DFC

125 Wing – Ophoven   W/Cdr F.D.S. Scott-Malden DSO, DFC
41 Squadron   Spitfire XIV   S/Ldr D.I. Benham DFC, AFC
130 Squadron   Spitfire XIV   S/Ldr P.V.K. Tripe
350 Squadron   Spitfire XIV   F/Lt J. Lavigne (Acting)
610 Squadron   Spitfire XIV   S/Ldr R.A. Newbury DFC*

126 Wing – Heesch   W/Cdr B.D. Russel DSO, DFC*
401 Squadron   Spitfire IX   F/Lt J. MacKay (Acting)
402 Squadron   Spitfire XIV   S/Ldr J.B. Lawrence
411 Squadron   Spitfire IX   S/Ldr J.N. Newell
412 Squadron   Spitfire IX   S/Ldr D.H. Dover DFC*
442 Squadron   Spitfire IX   S/Ldr M.E. Jowsey DFC

127 Wing – Evere   W/Cdr J.E. Johnson DSO*, DFC*
403 Squadron   Spitfire XVI   S/Ldr J.E. Collier
416 Squadron   Spitfire XVI   S/Ldr J.D. Mitchener DFC

143 Wing – Eindhoven   W/Cdr F.G. Grant DSO, DFC
  168 Squadron   Typhoon 1B   S/Ldr L.H. Lambert DFC
  438 Squadron   Typhoon 1B   F/Lt P. Wilson
  439 Squadron   Typhoon 1B   S/Ldr R.G. Crosby
  440 Squadron   Typhoon 1B   S/Ldr H.O. Gooding

39 Recce Wing – Eindhoven
  400 Squadron   Spitfire IX   S/Ldr M.G. Brown
  414 Squadron   Spitfire IX   S/Ldr G. Wonnacott DFC
  430 Squadron   Spitfire XIV   S/Ldr J. Watts

84 GROUP

123 Wing – Moving from Gilze Reijen to Chièvres

131 Wing – St Denis Westrem   W/Cdr T. Sawica DFC
  302 Squadron   Spitfire IX/XVI   S/Ldr M. Duryasz KW, DFC
  308 Squadron   Spitfire IX   S/Ldr K. Pniak, VM, KW, DFC
  317 Squadron   Spitfire IX   S/Ldr M. Chelmecki KW

132 Wing – Woensdrecht   W/Cdr R.A. Berg DFC
  66 Squadron   Spitfire XVI   S/Ldr R. Easby
  127 Squadron   Spitfire XVI   S/Ldr S.F. Sampson DFC
  322 Squadron   Spitfire IX   S/Ldr H.F. O'Neill DFC
  331 Squadron   Spitfire IX   Maj M. Gran DFC**
  332 Squadron   Spitfire IX   Maj J. Tvedte

135 Wing – Maldegem
  349 Squadron   Spitfire IX   S/Ldr A.A. van der Velde
  485 Squadron   Spitfire IX   S/Ldr J.G. Pattison

145 Wing – Deurne   W/Cdr W.V. Crawford-Compton DSO,
                                                      DFC
  341 Squadron   Spitfire IX   Capt J. Schloesing DFC
  74 Squadron   Spitfire IX   S/Ldr A.J. Reeves DFC
  345 Squadron   Spitfire IX   Cdt. Guizard
  329 Squadron   Spitfire IX   Cdt. J. Ozanne

146 Wing – Deurne   W/Cdr D.E. Gillam DSO*, DFC*, AFC
  193 Squadron   Typhoon 1B   S/Ldr C.D. Erasmus
  197 Squadron   Typhoon 1B   S/Ldr A.H. Smith DFC
  257 Squadron   Typhoon 1B   S/Ldr A.G. Todd DFC
  263 Squadron   Typhoon 1B   F/Lt R.E.G. Sheward (Acting)
  266 Squadron   Typhoon 1B   S/Ldr J.H. Deall

35 Recce Wing – Gilze Reijen
  2 Squadron   Mustang II/
                          Spitfire XIV   S/Ldr C.E. Maitland DFC

| 4 Squadron | Spitfire IX | S/Ldr C.D.H. St John DFC* |
| 268 Squadron | Mustang IA/II | S/Ldr C.T.P. Stephenson DFC |

2 GROUP

139 Wing – Melsbroek

98 Squadron	Mitchell II	W/Cdr Hamer AFC
180 Squadron	Mitchell II	W/Cdr K.J. Powell
320 Squadron	Mitchell II	W/Cdr A.W. Witholt

HEADQUARTERS

34 Recce Wing – Melsbroek

16 Squadron	Spitfire XI	S/Ldr A.N. Davis DFC
69 Squadron	Wellington XIII	W/Cdr M.J.A. Shaw DSO
140 Squadron	Mosquito XVI	W/Cdr F.O.S. Dobell

Royal Air Force Regiment Squadrons

Volkel

2809 Squadron –	1 Me109 destroyed	
2834 Squadron –	3 Ea destroyed, 2 damaged	
2874 Squadron –	1 Me109 destroyed, 2 damaged	108 rounds fired
Total: –	5 destroyed	Total 188

Eindhoven

2703 Squadron –		
2773 Squadron –	5 destroyed, several damaged	900 rounds fired
2817 Squadron –		170 rounds fired
2806 Squadron –		
Total: –	6 destroyed	Total 2750

Grimbergen

2719 Squadron –	3FW190s destroyed, 2 damaged	
2777 Squadron –		
		Total 230 SAA fired

Evere

2742 Squadron –		2600 rounds of Bren
2800 Squadron –	3 destroyed, 8 damaged	350 rounds of 40 mm

Heesch

2734 Squadron –	4 destroyed, 2 damaged	198 rounds fired
2819 Squadron –	3 destroyed	148 rounds fired
Total: –	7 destroyed	Total 344

Melsbroek

2701 Squadron –	4 destroyed, 4 damaged	197 rounds fired
2717 Squadron –	(One Flight only) Brens.	

2871 Squadron –
    Total: –   4 destroyed

Deurne
  2880 Squadron –   1 Me109 damaged   1270 rounds fired

Gilze Reijen
  2736 Squadron –   3 destroyed, 5 damaged   806 rounds fired
  2845 Squadron –

Woensdrecht
  2872 Squadron –   1 Me109 & 1 FW190 destroyed,   44 rounds fired
                   1 damaged

Ophoven
  2876 Squadron –   1 FW190 & 2 Me109s destroyed,   437 rounds fired
                   4 FW190s & 7 Me109s damaged
  2794 Squadron –   1 FW190 destroyed   250 rounds fired

Helmond
  2873 Squadron –   3 destroyed, several damaged   585 rounds fired
  2875 Squadron –   3 destroyed
  2881 Squadron –   1 shared destroyed, 4 damaged 2000 40 mm fired

      Total: –   6 destroyed

Luftwaffe Units involved in Operation Bodenplatte

Jagdgeschwader 1 (Oesau)
    I Gruppe   FW190A-8   Oberst Herbert Ihlefeld
    II Gruppe   FW190A-8   Hauptmann Georg Hackbarth
    III Gruppe   ME109G-14   Hauptmann Hermann Staiger

Jagdgeschwader 2 (Richthofen)
    I Gruppe   FW190A-8/A-9   Oberstleutnant Kurt Bühligen
    II Gruppe   Me109G-14/K-4   Hauptmann Franz Hrdlicka
    III Gruppe   FW190D-9   Hauptmann Schröder
        Hauptmann Siegfried Lemke

Jagdgeschwader 3 (Udet)
    I Gruppe   Me109G-10/G-14   Oberstleutnant Heinz Bär
    III Gruppe   Me109G-14/K-4   Oberleutnant Alfred Seidel (Acting)
    IV Gruppe   FW109A-8   Hauptmann Karl-Heinz Langer
        Leutnant Müller (Acting)

Jagdgeschwader 4
    I Gruppe   Me109G-14/K-4   Major Gerhard Michalski
    II Gruppe   FW190A-8   Major Wilhelm Steinmann
    IV Gruppe   Me109G-14/K-4   Major Schröder

Jagdgeschwader 6
    I Gruppe   FW190A-8   Oberstleutnant Johann Kogler
    II Gruppe   FW190A-8   Hauptmann Ewald Trost
    III Gruppe   Me109G-10/G-14   Hauptmann Johannes Naumann
        Major Helmut Kühle

Jagdgeschwader 11
    I Gruppe   FW190A-8   Oberstleutnant Günther Specht
    II Gruppe   Me109G-14/K-4
    III Gruppe   FW190A-8   Hauptmann Horst-Gunther von Fassong

Jagdgeschwader 26 (Schlageter)
    I Gruppe   FW190D-9   Oberstleutnant Josef Priller
    II Gruppe   FW190D-9   Major Karl Borris
    III Gruppe   Me109G-14/K-4   Major Anton Hackl
        Hauptmann Walter Krupinski

Jagdgeschwader 27		Major Ludwig Franzisket
I Gruppe	Me109G-14/K-4	Hauptmann Eberhard Schade
II Gruppe	Me109G-14	Hauptmann Gerhard Hoyer
III Gruppe	Me109K-4	Hauptmann Emil Clade
IV Gruppe	Me109G-10	Hauptmann Heinz Dudeck

Jagdgeschwader 53		Oberstleutnant Helmut Bennemann
II Gruppe	Me109G-14/K-4	Hauptmann Julius Meimberg
III Gruppe	Me109G-14	Hauptmann Luckenbach
IV Gruppe	Me109G-14	Hauptmann Müer

Jagdgeschwader 54		
III Gruppe	FW190D-9	
IV Gruppe	FW190A-8/A-9	

Jagdgeschwader 77		Major Erich Leie
I Gruppe	Me109G-14	
II Gruppe	Me109K-4	
III Gruppe	Me109K-4	Hauptmann Armin Köhler

Schlachtgeschwader 4		Oberst Alfred Druschel
III Gruppe	FW190A-8	

Kampfgeschwader 51		
(Fighters)	Me262A	

Allied Fighter Claims

83 Group		Destroyed	Probable	Damaged
3 Sqn	F/Sgt M.J.A. Rose	Me109		
	F/O D.J. Butcher			
	W/O D.R. Worley	Me109		
	F/O D.J. Butcher			FW190D
	W/O D.R. Worley			FW190D
56 Sqdn	F/O D.E. Ness			
	P/O H. Shaw	Me109		
137 Sqn	F/L G. Clubley			
	F/O D. Martyn	He111		
168 Sqn	F/L J.D. Stubbs			Me109
	F/L H.P. Gibbons	FW190		
80 Sqdn	F/O J.W. Garland	FW190		
	F/O J.W. Garland	FW190		
401 Sqdn	F/O G.D. Cameron	Me109		
	F/O G.D. Cameron	Me109		
	F/O G.D. Cameron	Me109		
	F/L J. MacKay	Me109		
	F/L J. MacKay	Me109		
	F/L J. MacKay	FW190		
	F/L J.C. Lee	Me109	Me109	
	F/O D.F. Church	Me109		**Me109**
	P/O D.M. Horseburgh	Me109		
	F/L W.E. Foster			FW190
	F/L J. MacKay			
	F/Sgt A.K. Woodill			Me262
403 Sqdn	P/O S. Butte	Me109		
	P/O S. Butte	Me109		
	P/O S. Butte	FW190		
	F/O M. Reeves	FW190		
	F/O M. Reeves	FW190		
	F/Sgt G.K. Lindsay	Me109	Me109	
411 Sqdn	F/L R.J. Audet	FW190		
	F/L R.J. Audet	FW190		
412 Sqdn	F/L J.P. Doak	FW190		
	F/O V. Smith	FW190		
	F/L B.E. Macpherson	FW190		

Sqdn	Pilot			
	F/L B.E. Macpherson	FW190		
	F/L W.J. Banks	Ju88		
	S/L D.H. Dover			
	F/O E.D. Kelly	FW190		
	S/L D.H. Dover	Me109		
	F/L J.A. Swan	Me109		
414 Sqdn	S/L G. Wonnacott	Me109		
	S/L G. Wonnacott	Me109		
	S/L G. Wonnacott	FW190		
	F/O L. Woloschuk	FW190		Me109
416 Sqdn	F/L D.W.A. Harling	Me109		
439 Sqdn	F/O R. Laurence	FW190		
	F/O R. Laurence	FW190		
	F/O A.H. Fraser	FW190		
	F/O A.H. Fraser	FW190		
442 Sqdn	F/L R.C. Smith	Me109		Me109
	F/L D.C. Gordon	Me109		
	F/L D.C. Gordon	Me109		
	F/L D.M. Pieri	FW190		FW190
	F/L D.M. Pieri	FW190		FW190
	F/L N.A. Keene	FW190		
	F/L J.B. Lumsden			FW190
	F/L J.B. Lumsden			
	F/O J.A. Cousineau			FW190
	F/L R.K. Trumley			
	F/O W.K. Dunne			
	F/L J.N.G. Dick			Me262
	P/O E.C. Baker			
486 Sqdn	S/L A.E. Umbers	FW190		
	S/L A.E. Umbers	Me109		
	F/O W.A.L. Trott	FW190		Me109
	P/O G.J. Hooper	FW190		Me109
	P/O C.J. Sheddan	FW190		
	P/O C.J. Steedman		FW190	
610 Sqdn	F/L A.F.O. Gaze	FW190		

84 Group

Sqdn	Pilot			
2 Sqdn	F/L E.J. Packwood	Me109		
268 Sqdn	F/L A.D. Mercer	Ju188		
	F/L J.B. Lyke			FW190
308 Sqdn	F/L I. Olszerwski	FW190		
	F/L B. Mach			
	W/O Bednarczyk	FW190		
	F/L B. Mach	FW190		FW190
	F/O T. Szlenkier	FW190		
	P/O Z. Soczynski	FW190		
	P/O A. Dromlewicz	FW190		
	F/Sgt J. Stanowski	FW190		
	F/Sgt J. Stanowski	FW190		

	W/O S. Bednarczyk	FW190		
	Sgt S. Breyner	FW190		
	Sgt S. Breyner	FW190		
	Sgt J. Glowczewski			FW190
	F/L W. Chojnacki	FW190		
317 Sqdn	S/L M. Chelmecki	FW190		
	Sgt K. Hubert	FW190	FW190	
	F/L C. Mroczyk	FW190		
	F/L R. Hrycak	FW190		
	W/O S. Piesik	FW190		FW190
	W/O Z. Wdowczynski	FW190		
	F/L Z. Zmigroddski		FW190	FW190
	F/Sgt S. Iwanowski			FW190

USAAF

422nd NFS	Lt Eugene D. Axtell	Ju188	
415th NFS	Lt Edward A. Schlueter	Me110	
391st FS	Lt John F. Bathurst	Me109	
	Lt Donald G. Holt	Me109	
390th FS	Lt Robert V. Brulle	Ea	
	Lt John W. Feeney	Ea	
	FO David C. Johnson Jr	Ea	
	Lt Melvyn R. Paisley	3/Ea	
	Capt Lowell B. Smith	Ea	
487th FS	Lt Walker G. Diamond	FW190	FW 190
	Maj William T. Halton	Ea'	
	Lt Dean M. Huston	FW190	
	Lt Nelson R. Jesup	Ea	
	Lt Raymond H. Littage	Ea	
	Lt Raymond H. Littage	Ea	
	Col John C. Meyer	FW190	
	Col John C. Meyer	FW190	
	Lt Sanford K. Moats	4/Ea	
	Lt Alden P. Rigby	FW190	
	Lt Alden P. Rigby	FW190	
	Lt Alden P. Rigby	Me109	
	Lt Alexander F. Sears	Me109	
	Capt Henry M. Stewart	Me109	
	Capt Henry M. Stewart	Me109	
	Capt Henry M. Stewart	Me109	
	Capt William T. Whisner	Me109	
	Capt William T. Whisner	Me109	
	Capt William T. Whisner	FW190	
	Capt William T. Whisner	FW190	

Some Statistics

From 83 Group HQ – Eindhoven

In the British area the results achieved by the attacks were by no means negligible, 127 operational aircraft being destroyed and 133 more damaged. In addition to that a considerable number of vehicles, petrol dumps and other stores destroyed or damaged. Personnel casualties were 40 killed and 145 injured. In the air the Allies lost six pilots and eight aircraft. The total number of pilots killed in the air and on the ground was eleven. These losses were, however, small in comparison with those the enemy suffered. 160 aircraft were claimed shot down in the air and nearly 300 were claimed by AA. These figures, including American claims, in every case the loss of an aircraft meant the loss of a pilot, except where the aircraft fell in enemy territory. So far over 60 pilots have been taken prisoner.[1]

The claims for the British area were, by fighters – 50, ground defences 89 = 139. While it is difficult to assess claiming in an operation like this as between fighters and AA, in formation collected by Air Technical Intelligence gives some guidance as to the accuracy. This analysis which limits itself to the British area and therefore excludes American claims, show 96 aircraft attributable to this operation have been found and examined. There are undoubtedly a good number more which crashed beyond our lines, in the Scheldt, and in swamps and woods that will never be found.[2] While it is not always possible to be certain of the cause of crashes, the examiners are of the opinion that the percentage attributed to the different arms are as follows:

[1] Both sides overclaimed at this early stage – the Germans claimed around 400 Allied aircraft destroyed on the ground, and nearly 80 shot down in air combat!

[2] By the mid-1970's some 40 pilots had still not been traced to a crash site.

Fighter action	36%
Ground defences	52%
Cause unknown	12%

As far as types of aircraft are concerned, the following proportions were examined:

Messerschmitt 109	38.5%
Focke Wulfe 190 As	38.5%
Focke Wulfe 190 DS	23%

*

Later in the day the German Air Force reacted strongly to Bomber Command's attack on the Dortmund-Ems Canal providing further air targets for the Group. Ground targets were suitably attacked throughout the day. The enemy had failed entirely to ground our Tactical Air Force.

Sorties flown:
  Armed Recces: 54 – 394 sorties
  Support: 2 – 20 sorties
  Recce ops: 13 – 22 sorties
  Fighter ops: 31 – 123 sorties
Claims:
  Motor transport: 9 destroyed, 10 damaged
  Trains: 21 destroyed, 29 damaged.
  Rail trucks: 55 destroyed, 180 damaged
  Enemy aircraft: 47 destroyed, 2 probables, 17 damaged.

*

9th TAC
Mounted 30 missions during the day totalling 297 sorties plus nearly 50 reconnaissance missions. The following offensive claims were made:

Motor transport:	156 destroyed
Armoured vehicles:	26 destroyed.
Trucks:	36 destroyed.
Gun positions:	1 destroyed.
Rail Cuts:	3
Enemy aircraft:	37 destroyed, 3 probables, 7 damaged.

RAF Pilot Casualties – 1st January, 1945 – 2nd TAF

168 Squadron			
F/L H.P. Gibbons	Killed	Typhoon	Shot down by Me109s over Eindhoven aerodrome 9.25 a.m.
438 Squadron			
F/L P. Wilson	Killed	Typhoon	Strafed on Eindhoven airfield, 9.20 a.m.
438 Squadron			
F/O R.W. Keller	Killed	Typhoon	Strafed on Eindhoven airfield, 9.20 a.m.
440 Squadron			
P/O E.T. Flanagan	Wounded	Typhoon	Strafed on Eindhoven airfield, 9.20 a.m.
137 Squadron			
F/Sgt L.A.V. Burrows	Killed	Typhoon	Strafed on Eindhoven airfield, 9.30 a.m.
439 Squadron			
F/O S. Angelini	Killed	Typhoon	Shot down in combat with enemy fighters, 9.30 approx.
308 Squadron		Spitfire	Shot down in combat over St Denis Westrem, 9.30 a.m.
F/L W. Chojnacki	Killed		
317 Squadron			
F/L T. Powierza	Killed	Spitfire	Shot down in combat over St Denis Westrem, 9.35 a.m.
416 Squadron			
F/L D.W.A. Harling	Killed	Spitfire	Shot down in combat over Brussels, 9.35 a.m. approx.
442 Squadron			
F/L D.C. Gordon	Wounded	Spitfire	Crash landed south of Heesch after combat, 9.40 approx.
442 Squadron			
F/O D.A. Brigden	Killed	Spitfire	Shot down over Venlo in dog-fight, 9.45 approx.

3 Squadron

P/O R. Pottinger	POW	Tempest	Hit by flak over Dulman, crash landed approx. 2 p.m.

183 Squadron

F/O D. Webber	Killed	Typhoon	Shot down by Mustang, 3 p.m. approx. over Gilze Reijen

2 Squadron

F/L P.J. Garland	Killed	Spitfire	Landing accident at Gilze Reijen, 3 p.m.

412 Squadron

F/L J.P. Doak	Killed	Spitfire	Shot down in combat near Osnabruck, 4 p.m.

Luftwaffe losses – 1st January, 1945

Unit	Killed/ missing	PoW	Commanders lost	Wounded
I/JG1	7	3	2	
II/JG1	10	1		1
III/JG1	1	2		
Stab/JG2		1		
I/JG2	10	5		1
II/JG2	3	1	1	1
III/JG2	10	3		2
I/JG3	3	5		
III/JG3	3		2	2
IV/JG3	4	1		
I/JG4	3			
II/JG4	8	3		1
IV/JG4	5	3		
Stab/JG6		1	1	
I/JG6	5	1	1	
II/JG6	6	1	1	
III/JG6	6	3	3	
Stab/JG11	2		1	
I/JG11	3			
II/JG11	6	2		
III/JG11	10	2	1	
I/JG26	5	3	1	2
II/JG26	4	4		1
III/JG26	3	1		1

I/JG27	6	1	1	
II/JG27	1	1		
III/JG27	2			1
IV/JG27	2	1	1	
II/JG53	5	2		1
III/JG53				2
IV/JG53	5	2		1
III/JG54	5	4	1	1
IV/JG54	2	1		
I/JG77	2	1		
II/JG77	1	1		
III/JG77	3	3	1	
	151	63	18	18

The Losses on the Airfields

Compiled by Chris Thomas, author of *The Typhoon File* and co-author of *The Typhoon and Tempest Story* with C.F. Shores

A full report detailing losses on each airfield, or by unit and type has not been located, if indeed such a report ever existed. The following list gives the losses as stated in unit ORBs (in quotation marks) together with the identities of the actual losses as revealed by research. Unfortunately, owing to the nature of surviving records (see Appendix K), neither of these totals are likely to be complete. In particular it is not possible to identify the aircraft which were slightly damaged and were repaired by the parent unit's repair section, nor many of those which were at Repair and Salvage Units under or awaiting repair and which were written off as a result of the attack.

It is impossible to reconcile the figures below with the loss totals given by 2nd TAF reports as it is not known if the 'destroyed' figures are for those aircraft declared 'Cat E' immediately, or whether they include those at first thought repairable but were 'reCat E' a few days later, or indeed those which were repairable but were 'reCat E' owing to approaching obsolescence (eg: 430 Squadron's Mustangs) or the end of the war. These, where identified, are shown below at 'Cat B/E'. For an explanation of damage categories, please see Appendix K.

Diest
409 R&SU
  "19 Cat E, 18 Cat B, 6 Cat Ae"

410 R&SU

  "10 Cat E, 11 Cat B, 4 CatAc"

Deurne
146 Wing – "8 aircraft received superficial damage"
  193 Squadron – Typhoon IB
  "a few kites destroyed or damaged"

197 Squadron – Typhoon IB
"3 destroyed or damaged"

257 Squadron – Typhoon IB
"2 damaged" – MN698/P – Cat B/E

263 Squadron – Typhoon IB – no details of losses
"2 damaged" – MN698/P – Cat B/E

266 Squadron – Typhoon IB
"1 lost" – MN364 – Cat B

Eindhoven

124 Wing – "4 destroyed and 10 damaged"
137 Squadron – Typhoon IB
"2 damaged – 1 Cat B, 1 Cat Ac, 11 serviceable"
JR261/Z – Cat B/E; Hurricane (hack) V7752 – Cat E

181 Squadron – Typhoon IB
"1 destroyed, 8 serviceable" – EK172 Cat E

182 Squadron – Typhoon IB
"all aircraft more or less damaged"
MN768/T – Cat E
JP397, JP654, JR328, MN823 – Cat B/E
JP736, MN340, MN422, MN693, PD450, RB193, RB254, RB256 – minor damage, all repaired

247 Squadron – Typhoon IB
"5 aircraft serviceable" and "2 badly damaged"
(ie: total damaged approximately 6)
EK371/P, JP437/W, JR129/R, PD495/B, RB225 (minor damage, all repaired)

143 Wing – no detail on losses
168 Squadron – Typhoon IB
"1 aircraft shot down, 1 damaged on the ground"
MN486/D – Cat E; RB209 – Cat A

438 Squadron – Typhoon IB
"3 aircraft burned, 1 crashed and broke up, 1 Cat Ac, slightly damaged but repaired at section"
MN607/G, MN816/Y, MP171/F, PD503/R, PD556/Q – Cat E

439 Squadron – Typhoon IB
"1 lost on recce, 1 destroyed and 1 slightly damaged on ground"
MN589 (shot down), MN869/A – Cat E
PD554, RB257/S – Cat B/E; MN144, PD608/J – Cat Ac

440 Squadron – Typhoon IB
"8 destroyed, 4 damaged"
MN940/M, MN984, MP139/W, MN569, PD621, RB192* – Cat E
JR530/Y – Cat B/E; PD595/X – Cat Ac/E; PD589/R – Cat B; MN380 Cat Ac
(* newly delivered, believed with 440 Sqdn)

39 Wing – "3 Mustangs destroyed, 1 damaged; 2 Spitfire XIV destroyed, 7 damaged; 5 Spitfire XI destroyed, 7 damaged; 5 Spitfire IX damaged"
400 Squadron – Spitfire XI – "5 destroyed, 4 Cat B, 1 Cat Ac"
PA894, PL786, PL883, PL911, PL989 – Cat E
MB942, PA887, PL950, PM128 – Cat B/E
PL828 – Cat Ac

414 Squadron – Spitfire FR IX – "4 Cat B and 1 Cat Ac"
MK290/U, MK374 – Cat B/E
MJ633/F, MJ910 – Cat B

430 Squadron – Spitfire FR XIV and Mustang I – "4 Cat E and 3 Cat B"
RM848/S, RM883 – Cat E
RM856/R, RM857/E – Cat B
AG544/H, AL966/E, AP194/L – Cat E; AG628 – Cat B/E

83 Group Communications Squadron
Anson XI – NK990, NK998, NL129 – Cat E
Spitfire IX – MK240, ML133 – Cat E
Auster – possibly three destroyed, not identified

403 R&SU
No detail on losses, but one Typhoon, RB205, Cat E

Air Fighting Development Unit (visiting)
Anson, MG184, Cat E

Unofficial sources also report a B17 (USAAF), 3 Bostons and a Hudson under repair by working parties, also destroyed.

Evere
"34 Cat E, 10 Cat B, 7 Cat Ac, 12 Cat A"

127 Wing
"1 shot down, 11 Cat E and 12 Cat B on the ground"

403 Squadron – Spitfire XVI – no detail on losses
SM206 – Cat E; SM258 – Cat B/BE;

416 Squadron – Spitfire XVI – "1 shot down, 3 shot-up taxying"
ML153 (Mk IX), SM304 (shot down), SM130, SM369, SM403 – Cat E
SM274, SM349 – Cat B/E

443 Squadron – Spitfire IX (most aircraft away at APC)
MK730 – Cat E

SM368 – Cat E – Squadron allocation not known

2nd TAF Communications Squadron
Dakota: NK736 – Cat E
Anson XI: NL193, NL194, NL195, NL196, NL201 – Cat E
Auster: RT639 – Cat E

147 Squadron – visiting
Dakota: KG796, KG800, KJ803 – Cat E

271 Squadron – visiting
   Dakota: KG488 – Cat E

Prince Bernhard
   Beech 18 – Cat E

Gilze-Reijen
   164 Squadron – Typhoon IB – "1 written off"
   RB969/P – Cat B

Maldegem
135 Wing
   349 Squadron – Spitfire IX – "1 destroyed"
   PT830 – Cat E

   485 Squadron – Spitfire IX – "12 destroyed, inc WCF's, 2 damaged beyond repair"
   MK722, MK921, ML361, NH321, NH421, NH432, NH530, PL251, PT885, PT857, PT890, PV156 – Cat E
   ML368, PT525 (possibly) Cat B

Melsbroek
34 Wing
   16 Squadron – Spitfire XI – "3 destroyed, 3 damaged, 2 on loan from 106 Group destroyed"
   PL765, PL905, PL976 – Cat E
   PL978, PL912 – Cat Ac

   69 Squadron – Wellington XIII – "11 destroyed, 2 severely damaged"
   HZ723, HX769, HZ794, HZ862, HZ885, JA584, JA629, ME950, MF128, MF129, NC534, NC540 – Cat E; and possibly HZ886 (damaged on 27 Dec 1944 and written off 11 Jan 1945)

   140 Squadron – Mosquito XVI – no detail on losses
   MM284, MM349, NS567 – Cat E; NS746 – Cat B/E

139 Wing
   98 Squadron – Mitchell – "6 badly damaged"
   FV903, FV945, FW199, FW202, FW206 – Cat E

   320 Squadron – Mitchell – "2 damaged"

271 Squadron – Harrow – "7 destroyed"
   K6943, K6973, K6986, K6993, K6994, K6998, K7024 – Cat E

416 ARF
   Mitchell: FV961, HD382 – Cat E
   Boston: BZ444 – Cat E
   Stirling: LJ954 – Cat E

2nd TAF Communications Squadron
   Anson: NK986, NK988 – Cat E
   Auster: MS937, MT114, NJ622, NJ869 – Cat E
   Proctor: P6232 – Cat E

85 Group Communications Squadron
  Anson: NK725 – Cat E
  Oxford: R6147 – Cat E

Air Marshal Coningham
  Mosquito: Cat E

Nivelles
48 Squadron
  Dakota: KG331 – Cat E

Ophoven
125 Wing
  41 Squadron – Spitfire XIV – "no damage"

  130 Squadron – Spitfire XIV – "3 damaged"

  350 Squadron – Spitfire XIV – "7 damaged"
  RM622 – Cat E; NH710, RM728 – Cat B

  610 Squadron – Spitfire XIV – "no damage"

St Denis Westrem
131 Wing – "17 Cat E, 4 Cat B, 6 Cat Ac" (according to 411 R&SU ORB)
  302 Squadron – Spitfire IX – "9 destroyed"
  MA645, MH938, ML136, NH410, NH463, PL267 – Cat E
  NH712 – Cat B/E; MJ801 – Cat Ac

  308 Squadron – Spitfire IX – "several force-landed due to lack of fuel"
  MJ281, MJ467 – Cat E (combat)
  MJ998 – Cat Ac/E; MK346 – Cat B/E (combat)
  MJ888 – Cat B (combat); MK756 – Cat Ac (combat); MK247, MK256,
  MK940 (not conf), MK984, ML112 – Cat E

  317 Squadron – Spitfire IX – "6 destroyed on the ground"
  MK190 – Cat E (combat)
  MK264, MK610, MJ797, PL284 – Cat E

85 Group Communications Squadron
  Anson: NK544, NK608, NK875, NL190 – Cat E
  Mosquito XIII: HK365 – Cat E
  Spitfire Vb: BM – Cat Ac/E
  Auster: RT481 – Cat E

295 Squadron
  Stirling: LJ954 (under repair) – Cat E

Ursel
417 R&SU
  Mosquito XIII: HK965 – Cat E
  Lancaster: LL777/S (ex-61 Sqdn), ME850 (ex-15 Sqdn) – Cat E

Location not known
ATA
    Anson: AW928, NK809, NK905, NK970 – Cat E

575 Squadron
    Anson: NK493 – Cat E

Grimbergen
    4 USAAF B17 Fortresses destroyed
    1 USAAF P51 Mustang destroyed
    1 twin-engined aeroplane damaged

Heesch
126 Wing
    442 Squadron – Spitfire IX
    MK420 – Cat E (combat)

Asch
    352nd FG USAAF – 4 P51 Mustangs shot down in combat
                   – 1 P51 Mustang damaged on the ground

    366th FG USAAF – 1 P47 Thunderbolt shot down in combat

Metz
    365th FG USAAF – (22 P47 Thunderbolts destroyed on the ground and
    8/11 damaged)

    386th FS USAAF – 12 P47 Thunderbolts destroyed on the ground
                   – 7 P47 Thunderbolts damaged

    387th FS USAAF – 9 P47 Thunderbolts destroyed on the ground
                   – 1 P47 Thunderbolt damaged

    388th FS USAAF – 1 P47 Thunderbolt destroyed on the ground
                   – 3 P47 Thunderbolts damaged

Taking the worst of the conflicting figures from the various sources, the total
RAF losses could be as high as 221 destroyed and 143 damaged. However,
as, for example, some of the communications aircraft could be among the
gross totals for Evere, the total destroyed may be less than this figure.

Known Personnel Ground Casualties

Eindhoven

124 Wing:	2 killed, 6 seriously wounded, 9 slightly wounded (inc Cpl Bradley, Wing HQ)		
137 Squadron:	F/Sgt R. Bazley	6137 SE	Killed
	AC1 R.A. Norris	„	Died of Wounds
	LAC Hockaday	„	Wounded
	LAC Dughan	„	Wounded
	Cpl Wattercamps	„	Wounded

| 182 Squadron: | Cpl C.A. Rabbitt | 6182 SE | Died of Wounds |
| | LAC Hodges | „ | Wounded |

143 Wing:

168 Squadron:	Sgt J.R. Gosney	6168 SE	Killed
	LAC C. Nicholson	„	Killed
	LAC A.E. Davids	„	Killed
	LAC A. Eardley	„	Killed

438 Squadron:	P/O B.J. Macklon	438 Sqdn	Wounded
	P/O A.B. Harle	„	Injured
	F/O R.W. Keller	„	Killed
	F/L P. Wilson	„	Killed – taking off

439 Squadron:	Sgt R.M. Capelman		Injured
	Col M. Singerman		Injured
	LAC J.T. Bews		Injured
	LAC Crinklaw	6439 SW	Injured
	F/L H.P.V. Massey		Wounded

| 440 Squadron: | P/O E.T. Flanagan | | Wounded |
| | 3 airmen of | 6440 SE | Injured |

39 Wing: 2 other ranks killed
10 other ranks injured
4 officer pilots injured
1 ALO injured

| 400 Squadron: | Cpl Trevelyan | | Wounded |

414 Squadron:	LAC J.L.E Williams	6414 SE	Killed
	LAC G.B. Bell	„	Killed
	LAC H.J. Frayne	„	Wounded
	LAC A.T. Firth	„	Wounded
	LAC G.C. Butler	„	Wounded
	F/L D.L. Fuller		Wounded
	F/O F.R. Lovelace		Injured
	LAC J.H. Harding		Wounded

430 Squadron:	F/L R.F. Gill		Wounded
	F/O W.P. Golden		Wounded
	Sgt J.L.A. Smith	6430 SE	Wounded
	Cpl J.L.G. Cook	„	Wounded
	AC1 T.M. Robinson	„	Wounded

St Denis Westrem

131 Wing:	Cpl J. Koczwara		Killed
	Cpl J. Sikora		Killed
	14 officer and other ranks injured		

Grimbergen   1 airman killed and two wounded

Evere
| 127 Wing: | LAC R.C. Medforth | Killed |
| | 9 airmen wounded, one mortally | |

Melsbroek
| 69 Squadron: | 5 airmen of 6069 SE killed and 25 airmen wounded |
| 271 Squadron: | LAC J. Hymans | Killed |

Ophoven   2 airmen wounded
| 350 Squadron: | 1 airman of 6130 SE wounded |

Metz
386th FS:	S/Sgt R.A. Gabarine	Wounded
	S/Sgt K. Garner	Wounded
387th FS:	Pfc F. Williams	Wounded
	Lt R.S. Maney	Wounded
388th FS:	Cpl L. Welden	Wounded
	2/Lt C. Riggs	Injured

The Typhoons on Eindhoven

Compiled by Chris Thomas

Despite the passage of fifty years since 'Bodenplatte', there is still controversy regarding the actual extent of Allied losses. Some authors have hinted at a conspiracy to hide the true, unacceptable, total of aircraft destroyed. This theory has been aided by the conflicting totals quoted in various official records and the apparent lack of a surviving detailed report.

So what records are available to today's researcher in his quest for the truth? When it comes down to individual aircraft there are two prime sources (i) the Forms 78, more usually known as the 'movement cards' and (ii) the Squadron ORBs (Operational Records Books). Unfortunately both these sources are far from perfect.

The Forms 78 were manually updated records of each aircraft's movement from unit to unit with annotations recording significant damage and allocation to repair units. These relied on information from the aircraft's users and this was not always forthcoming. The sheer volume of information and its nature led to many errors. For example, there were Typhoons with JP and JR, MM and MN serials which shared the same numbers, so movements and sometimes entries were made on the wrong record card.

The Squadron ORBs consist of two Forms, the 540 and the 541. The former was a daily narrative of significant events on the unit, whereas the latter was a record of operational sorties, normally detailing aircraft and crews involved, times, targets and results. The quantity and accuracy of the detail varies very much from unit to unit and period to period. As far as aircraft identity is concerned, the majority recorded the serial numbers of each aircraft involved in an operation but some recorded neither! However, by combining Form 78 and Form 541 information, a more accurate picture of aircraft on strength at any given time emerges.

There are further sources, unfortunately fragmented, which provide useful confirmation or added detail. From May 1944 to January 1945, 2nd TAF squadrons were required to submit a variety of monthly statistical reports on such items as hours flown, ammunition expended, and aircraft status. The latter was declared on Form OR101 which gave the serial number and arrival/departure dates of each aircraft, together with a very accurate but unfortunately they have been traced for only a small proportion of the units involved. Pilots' log books, when they can be traced, are helpful but vary in much the same way as the ORBs. Accident records also provide a useful spot date for the presence of an aircraft on a specified unit.

To test the accuracy of the ORBs which were the main source of the totals for losses given in Appendix J, the fate of the Typhoons at Eindhoven on 1 January 1945 has been examined in as much detail as records currently located allow. One recent chronicler of the Typhoon has claimed to have calculated these losses as 141 Typhoons 'written off'! Written off in RAF parlance meant 'of no further use as an airframe' and covered many circumstances, from totally burnt out or damaged beyond economical repair, through to scrapping due to obsolescence. It should be noted that many aircraft declared 'written off' by an operational unit were in fact repaired and put back into service. Damage to aircraft was categorised according to the repair unit which would be required to carry out the repair. In 2nd TAF, and specifically in the case of Typhoons at Eindhoven, damage can be defined as follows:

Category A: Damage repairable by a local unit, ie: the Repair and Inspection section of the Squadron Servicing Echelon. This damage was not usually recorded on Form 78s.

Category Ac: Damage beyond the capacity of the parent unit. For Typhoons at Eindhoven this would mean a trip round the peri-track to 403 Repair and Salvage Unit. If repair could not be effected within 28 days, the aircraft was transferred to 151 Repair Unit at Courtrai.

Category B: Damage requiring repair by a Maintenance Unit or civilian contractor. For Typhoons at this stage of the war this meant transportation back to the UK and repair by Taylorcraft at Rearsby or Marshall at Cambridge.

Category E: Totally destroyed, scrap value only.

On 1 January 1945, eight Typhoon squadrons were resident at Eindhoven. The established aircraft strength for each squadron was 18 aircraft; a report dated 5 November 1944 gives their actual strength as follows:

124 Wing:	137 Squadron – 19	181 Squadron – 19	
	182 Squadron – 17	247 Squadron – 16	
143 Wing:	168 Squadron – 19	438 Squadron – 20	
	439 Squadron – 19	440 Squadron – 20	Total: 149

However, after a period of bad weather, intensive operations in support of Allied forces in the Ardennes commenced on 24 December. In the following week, Typhoon losses were high, the following being totals of losses from the squadrons as Cat Ac, B or E:

124 Wing:	137 Squadron – 7	181 Squadron – 5	
	182 Squadron – 7	247 Squadron – 6	
143 Wing:	168 Squadron – 6	438 Squadron – 3	
	439 Squadron – 9	440 Squadron – 3	Total: 46

Replacement Typhoons had to be flown out from 83 Group Support Unit at

Westhampnett and demand exceeded supply during this period. Delivery quantities and dates are not known but 438 and 440 Squadrons, whose losses had been the lightest, both reported their strengths as only 16 Typhoons on 31 December. Research indicates that the squadron strengths and losses (on the ground unless noted otherwise) on 1 January were as follows:

124 Wing: 137 Squadron

Survived: DN492/W, EK128, EK270, JR247/J, JR305/Y, MN198/L, MN455/D, MN575/H, MN922/P, MN980/C, PD611/R, RB252/Q

Cat B: JR261/Z (recategorised as Cat E 23 Oct 1945)

Thirteen aircraft on strength. In addition to one Cat B, the ORB reports one Cat Ac which has not been identified; it was probably one of the above as 247 Squadron's ORB records 137 Squadron as having 11 serviceable after the attack. Therefore, 13 aircraft on strength, one damaged and one effectively destroyed.

181 Squadron

Survived: R8725, JP672/H, JP922, JR265/A, JR337, JR438, MN199, MN688, MN757, MN875/B, MN980/C, RB208*

Cat E: EK172/H
NP129 – fate obscure; possibly damaged beyond repair
* Wing Commander Flying's aircraft – coded KNL

Therefore, 15 or 16 aircraft on strength, of which one was destroyed, one possibly damaged beyond repair, and (as 181 was reported to have 8 serviceable) six apparently slightly damaged and repaired locally.

182 Squadron

Survived: JP736, MN340, MN422, MN693, PD450, RB193, RB254, RB256

Cat E: MN768/T
Cat B: JP397/S, JP654/P, JR328, MN823/W (all re-Cat E)

Thirteen aircraft on strength; one destroyed, four damaged beyond repair and (as all 182 Squadron's aircraft were reported damaged to some degree, eight slightly damaged).

247 Squadron

Survived: RB688/X, EK371/P, JP437/W, JP538/H, JR129/R, MN471/G, MN585/Z, MN606/T, MP201/O, PD495/B, RB225

Eleven aircraft on charge; those marked * were flown later in the day and were presumably the five reported serviceable plus one which had been rapidly repaired. All the remainder were either damaged but apparently repaired locally, or just requiring normal service.

143 Wing: 168 Squadron

Survived: EK140/K, EK382, JP515, JR308, JR308, JR444, MN265, MN267/L, MN366, MN999, PD163

Cat E: MN486/D

Eleven aircraft on strength. One shot down and one (unidentified) damaged and repaired locally.

438 Squadron

Survived: MM989, MN716/A, MN758, MP128/X, MP181, PD446/E,
PD476/E, PD592, RB207/T
Cat E: MN607/G, MN816/Y, MP177/F, PD503/R, PD556/Q
Cat Ac: ? /K

Sixteen aircraft on charge; five destroyed, one damaged (fate unknown), one (PD569/D) with minor damage repaired.

439 Squadron

Survived: MN691, MP134, MP151/R, RB223/F, RB281/X
Cat E: MN589, MN869/A
Cat B: PD554/T (re-Cat E)
Cat Ac: PD461, PD608/J, MN144 (in combat)

Eleven aircraft on strength; one shot down, one destroyed and one damaged beyond repair, three damaged and repaired.

440 Squadron

Survived: MN626/B, MN777/D, MP138/V, PD497/K, RB202, RB203
Cat E: MN569, MN940/M, MN984, MP139/W, PD621, RB192
Cat B: PD589/R, JR530/V (re-Cat E)
Cat Ac: MN380, PD595/X (re-Cat E)

Sixteen aircraft on strength; six destroyed, two damaged beyond repair, two seriously damaged but repaired, and two (unidentified) with minor damage, repaired locally.

Also on the airfield were a number of Typhoons under repair by 403 R&SU. These are believed to have included: JP920, JR513, MM976, MN134, MN306, MN424, MN581, MN822, MP120, MP172, PD536, PD599, RB198, RB204, RB205, and RB217. Of these, only RB205/FGG, Wing Commander F.G. Grant's aircraft, was destroyed during the attack.

Taking the maximum figures in each case we have a total of 107 operational Typhoons on the airfield, plus approximately 16 more under repair. Of this total, 17 were destroyed outright and a further 9 badly damaged aircraft were never repaired, 10 were badly damaged but repaired off unit, and 24 slightly damaged and repaired locally, ie: a grand total of 60 Typhoons destroyed or damaged. Furthermore, it can be seen that the totals of Typhoons destroyed or badly damaged are of similar order to the figure given in the ORBs.

Luftwaffe Casualties – 1 January 1945

Name	Staffel	Machine	A/C Nr.	A/C Code	Brought down	Fate	Note
Jagdgeschwader Nr.1							
Hptm. Georg Hackbarth	Stab	FW190 A-8			Ghent Rly Stn	Killed	G/Kdr
Uffz. Egon Comtesse	1	FW190 A-8	960729	White 3	Ghent	Wounded	
Uffz. Paul Wunderlich	2	FW190 A-8	739228	Black 6	Scheldt	POW	
Gefr. Karl Heinz Bauch	2	FW190 A-8	960709	Black 9	Ghent	Killed	
Uffz. Heinz Bohmer	3	FW190 A-8	173929	Yellow 15	Ghent	Killed	
Fw. Heinz Jurgen Killian	3	FW190 A-8	738159	Yellow 6	Ghent	Killed	
Fw. Fritz Hoffmann	3	FW190 A-8	175044	< 1	Ghent	POW	
Oblt. Hans Gottfried Meinhof	4	FW190 A-8	961052	Red 8	Breda	Killed	St. Kpn
Uffz. Alfred Fritzche	4	FW190 A-8	739269	Red 1	Ghent	POW	
Ltn. Ernst von Johannides	5	FW190 A-8	739429	White 1	Ghent	Killed	
Ltn. Walter Holick	5	FW190 A-8	739230	White 6	Ghent	Killed	
Uffz. Otto Kuntzsch	5	FW190 A-8	960679	White 4	Ghent	Killed	
Uffz. Erich Wenniges	5	FW190 A-8	960475	White 15	Ghent	Killed	960473?
Uffz. Edgar Ardner	5	FW190 A-8	171513	Black 4	Ederkamp	POW	
Fw. Karl Hahn	II Gp	FW190 A-8	352518	White 8	B.61	Killed	
Fw. Harry Klints	II Gp	FW190 A-8	739235	Black 5	St Denis A/F	KIA	
Ofhr. Himar Kreb	II Gp	FW190 A-8	960659	Yellow 4	Ghent	Killed	
Ofw. Kurt Niedereicholz	7	FW190 A-8	173932	Yellow 14	Ghent	Killed	
Uffz. Oskar Vetter	7	FW190 A-8	173813	Yellow 16	Ghent	Killed	
Fw. Paul Mayr	8	FW190 A-8	960547	Blue 10	Ghent	Killed	
Uffz. Gerhard Behrens	8	FW190 A-8	960677	Blue 14	Ghent	Killed	

Name	Staffel	Machine	A/C Nr.	A/C Code	Brought down	Fate	Note
Jagdgeschwader Nr.1 (continued)							
Uffz. Reinhold Schober	8	FW190 A-8	733978	Blue 15	Ghent	Killed	
FjFw. Willi Wichardt	9	Me109 G-14	782402	White 19	Scheldt Estuary	POW	
Ltn. Anton Guha	10	Me109 G-14	780375	Grey 22	Nr Biervliet	POW	
Fw. Wilhelm Krauter	10	Me109 G-14	784090	Grey 23	S Holland	KIA	
Jagdgeschwader Nr.2							
Ltn. Werner Edelhoff	Stab	FW190 D-9	600382		St Trond	POW	
Uffz. Helmut Breitweg	1	FW190 A-8	173188		Liege	POW	
Uffz. Otto Dost	1	FW190 A-8	737371		Liege	Killed	
Fhr. Richard Storkan	1	FW190 D-9	210288		Liege	MIA	
Ogfr. Hubert Schyma	2	FW190 D-9	210214		Liege	POW	
Fw. Karl Tschelesnig	2	FW190 D-9	500385		Liege	MIA	
Uffz. Hans Wyssola	2	FW190 D-9	210244		Liege	POW	
Gefr. Fritz Buscher	3	FW190 D-9	210250		Liege	Killed	
Ogfr. Franz Dworak	3	FW190 D-9	210117		Liege	MIA	
Uffz. Herbert Korber	3	FW190 D-9	500111		Liege	Injured	
Hptm. Georg Schroder	II Gp	Me109 G-14	510885		St Trond	POW	GrKdr
Uffz. Wilhelm Eggert	4	FW190 D-9	210277		Liege	MIA	
Fw. Werner Hohenberg	4	FW190 D-9	210194	< 11	Liege	POW	
Uffz. Erwin Katzer	4	FW190 D-9	500387		Liege	MIA	
Uffz. Friedrich Optenhostert	4	DW190 D-9	500390		Liege	Killed	
Gefr. Werner Piesker	4	FW190 D-9	500116		Liege	MIA	
Uffz. Georg Wilkens	4	FW190 D-9	500124		Liege	POW	
Uffz. Helmut Bollwerk	5	Me109 G-14	462781		St Trond	MIA	
Ltn. Helmut Wagner	5	Me109 G-14	461328		St Trond	Injured	
Ofhr. Rudolf Aickelin	7	Me109 K-4	330412		St Trond	Killed	

Name	Staffel	Machine	A/C Nr.	A/C Code	Brought down	Fate	Note
Jagdgeschwader Nr.2 (continued)							
Fw. Fritz Keppler	8	Me109 K-4	330431		St Trond	Killed	
Uffz. Werner Hilbert	9	FW190 D-9	210211		Bad Nauheim	Injured	
Uffz. Siegfried Binger	10	FW190 D-9	210290		St Trond	POW	
Ogfr. Albert Buttner	10	FW190 D-9	500394		Liege	MIA	
Ltn. Christfried Clemens	10	FW190 D-9	600380		St Trond	Killed	
Ltn. Martin Enge	10	FW190 D-9	400223	Black 9	St Trond	Killed	
Uffz. Ernst Klein	10	FW190 D-9	600372		St Trond	Killed	
Fw. Josef Peschak	10	FW190 D-9	400222		St Trond	POW	
Ofw. Otto Wylezick	10	FW190 D-9			Giessen	Injured	
Uffz. Fritz Altpeter	11	FW190 D-9	600145	Yellow 4	Diersdorf	Killed	
Uffz. Richard Ruppel	11	FW190 D-9	600407	Yellow 3	St Trond	Killed	
Uffz. Wilhelm Scherwadt	11	FW190 D-9	210132	Yellow 6	St Trond	POW	
Ltn. Fritz Swoboda	11	FW190 D-9	210205	Blue 16	St Trond	KIA	
Uffz. Johann Jager	12	FW190 D-9		White 2	St Trond	Killed	
Uffz. Adolf Redlich	12	FW190 D-9	210145	Blue 1	St Trond	MIA	
Ofw. Fritz Schuler	12	FW190 D-9	210122	Blue 7	St Trond	Killed	
Uffz. Michael Speiss	12	FW190 D-9	210162	Blue 12	St Trond	MIA	
Jagdgeschwader Nr.3							
Uffz. Helmut Reinecke	1	Me109 G-14	783846	Yellow 7	Eindhoven	POW	
Fhr. Friedrich Tazreiter	1	Me109 G-14	783898	Green 6		POW	
Fw. Paul Fischer	2	Me109 G-14	780744	Black 18		POW	
Fw. Theodor Schmitt	3	Me109 G-10	490751	Yellow 20		Killed	
Uffz. Horst Schone	3	Me109 G-14	782380	Yellow 9		MIA	
Ogfr. Siegfried Reuther	I Gp	Me109 G-14		Green 1		MIA	
Ofw. Friedrich Hameister	4	Me109 G-14	785966	Green 7	Eindhoven	POW	

Name	Staffel	Machine	A/C Nr.	A/C Code	Brought down	Fate	Note
Jagdgeschwader Nr.3 (continued)							
Fw. Walter Rutowski	4	Me109 G-10	490195	Green 5	Eindhoven	POW	
Gfw. Rudolf Wieschhoff	4	Me109 G-14	785944	Green 16		Killed	
Uffz. Alfred Dors	10	Me109 G-14	462809	Black 15		Injured	St. Kap
Ltn. Hans Jung	10	Me109 G-14	464162	Black 3		Killed	
Ofw. Robert Reiser	10	Me109 G-14	664076	Black 1		Injured	
Ofhr. Uwe Naumann	11	Me109 K-4	330469	Yellow 1		Killed	
Oblt. Eberhard Graf von Treuberg	12	Me109 G-14	464297	Yellow 6		MIA	
Uffz. Erich Busch	14	FW190 A-8	682312	Black 12	Eindhoven	Killed	
Fw. Gerhard Leipholz	14	FW190 A-8	682253	Black 16	Eindhoven	Killed	
Uffz. Hans-Joachim Grell	15	FW190 A-8	682751	Yellow 10	Siegburg	Killed	
Uffz. Gerhard Schmidt	15	FW190 A-8	960320	Yellow 12	Eindhoven	POW	
Uffz. Alois Schmidt	16	FW190 A-8	682769	Red 9		MIA	
Jagdgeschwader Nr.4							
Gefr. Kurt Lack	3	?				MIA	
Fw. Franz Schneider	4	?				MIA	
Uffz. Werner Zetschke	4	?				Killed	
Uffz. Hans Gustav Dierks	5	FW190 A-8	681870	White 7		Killed	
Uffz. Erich Keller	5	FW190 A-8	682276	White 4		MIA	
Ogfr. Hans Peschel	5	FW190 A-8	682738	White 14		MIA	
Ofhr. Franz Schaar	5	Me109 G-14	682676	White 18		Killed	
Gfr. Walter Wagner	5	FW190 A-8/R2	681497	White 11	St Trond A/F	POW	
Uffz. Heinz Richter	II Gp	?				MIA	
Uffz. Willi Breves	7	FW190 A-8	175292	Yellow 6		MIA	
Uffz. Erich Guldenpfennig	7	Me109 K-4	331473	Black 5		Killed	
Uffz. Walter Huber	7	FW190 A-8	682673	Yellow 14	Babenhausen	Killed	

Name	Staffel	Machine	A/C Nr.	A/C Code	Brought down	Fate	Note
Jagdgeschwader Nr.4 (continued)							
Ltn. Gottfried Morio	7	FW190 A-8	682657	Yellow 8	Wesel	Injured	
Uffz. Gunther Schwarzenau	8	FW190 A-8	682763	Blue 15		POW	
Uffz. Horst Tharann	8	FW190 A-8	960324	Blue 3		POW	
Uffz. Walter Anetzhuber	13	Me109 G-14	785786	White 2		Killed	
Uffz. Hermann Holtkotter	13	Me109 G-14	785819	White 5		Killed	
Gfr. Karl Noppener	13	Me109 K-4	331477	Black 1		Killed	
Fw. Karl Berg	15	Me109 K-4	331418	Yellow 3		MIA	
Ofhr. Horst Gruner	15	Me109 K-4	331473	Black 5		Killed	
Ofhr. Arnulf Russow	15	Me109 G-14	461200	Yellow 13		POW	
Uffz. Lothar Schmidt	15	FW109 A-8	331450	Black 4		POW	
Ltn. Elmer Ecker	16	Me109 G-14	461533	Blue 12		Killed	
Jagdgeschwader Nr.6							
Obstlt. Johann Kogler	Stab	FW190 D-9	980543	< - + -	Volkel	POW	G. Kdor
Hptm. Ewald Trost	I Gp	FW190 A-8	373414	Red 12	Lingen	POW	
Uffz. Willi Voss	1	FW190 A-8	380349	White 12	Ziegenhain	Killed	
Uffz. Josef Zangerle	1	FW190 A-9	960224	White 9	Isselmeer	Killed	
Ofw. Walter Jung	2	FW190 A-8	460542	Yellow 1		MIA	
Oblt. Eberhard Pfleiderer	3	FW190 A-8	960542	Yellow 1	Delmenhorst	Killed	
Uffz. Karl Fries	4	FW190 A-8	737405	Blue 13	Nijmegen	Killed	
Ltn. Karl Grabmair	5	FW190 A-8	175049	White 7	Volkel	Killed	
Fw. Helmut Grislawski	5	FW190 A-8	738173	White 16	Volkel	MIA	
Hptm. Norbert Katz	5	FW190 A-8	69221	White 1	Volkel	Killed	St. Kpt
Maj. Helmut Kuhle	III Gr	Me109 G-14	460339	<<		Killed	Gr. Kdr
Uffz. Karl-Heinz Riedel	7	FW190 A-8	738167	Yellow 16	Volkel	MIA	
Uffz. Paul Schneider	7	FW190 A-8	171605	Yellow 12	Volkel	MIA	

Name	Staffel	Machine	A/C Nr.	A/C Code	Brought down	Fate	Note
Jagdgeschwader Nr.6 (continued)							
Uffz. Franz Schrottle	8	FW190 A-8	171557	Blue 13	Kirchellen	Killed	
Ltn. Hans Wulff	8	FW190 A-9	960224	Blue 4	Volkel	POW	
Oblt. Lothar Gerlach	9	Me109 G-14	784778	White 10		Killed	St. Kpt
Uffz. Hans-Joachim Rose	9	Me109 G-14	785763	White 4		POW	
Uffz. Rudolf Schlossborn	9	Me109 G-10	490704	White 14	Holland	POW	
Uffz. Karl Betz	10	Me109 G-10	490719	Black 12	Nijmegen	Killed	
Uffz. Hans Schaupp	10	Me109 G-14	784986	Black 5		Killed	
Hptm. Wilhelm Kindler	11	Me109 G-10	491282	< –		POW	St. Kpt
Ofw. Paul Schwerdtfeger	11	Me109 G-14	784986	Yellow 19		Killed	
Ofhr. Johann Krumm	12	Me109 G-14	784946	Green 8		Killed	
Jagdgeschwader Nr.7							
Ltn. Heinrich Lonnicker	9	Me262 A-1	500021		Nr Fassberg	Killed	G. Kdor
Jagdgeschwader Nr.11							
Maj. Gunther Specht	Stab	FW190 A-9	205033	Black 4	Brussels	MIA	
Uffz. Sophus Schmidt	Stab	FW190 A-8	737946			MIA	
Ogfr. Karl-Heinz Sistenich	1	FW190 A-8	738231	Yellow 5		Killed	
Ofhr. Heinrich Wiethoff	3	FW190 A-8	171742	White 10		MIA	
Ltn. Alwin Doppler	I Gr	FW190 A-8	960728	White ?		MIA	
Fhr. Gunter Hoffmann	II Gr	Me109 K-4	331510			MIA	
Fhr. Herbert Huss	6	Me109 K-4	330474	Black 3		MIA	
Fw. Peter Reschke	6	Me109 G-14	785119	Black 5		Killed	
Hptm. Horst-Gunther von Fassong	III Gr	FW190 A-8	682792	<<8	Maastricht	MIA	
Maj. Gunter Vowinkel	III Gr	FW190 A-8	960552	<4		MIA	
Oblt. Hans Fiedler	III Gr	FW190 A-8	739250	Yellow 9	Maastricht	POW	

Name	Staffel	Machine	A/C Nr.	A/C Code	Brought down	Fate	Note
Jagdgeschwader Nr.11 (continued)							
Ltn. Gerhard Neumann	III Gr	FW190 A-8	737932	<2		MIA	
Fw. Harald Schwartz	7	Me109 G-14	785751	Yellow 5		Killed	
Oblt. August Engel	8	Me109 G-14	784958	Blue 14		Killed	
Fw. Herbert Kraschinski	8	Me109 G-14		Yellow 3		Killed	
Ofw. Franz Meindl	8	Me109 G-14	784765	Blue 11		MIA	
Fw. Alfred Tempel	8	Me109 G-14	785770	Blue 3		MIA	
Gef. Gerhard Bohm	9	FW190 A-8	172663	White 3	Maastricht	Killed	
Uffz. Kurt Nussle	9	FW190 A-8	734007	White 13	Maastricht	MIA	
Uffz. Walter Gattner	10	FW190 A-8	732208	Black 3		MIA	
Ofw. Xaver Giese	10	FW190 A-8	733208	Black 11		MIA	
Uffz. Ernst Noreisch	10	FW190 A-8	681063	Black 10	Maastricht	Killed	
Uffz. Hermann Barion	12	FW190 A-8	738271	<6	Maastricht	Killed	
Ofw. Karl Hiller	12	FW190 A-8	960298	Blue 11	Maastricht	POW	
Uffz. Max Milkreiter	12	FW190 A-8	732210	Blue 15	Maastricht	MIA	
Jagdgeschwader Nr.26							
Oblt. Franz Kunz	2	FW190 D-9	510105	White 1	NE Rotterdam	WIA	St. Kpt
Uffz. Heinz Schulz	2	FW190 D-9	400234	Black 11	In Scheldt	MIA	
Uffz. Willy Sydow	2	FW190 D-9	600147	Black 6	SW Eindhoven	Killed	
Ogfr. Bodo Vogel	2	FW190 D-9	400237	Black 3	Walcheron Is	Killed	
Ogfr. Dieter Kraegeloh	3	FW190 D-9	500093	Yellow 13	Scheldt	POW	
Ogfr. Manfred Niessen	3	FW190 D-9	400233	Yellow 5	Utrecht	Unhurt C/landed	
Fhr. Hans-Joachim Werner	3	FW190 D-9	600168	Yellow 8	Grimbergen A/F	POW	
Ogfr. Karl-Heinz Braunert	4	FW190 D-9	210955	Black 10	Antwerp	Killed	
Fw. Karl-Heinz Hartmann	4	FW190 D-9	210126	Black 8	Grimbergen A/F	POW	
Uffz. Heinz Wodarczyk	4	FW190 D-9	210936		Wijhe/SE Zwolle	Killed	

212   *The Battle of the Airfields*

Name	Staffel	Machine	A/C Nr.	A/C Code	Brought down	Fate	Note
Jagdgeschwader Nr.26 (continued)							
Uffz. Karl-Erich Zeidler	4	FW190 D-9	600170	Black 2	Lengerich	WIA	
Uffz. Ernst Lampferhoff	5	FW190 D-9	210193	White 7	S Goes	POW	
Ogfr. Hubert Lott	5	FW190 D-9	500102	White 11	Zuider Zee	Killed	
Ofhr. Helmut Heuser	6	FW190 D-9	500034	Black 16	Tholen Is	POW	
Fw. Karl Hoett	6	FW190 D-9	400207	Black 2	Brielle	WIA	
Uffz. Norbert Risky	6	FW190 D-9			Zwolle	Unhurt C/landed	
Uffz. Wilhelm Schmitz	6	FW190 D-9	210274	Black 14	Wieze, Belg	Killed	
Fw. Erich Ahrens	7	FW190 D-9	210186	Brown 6	Beveland	POW	
Gefr. Hans-Karl Goetz	7	FW190 D-9	600161	Black 2	Gilze-Reijen A/F	POW	
Gefr. Willi Kunz	7	FW190 D-9	500105	Black 1	W Borger	Killed	
Iffz. Leopold Speer	7	FW190 D-9	210165	Brown 5	Zuider Zee	Killed	
Ltn. Gottfried Meyer	9	Me109 K-4	330404	White 15	Evere A/F	Killed	
Ltn. Rudolf Leinberger	11	Me109 K-4	330354	Black 18	Kirchellen A/F	WIA	
Oblt. Harald Lenz	11	Me109 K-4	330385	Yellow 18	Harderwijk	Killed	
Uffz. Walter Tepperis	11	Me109 G-14	413550	Black 8	Schouwen Is	Unhurt/WIA?	
Uffz. Karl-Heinz Berndt	12	Me109 K-4	330426	Black 30	St Martensdijk	POW	
Gefr. Horst Sengpiel	12	Me109 K-4	330404	White 15	Scheldt Est	Killed	
Jagdgeschwader Nr.27							
Fj.Uffz. Ferdinand Fink	1	Me109 G-14	402677		Melsbroek A/F	Killed	
Uffz. Heinrich Braun	2	Me109 K-4	331344		Melsbroek A/F	Killed	
Ltn. Joachim von Stechow	2	Me109 K-4	331401		Melsbroek A/F	Killed	St. Kpt
Fhr. Otto Theisen	2	Me109 K-4	331493		Melsbroek A/F	POW	
Ltn. Heinrich Weise	2	Me109 K-4	330285		Melsbroek A/F	Killed	
Fw. Gert Gabel	3	Me109 K-4	331502		Melsbroek A/F	Killed	
Gefr. Arno Diesing	4	Me109 K-4	331395		Melsbroek A/F	Killed	

Name	Staffel	Machine	A/C Nr.	A/C Code	Brought down	Fate	Note
Jagdgeschwader Nr.27 (continued)							
Uffz. Peter-Michel Gisevius	7	Me109 K-4		White 7	Thielen, Belg	Killed	
Uffz. Johannes Hartlein	7	Me109 G-14				POW	
Hptm. Hans-Heinz Dudeck	IV Gr	Me109 G-10			Melsbroek A/F	POW	Gr. Kdr
Ogfr. Erich Heymann	10	Me109 G-10				MIA	
Uffz. Heinrich Frickmann	11	Me109 G-10				Killed	
Uffz. Heinrich Maus	12	Me109 G-10				Injured	
Uffz. Karl Rehak	12	Me109 G-10				Killed	
Fw. Alfred Mannchen	16	Me109 G-10				Killed	
Jagdgeschwader Nr.53							
Oblt. Helmut Bennemann	Stab	Me109 G-14AS			Frescaty area	WIA	Damaged
Oblt. Rudolf Schumer	Stab	Me109 G-14AS	166288	Black <3	Frescaty	Safe	Damaged
Fw. Friedrich Meyer	Stab	Me109 G-14AS			C/L Koblenz	Safe	Petrol
Uffz. Rudolf Konitzer	5	Me109 G-14AS	783900	Black 12	S Metz	MIA	
Fj.Ofw. Karl Opitz	5	Me109 G-14AS	785813	Black 3+−	Metz area	MIA	
Uffz. Erich Ernst	6	Me109 G-14AS			C/L Huchenfeld	Safe	
Fw. Ernst Nachotsky	6	Me109 G-14AS	785922	Yellow 9	Metz area	Killed	
Uffz. Florian Juszczak	7	Me109 G-14AS	785952	White 11	Metz area	MIA	
Fw. Johannes Muller	7	Me109 G-14AS	785939	White 14	Metz area	DOW 2 Jan	
Gefr. Franz Reichart	7	Me109 G-14AS	784928	White 17	Metz area	MIA	
Fw. August Bermpohl	8	Me109 K-4	332362	Blue 8	Metz area	Injured	
Fw. Ernst Off	8	Me109 G-14AS	785056	Blue 9	Speyer	Killed	
Uffz. Hermann Heck	9	Me109 G-14		Yellow 9	Pirmasens	Safe	W/off
Fw. Stein	9	Me109 G-14			Pirmasens	Safe	W/off
Fw. Heinz Plettner	11	Me109 G-14	462797	Black 3+	Pirmasens	Injured	W/off
Ofw. Wilhelm Scheer	11	Me109 G-14			Pirmasens	Safe	W/off

Name	Staffel	Machine	A/C Nr.	A/C Code	Brought down	Fate	Note
Jagdgeschwader Nr.53 (continued)							
Uffz. Karl Goller	12	Me109 G-14	464112	Blue 7	Kaiserslautern	Injured	W/off
Hptm. Siegfried Luckenbach	12	Me109 G-14			Pirmasens	Safe	St. Kpt
Oblt. Otto Benz	13	Me109 G-14	461516	White 3	Metz area	Killed	
Ofw. Stefan Kohl	13	Me109 G-14	461340	White 11	Marly	POW	
Uffz. Herbert Maxis	13	Me109 G-14	784993	White 13	Nr Marly	Killed	
Fhr. Siegried Leese	14	Me109 G-14	464137	Black 6	Metz area	Killed	
Fj.Fw. Werner Jaschek	15	Me109 G-14	464092	Yellow 2	Nr Waldwisse	Killed	
Fhr. Wolfgang Rosenberger	15	Me109 G-14	462828	Yellow 12	Metz area	Killed	
Gefr. Alfred Michel	16	Me109 G-14	462892	Blue 2	Metz area	MIA	
Uffz. Horst Pechardscheck	16	Me109 G-14	464186	Yellow 9	C/L Echterdingen	Injured	Damaged
Oblt. Georg Schwidtal	16	Me109 G-14			C/L Saarbruken	Sage	Damaged
Jagdgeschwader Nr.54							
Fw. Paul Deutschmann	9	FW190 D-9	210102	White 3	Belgium	POW	
Uffz. Gerhard Kroll	9	FW190 D-9	210960	White 19	W Rotterdam	Injured	
Ltn. Theo Nibel	10	FW190 D-9	210079	Black 12	Nr Brussels	POW	
Hptm. Willi Bottlander	11	FW190 D-9	210045	Yellow 2	Grimbergen	MIA	St. Kpt
Ofw. Walter Eckert	11	FW190 D-9	210071	Yellow 7	Belgium	Killed	
Fw. Gunther Egli	11	FW190 D-9	210084	Yellow 14	Belgium	POW	
Uffz. Gerhard Thoss	11	FW190 D-9	210120	Yellow 15	Belgium	MIA	
Uffz. Aloysius von Hooven	12	FW190 D-9	210957	Blue 18	Belgium	Killed	
Ltn. Jurgen Ratzlaff	12	FW190 D-9	600346	Yellow 6	Grimbergen	MIA	
Fw. Hans-Joachim Steinkamp	12	FW190 D-9	210028	Red 2	Belgium	POW	
Uffz. Werner Kopp	13	FW190 D-9	734038		Nijmegen	Killed	
Fw. Fridolin Bachhuber	15	FW190 A-8	750093		Brussels	MIA	

Name	Staffel	Machine	A/C Nr.	A/C Code	Brought down	Fate	Note
Jagdgeschwader Nr.54 (continued)							
Uffz. Gerhard Ohlenschlager	15	FW190 A-8	732088		Brussels area	POW	
Jagdgeschwader Nr.77							
Oblt. Karl-Heinz Bartels	3	Me109 G-14	511893	Yellow 1	Antwerp area	MIA	
Gefr. Helmut Kofler	3	Me109 G-14	512314	Yellow 5	Antwerp area	Killed	
Gefr. Edwin Mannweiler	4	Me109 G-14	512426	White 17	Antwerp area	POW	
Fw. Paul Tanck	8	Me109				MIA	
Ltn. Heinz Abendroth	9	Me109 K-4	330204	1	Rosendaal	POW	
Uffz. Heinrich Munninger	10	Me109 K-4	330230	Red 17	Tilburg	Killed	
Ltn. Hans-Jurgen Schumacher	10	Me109 K-4	330119	Red 7	Antwerp	Killed	
Uffz. Johann Tweitmeyer	10	Me109 K-4	330163	Red 7	Antwerp	POW	
Fhr. Rolf Braband	11	Me109 K-4	330174	Yellow 12	Antwerp	Killed	
Ltn. Heinrich Hackler	11	Me109 K-4	330196	Yellow 1	Antwerp	Killed	St. Kpt
Schlachtgeschwader Nr.4							
Oberst. Alfred Druschel	Stab	FW190 F-8	584400		Aachen	MIA	G/Kdor
Fw. Richard Heinz	7	FW190 F-8	586450	White 3	St Trond	MIA	
Ofw. Hans Schmieder	7	FW190 F-8	933433	Yellow 14	St Trond	POW	
Fw. Rudolf Fye	9	FW190 F-8	584233	Brown 12	St Trond/Antwerp	Killed	

Bibliography

Six Months to Oblivion, Werner Gerbig. Ian Allan Ltd, 1975.
2nd Tactical Air Force, C.F. Shore. Osprey Ltd, 1970.
The RCAF Overseas – The Sixth Year. Oxford Press, 1949.
Heaven Next Stop, Gunther Bloemertz. Wm Kimber Ltd, 1953.
Alert in the West, Willi Heilmann. Wm Kimber Ltd, 1955.
For Valour – The Air VCs, Chaz Bowyer. Wm Kimber Ltd, 1978.
American Aces of WWII, Edward H. Sims. Macdonald Ltd, 1958.
Jagdgeschwader 27, H. Ring & W. Gerbig. Motorbuch Verlag, 1971.
Fighter Squadrons of the RAF, J. Rawlings. Macdonald & Janes, 1976.
Die Ritterkreuztrager der Luftwaffe, Ernest Obermaier. Verlag Dieter Hoffman, 1966.,
2 Group RAF, M.J.F. Bowyer. Faber & Faber, Ltd, 1974.
History of the Hell Hawks, by Charles R. Johnson, USA, 1975

Articles:
'The Final Gamble', John Weal, *Air International*, 1975.
'Bodenplatte 1945', Martin Windrow, *War Monthly*.

Index

A separate index to Places and Squadrons follows the index of Personal Names

Places

RAF Squadrons
(including RCAF, Polish, French, Dutch, Belgian, Norwegian, RNZAF etc)